T
H

Other Books in the Turning Points Series:

Turning|Points

IN WORLD HISTORY

The Holocaust

Mitchell G. Bard, *Book Editor*

David L. Bender, *Publisher*
Bruno Leone, *Executive Editor*
Bonnie Szumski, *Editorial Director*
Stuart B. Miller, *Managing Editor*

Greenhaven Press, Inc., San Diego, California

Every effort has been made to trace the owners of copyrighted material. The articles in this volume may have been edited for content, length, and/or reading level. The titles have been changed to enhance the editorial purpose.

Library of Congress Cataloging-in-Publication Data

The Holocaust / Mitchell G. Bard, book editor.
    p.   cm. — (Turning points in world history)
    Includes bibliographical references (p.   ) and index.
    ISBN 0-7377-0575-2 (pbk. : alk. paper) —
ISBN 0-7377-0576-0 (lib. bdg. : alk. paper)
    1. Holocaust, Jewish (1939–1945) I. Bard, Mitchell Geoffrey, 1959–   II. Series. III. Turning points in world history (Greenhaven Press)

D804.3 .H62 2001
940.53'18—dc21   00-044286
                                                CIP

Cover photo: © Hulton Getty Picture Library/Stone
Dover, 62
Library of Congress, 102, 188
National Archives, 112, 207

©2001 by Greenhaven Press, Inc.
P.O. Box 289009, San Diego, CA 92198-9009

Printed in the U.S.A.

Contents

Chapter 1: Isolation and Dehumanization: Institutionalizing Persecution

Chapter 2: Evil Reaches New Lows: The Final Solution

tries made it difficult, if not impossible for them to
leave, and few countries would accept those who could.

Chapter 5: The Legacy of the Holocaust

Foreword

Certain past events stand out as pivotal, as having effects and outcomes that change the course of history. These events are often referred to as turning points. Historian Louis L. Snyder provides this useful definition:

> A turning point in history is an event, happening, or stage which thrusts the course of historical development into a different direction. By definition a turning point is a great event, but it is even more—a great event with the explosive impact of altering the trend of man's life on the planet.

History's turning points have taken many forms. Some were single, brief, and shattering events with immediate and obvious impact. The invasion of Britain by William the Conqueror in 1066, for example, swiftly transformed that land's political and social institutions and paved the way for the rise of the modern English nation. By contrast, other single events were deemed of minor significance when they occurred, only later recognized as turning points. The assassination of a little-known European nobleman, Archduke Franz Ferdinand, on June 28, 1914, in the Bosnian town of Sarajevo was such an event; only after it touched off a chain reaction of political-military crises that escalated into the global conflict known as World War I did the murder's true significance become evident.

Other crucial turning points occurred not in terms of a few hours, days, months, or even years, but instead as evolutionary developments spanning decades or even centuries. One of the most pivotal turning points in human history, for instance—the development of agriculture, which replaced nomadic hunter-gatherer societies with more permanent settlements—occurred over the course of many generations. Still other great turning points were neither events nor developments, but rather revolutionary new inventions and innovations that significantly altered social customs and ideas, military tactics, home life, the spread of knowledge, and the

9

human condition in general. The developments of writing, gunpowder, the printing press, antibiotics, the electric light, atomic energy, television, and the computer, the last two of which have recently ushered in the world-altering information age, represent only some of these innovative turning points.

Each anthology in the Greenhaven Turning Points in World History series presents a group of essays chosen for their accessibility. The anthology's structure also enhances this accessibility. First, an introductory essay provides a general overview of the principal events and figures involved, placing the topic in its historical context. The essays that follow explore various aspects in more detail, some targeting political trends and consequences, others social, literary, cultural, and/or technological ramifications, and still others pivotal leaders and other influential figures. To aid the reader in choosing the material of immediate interest or need, each essay is introduced by a concise summary of the contributing writer's main themes and insights.

In addition, each volume contains extensive research tools, including a collection of excerpts from primary source documents pertaining to the historical events and figures under discussion. In the anthology on the French Revolution, for example, readers can examine the works of Rousseau, Voltaire, and other writers and thinkers whose championing of human rights helped fuel the French people's growing desire for liberty; the French *Declaration of the Rights of Man and Citizen*, presented to King Louis XVI by the French National Assembly on October 2, 1789; and eyewitness accounts of the attack on the royal palace and the horrors of the Reign of Terror. To guide students interested in pursuing further research on the subject, each volume features an extensive bibliography, which for easy access has been divided into separate sections by topic. Finally, a comprehensive index allows readers to scan and locate content efficiently. Each of the anthologies in the Greenhaven Turning Points in World History series provides students with a complete, detailed, and enlightening examination of a crucial historical watershed.

Introduction

The Holocaust, or Shoah, refers to the period from January 30, 1933, when Adolf Hitler became chancellor of Germany, to May 8, 1945, when the war in Europe ended. During this time, Jews in Europe were systematically persecuted and, ultimately, approximately 6 million were murdered. It is difficult to comprehend the magnitude of this number. At the time, the figure represented two-thirds of European Jewry and one-third of world Jewry. Today, murdering 6 million people would be the equivalent of exterminating the entire population of Israel. And the Jews were not casualties of war, they were innocent civilians—men, women, and children.

It is not just the magnitude of the slaughter that made the Holocaust a turning point in history, it is the fact that the Germans were willing to go to such extreme lengths to exterminate the Jews that they undermined their military objectives at the height of the battles with the Allies to divert money, manpower, and transportation from the army to the concentration camps. Though this diversion alone did not bring about the defeat of the Nazis, it certainly contributed to their inability to maintain their offensives and withstand the onslaught of the Allied forces.

The Holocaust, which the Germans called the Final Solution, required the creation of an entire bureaucracy devoted to the isolation, deportation, dehumanization, and murder of Jews. The Holocaust was not a sudden act of mass murder. It was actually a gradual process of five phases that began with relatively minor restrictions on Jewish behavior and gradually escalated over a period of nearly a decade to the point where the official policy of the Nazis was the extermination of every Jew in Europe.

A number of factors contributed to the systematic escalation of the persecution of the Jews, including anti-Semitism in German society, the need for a scapegoat for Germany's economic problems and decline after the nation's humiliation in World War I, and the fear and weakness of average Germans, most of whom were unprepared to oppose the Nazis, who quickly learned that violence and intimidation could readily prevent most resistance.

Phase I: Isolation

At the time Hitler came to power, Germany was regarded as the most civilized country in the world, and Jews were among its most prominent citizens, holding positions of influence in every field. Jews had also fought with distinction in World War I and veterans considered themselves patriotic German citizens. Though many Jews remained committed to their faith, many others assimilated, partly because they believed this would make it easier for them to be accepted by their non-Jewish neighbors. It therefore came as quite a shock when a boycott against Jews was initiated early in 1933. This boycott was not only directed against Jewish businesses but also professionals such as doctors and lawyers. Jewish civil service employees, with the exception of World War I veterans, were dismissed from their posts.

The persecution of Jews in other ways and in other professions followed. In May, Nazis burned books written by Jews and opponents of Nazism. In July, a law was passed revoking the naturalization and cancelling the citizenship of Jews who had immigrated to Germany after 1918. Toward the end of the year, Jewish writers, artists, and journalists lost their jobs. A few months later Jews were denied the right to health insurance. By 1935 posters began to appear in the windows of shops, restaurants, and other public places that read, "Jews not wanted."

The legislated persecution of the Jews culminated in the adoption of the Nuremberg Laws in 1935. These laws excluded Jews from all public business life and reclassified the political rights of Jewish citizens. Under the National Citizens Law, Jews were denied voting rights and were forbidden to hold public office. Any remaining Jewish civil service employees, including World War I veterans, were dismissed. The Law for the Protection of German Blood and German Honor prohibited the marriage of Jews to non-Jews. Other bans prevented Jews from using the same facilities as non-Jews.

Virtually every institution of the government contributed to the anti-Jewish policy of the Nazis. Among the most important were the press and propaganda ministry. Throughout the early years of Hitler's rule, as his Nazi Party came to dominate the nation, the German people were fed a steady stream of anti-Semitic propaganda through official government channels and publications. The most vitriolic attacks on the Jews were issued by Hitler's minister of propaganda and public information, Joseph Goebbels, who also supervised a weekly publication, *Der Stürmer*, which was devoted primarily to promoting hatred against the Jews. Its motto was, "The Jews are our misfortune."

Phase II: Aryanization

During the early years of Hitler's rule, persecution of Jews was limited primarily to denying them certain rights and jobs. In 1937 the Nazis began to take away Jewish possessions. Jewish businessmen, for example, were forced to sell their businesses, usually at below-market prices. Industrialists and other wealthy property owners were required to register with the government and to declare their holdings. Professionals, most of whom had already lost their jobs, were stripped of their licenses in 1938. Doctors, for instance, were only allowed to serve as nurses, and then only for Jewish patients.

During the course of 1938 the Germans also continued to isolate Jews by instituting new methods for branding them. Jews were given identity cards, and their passports were confiscated and new ones, identifying them as Jews, were issued—at least to those who managed to navigate the bureaucratic obstacles created to make it more difficult. Jews also had their driver's licenses taken away and were required to change their names, adding either *Israel* for men or *Sara* for women to their names.

The Germans found still more rights to take away and limitations to place on Jews: Children were expelled from school, Jews were banned from cultural and sporting events and associations, and limits were placed on what Jews could do in public.

All of these various measures were based on Hitler's anti-Semitic views and his desire to ultimately rid Germany of Jews. From the beginning of his political career, Hitler made no secret of his intentions regarding the Jews. He repeatedly made public remarks that left little to the imagination, such as his January 1939 speech to parliament predicting the "extermination of the Jewish race in Europe" in the event of war. Yet, the Holocaust did not issue from the edicts of one man. The vast array of prohibitions was devised, implemented, and enforced by a growing number of people in an ever-expanding bureaucracy devoted largely to what became known as "the Jewish question."

Phase III: Violence Against Jews

The level of persecution against the Jews was ratcheted up significantly in 1938. As disconcerting, humiliating, and discriminating as the measures had been, they had not yet posed a physical danger to the well-being of German Jews. This began to change with the destruction of synagogues in Munich and Nuremberg and the so-called Night of Broken Glass, *Kristallnacht*. On November 9–10, the government organized attacks by mobs that destroyed 191 synagogues and looted 7,500 shops. At least ninety-one Jews were killed.

Another alarming new development was the arrest of more than twenty-six thousand Jewish men, who were then imprisoned in concentration camps at Dachau, Buchenwald, and Sachsenhausen. Though concentration camps are associated with the murder of Jews, the first one, Dachau, was actually established in June 1933 for non-Jewish opponents of the Nazi regime and other "criminals." After *Kristallnacht*, however, the camps increasingly became prisons for Jews.

Nazis continued to torment Jews, including making them pay for all of the damage done during *Kristallnacht*. Ominously, the Germans also began to impose anti-Semitic measures against non-German Jews as they seized control of Austria and Czechoslovakia. The importance of "the Jewish question" was also reinforced by the creation of a new bureaucracy, the National Central Office for Jewish Emigration, with central offices in Vienna and Prague.

Phase IV: Ghettoization

Germany's invasion of Poland on September 1, 1939, marked the unofficial start of World War II. One of the reasons Hitler said he went to war was to make room—lebensraum (living space)—for Germans. He believed that Eastern Europe had to be conquered to create a vast German empire with a greater population and new territory to supply food and raw materials.

Hitler's objective was complicated, however, by the fact that the conquest of Poland brought another 2 million Jews under his authority. The Nazis wasted little time in applying their anti-Semitic laws against the newly conquered Jews, but, once again, they escalated the severity of the measures. Heinrich Himmler created special task forces within the SS, the *Einsatzgruppen*, which were charged with liquidating all political enemies of the Reich. By the end of the war these mobile killing units would liquidate approximately 1.4 million Jews. Initially, however, the mass murder of Polish Jews was not practical, so while Hitler planned the creation of special camps for the extermination of the Jews, he decided to isolate them in ghettos.

The ghettos were enclosed areas—barbed wire at Lodz, a brick wall in Warsaw and Krakow—guarded by German soldiers. Living conditions in the ghettos were horrible. Malnutrition was widespread and death by starvation and disease was a daily occurrence.

Each ghetto was administered by a Jewish council (*Judenrat*), which was composed of influential members of the Jewish community. This was one of the many diabolical inventions of the Germans. The council members represented the Jewish community to the Nazi authorities, but their primary role was to implement German policy. They were put in the position of having to decide whether to help the Nazis or risk being murdered for their refusal. Many Jews believed they were in some way helping to improve the plight of Jews in the ghetto, but ultimately they were often the ones who had to choose who would be deported to the death camps. In the end, cooperating with the Nazis did not spare the *Judenrat* from sharing the same fate as the other Jews.

The ghettos provide yet another example of the unprecedented effort the Nazis devoted to disposing of the Jews. It was an enormous bureaucratic and logistical task to organize the segregation of more than 2 million people who were spread throughout Poland, and later to transport them in the most efficient manner to the death camps.

Phase V: Annihilation

Throughout 1940–1941, the German army marched through Europe, invading one country after another and, in the process, absorbing more and more Jews. Anti-Jewish laws would be instituted almost immediately, but this did not solve the problem of creating "living space," so the Jews were rounded up and deported to the growing number of concentration camps.

In 1941 the *Einsatzgruppen* began to commit large-scale massacres, particularly in Russian territories that came under German control as Hitler's army advanced into the Soviet Union. The most notorious of these massacres was at Babi Yar, where thirty-four thousand Jews were machine-gunned over the course of two days, but other mass killings of tens of thousands occurred in Kiev, Riga, Simferopol, and Kovno.

The Germans also opened a number of camps specifically for the purpose of murdering Jews and began testing various ways to kill more people more quickly and efficiently. While Germany was engaged in a world war, thousands of men who otherwise could be fighting were engaged in the administration of concentration camps and the cold-blooded murder of innocent men, women, and children. The technological know-how that might be devoted to developing weapons with which to fight opposing armies was instead directed toward figuring out ways to burn bodies more quickly and dispose of them more easily.

The Germans were not content with just killing people, however. They had tortured, dehumanized, and humiliated them. Prisoners' heads were shaved, their names were replaced with numbers, and, in Auschwitz, their arms were tattooed. The most sickening methods were used to kill people—gassing, hanging, clubbing, heart injections, driving inmates into electric fences, burying them alive. Prisoners were also used as guinea pigs for ghastly medical experiments. Some of these involved seeing how often bones could be broken before they could no longer be reset, observing how the body would react to extremes of heat and cold, and using X rays for sterilization.

By the beginning of 1942, hundreds of thousands of Jews were already dead. Still, the head of the SS, Heinrich Himmler, recognized that it would require greater coordination among the various Nazi institutions and officials to accomplish the goal of achieving the Final Solution to the Jewish question, namely the extermination of the 11 million Jews he believed to be living in Europe. On January 20 a meeting was held on the shores of a Berlin lake called Wannsee for this purpose. Afterward, the liquidation of the ghettos and the deportation of Jews from the occupied territories became a much more systematic process.

From that point until the surrender of Germany, the Nazis followed the course laid out at Wannsee and proceeded to murder approximately 6 million Jews as well as an almost equal number of non-Jews. And the killing continued unabated even when the course of the war turned against Germany. When every German was needed to fight, when food, oil, and transportation were in short supply, resources continued to be used to kill Jews rather than to be diverted for military use. As Emil Fackenheim has written, "The killing of Jews was not considered just a part of the war effort, but equal to it." It is an overstatement to say the Germans lost the war because of their dogged commitment to the Final Solution, but there is no question that the extermination campaign was a drain that weakened their ability to fight.

Conclusion

World War II was the most destructive human endeavor in history. Battles were fought on every continent and involved more than sixty countries, affecting roughly three-quarters of the world's population. The casualty figures were staggering: More than 57 million people were killed, and more than half of these people were civilians. Six million Jews were specifically singled out by the Nazis from all of the civilians in Europe for extermination. The Holocaust was the greatest single case of mass murder in history. It demonstrated what human beings were capable of doing to each other and how the most civilized society on Earth could use the latest scientific methods to exterminate another people. Though mass murders have occurred since World War II in places like Bosnia and Cambodia, the memory of the Holocaust has made the world more sensitive to genocide and has made atrocities more difficult to ignore.

After the Holocaust, new notions of wartime responsibility were adopted. The perpetrators of crimes against civilians could not use the excuse that they were merely following orders. At the trial of war criminals at Nuremberg, the precedent was set that officials who give orders to commit crimes against civilians, as well as those who carry them out, will be punished. Nuremberg also established the notion of a crime against humanity, the "murder, extermination, enslavement, deportation and other inhuman acts committed against any civilian population, before or during the war; or persecution on political, racial, or religious grounds." The precedents set at Nuremberg in the trials of Germans responsible for the Holocaust are being used today in war crimes trials of those accused of atrocities in the Balkans.

The Holocaust, of course, had a particularly powerful impact on the Jewish people, who vowed never to allow such a thing to happen again and to ensure that they would never become so powerless that they would have to depend on others for their safety. This feeling played an important role in the creation of Israel, a state where every Jew is welcomed with open arms, guaranteeing that no Jew will ever again have to worry about being turned away from a place of refuge.

Chapter 1

Isolation and Dehumanization: Institutionalizing Persecution

Turning|Points
IN WORLD HISTORY

A Brief History of the Holocaust

Holocaust Memorial Center

This article offers an overview of the history of the Holocaust, which traces its beginning to 1933 when Hitler came to power. It describes all of the elements of what we now call the Holocaust, starting with anti-Jewish propaganda and steadily escalating to the isolation of the Jews and the decision to exterminate them. This introduction was taken from the website of the Holocaust Memorial Center in West Bloomfield, Michigan.

The Holocaust (also called *Shoah* in Hebrew) refers to the period from January 30, 1933, when Adolf Hitler became chancellor of Germany, to May 8, 1945 (VE Day), when the war in Europe ended. During this time, Jews in Europe were subjected to progressively harsh persecution that ultimately led to the murder of 6,000,000 Jews (1.5 million of these being children) and the destruction of 5,000 Jewish communities. These deaths represented two-thirds of European Jewry and one-third of world Jewry. The Jews who died were not casualties of the fighting that ravaged Europe during World War II. Rather, they were the victims of Germany's deliberate and systematic attempt to annihilate the entire Jewish population of Europe, a plan Hitler called the "Final Solution" (*Endlösung*).

After its defeat in World War I, Germany was humiliated by the Versailles Treaty, which reduced its prewar territory, drastically reduced its armed forces, demanded the recognition of its guilt for the war, and stipulated it pay reparations to the allied powers. The German Empire destroyed, a new parliamentary government called the Weimar Republic was formed. The republic suffered from economic instability, which grew

Reprinted from the Holocaust Memorial Center, "History of the Holocaust—An Introduction," an online article found at www.us-israel.org/jsource/Holocaust/history.html. Reprinted with permission from the Holocaust Memorial Center.

worse during the worldwide depression after the New York stock market crash in 1929. Massive inflation followed by very high unemployment heightened existing class and political differences and began to undermine the government.

On January 30, 1933, Adolf Hitler, leader of the National Socialist German Workers (Nazi) Party, was named chancellor by president Paul von Hindenburg after the Nazi Party won a significant percentage of the vote in the elections of 1932. The Nazi Party had taken advantage of the political unrest in Germany to gain an electoral foothold. The Nazis incited clashes with the Communists, who many feared, disrupted the government with demonstrations, and conducted a vicious propaganda campaign against its political opponents—the weak Weimar government, and the Jews, whom the Nazis blamed for Germany's ills.

Propaganda: "The Jews Are Our Misfortune"

A major tool of the Nazis' propaganda assault was the weekly Nazi newspaper *Der Stürmer* (The Attacker). At the bottom of the front page of each issue, in bold letters, the paper proclaimed, "The Jews are our misfortune!" *Der Stürmer* also regularly featured cartoons of Jews in which they were caricatured as hooked-nosed and ape-like. The influence of the newspaper was far-reaching: by 1938 about a half million copies were distributed weekly.

Soon after he became chancellor, Hitler called for new elections in an effort to get full control of the Reichstag, the German parliament, for the Nazis. The Nazis used the government apparatus to terrorize the other parties. They arrested their leaders and banned their political meetings. Then, in the midst of the election campaign, on February 27, 1933, the Reichstag building burned. A Dutchman named Marinus van der Lubbe was arrested for the crime, and he swore he had acted alone. Although many suspected the Nazis were ultimately responsible for the act, the Nazis managed to blame the Communists, thus turning more votes their way.

The fire signaled the demise of German democracy. On the next day, the government, under the pretense of controlling the Communists, abolished individual rights and protections: freedom of the press, assembly, and expression were nullified, as well as the right to privacy. When the elections were held on March 5, the Nazis received nearly 44 percent of the vote, and with 8 percent offered by the Conservatives, won a majority in the government.

The Nazis moved swiftly to consolidate their power into a dictatorship. On March 23, the Enabling Act was passed. It sanctioned Hitler's dictatorial efforts and legally enabled him to pursue them further. The Nazis marshaled their formidable propaganda machine to silence their critics. They also developed a sophisticated police and military force.

The *Sturmabteilung* (S.A., Storm Troopers), a grassroots organization, helped Hitler undermine the German democracy. The Gestapo (*Geheime Staatspolizei*, Secret State Police), a force recruited from professional police officers, was given complete freedom to arrest anyone after February 28. The *Schutzstaffel* (SS, Protection Squad) served as Hitler's personal bodyguard and eventually controlled the concentration camps and the Gestapo. The *Sicherheitsdienst des Reichsführers SS* (S.D., Security Service of the SS) functioned as the Nazis' intelligence service, uncovering enemies and keeping them under surveillance.

With this police infrastructure in place, opponents of the Nazis were terrorized, beaten, or sent to one of the concentration camps the Germans built to incarcerate them. Dachau, just outside of Munich, was the first such camp built for political prisoners. Dachau's purpose changed over time and eventually became another brutal concentration camp for Jews.

By the end of 1934 Hitler was in absolute control of Germany, and his campaign against the Jews in full swing. The Nazis claimed the Jews corrupted pure German culture with their "foreign" and "mongrel" influence. They portrayed the Jews as evil and cowardly, and Germans as hardworking, courageous, and honest. The Jews, the Nazis claimed, who were heavily represented in finance, commerce, the press, literature, theater, and the arts, had weakened Germany's economy and culture. The massive government-supported propaganda machine created a racial anti-Semitism, which was different from the long-standing anti-Semitic tradition of the Christian churches.

The superior race was the "Aryans," the Germans. The word Aryan, [according to author Leni Yahil in *The Holocaust: The Fate of European Jewry*] "derived from the study of linguistics, which started in the eighteenth century and at some point determined that the Indo-Germanic (also known as Aryan) languages were superior in their structures, variety, and vocabulary to the Semitic languages that had evolved in the Near East. This judgment led to a certain conjecture about the character of the peoples who spoke these languages; the conclusion was that the 'Aryan' peoples were likewise superior to the 'Semitic' ones."

The Jews Are Isolated from Society

The Nazis then combined their racial theories with the evolutionary theories of Charles Darwin to justify their treatment of the Jews. The Germans, as the strongest and fittest, were destined to rule, while the weak and racially adulterated Jews were doomed to extinction. Hitler began to restrict the Jews with legislation and terror, which entailed burning books written by Jews, removing Jews from their professions and public schools, confiscating their businesses and property and excluding them from public events. The most infamous of the anti-Jewish legislation were the Nuremberg Laws, enacted on September 15, 1935. They formed the legal basis for the Jews' exclusion from German society and the progressively restrictive Jewish policies of the Germans.

Many Jews attempted to flee Germany, and thousands succeeded by immigrating to such countries as Belgium, Czechoslovakia, England, France and Holland. It was much more difficult to get out of Europe. Jews encountered stiff immigration quotas in most of the world's countries. Even if they obtained the necessary documents, they often had to wait months or years before leaving. Many families out of desperation sent their children first.

In July 1938, representatives of 32 countries met in the

French town of Evian to discuss the refugee and immigration problems created by the Nazis in Germany. Nothing substantial was done or decided at the Evian Conference, and it became apparent to Hitler that no one wanted the Jews and that he would not meet resistance in instituting his Jewish policies. By the autumn of 1941, Europe was in effect sealed to most legal emigration. The Jews were trapped.

On November 9–10, 1938, the attacks on the Jews became violent. [On November 7] Hershel Grynszpan, a 17-year-old Jewish boy distraught at the deportation of his family, shot Ernst vom Rath, the third secretary in the German Embassy in Paris, who died on November 9. Nazi hooligans used this assassination as the pretext for instigating a night of destruction that is now known as *Kristallnacht* (the night of broken glass). They looted and destroyed Jewish homes and businesses and burned synagogues. Many Jews were beaten and killed; 30,000 Jews were arrested and sent to concentration camps.

The Jews Are Confined to Ghettos

Germany invaded Poland in September 1939, beginning World War II. Soon after, in 1940, the Nazis began establishing ghettos for the Jews of Poland. More than 10 percent of the Polish population was Jewish, numbering about three million. Jews were forcibly deported from their homes to live in crowded ghettos, isolated from the rest of society. This concentration of the Jewish population later aided the Nazis in their deportation of the Jews to the death camps. The ghettos lacked the necessary food, water, space, and sanitary facilities required by so many people living within their constricted boundaries. Many died of deprivation and starvation.

The "Final Solution"

In June 1941 Germany attacked the Soviet Union and began the "Final Solution." Four mobile killing groups were formed called *Einsatzgruppen* A, B, C and D. Each group contained several commando units. The *Einsatzgruppen* gathered Jews town by town, marched them to huge pits dug earlier, stripped them, lined them up, and shot them with automatic weapons. The dead and dying would fall into the pits to be buried in mass graves. . . . In addition to their operations in the Soviet Union, the *Einsatzgruppen* conducted mass murder in eastern Poland, Estonia, Lithuania and Latvia. It is estimated that by the end of 1942, the *Einsatzgruppen* had murdered more than 1.3 million Jews.

On January 20, 1942, several top officials of the German government met to officially coordinate the military and civilian administrative branches of the Nazi system to organize a system of mass murder of the Jews. This meeting, called the Wannsee Conference, "marked the beginning of the full-scale, comprehensive extermination operation [of the Jews] and laid the foundations for its organization, which started immediately after the conference ended."

While the Nazis murdered other national and ethnic groups, such as a number of Soviet prisoners of war, Polish intellectuals, and gypsies, only the Jews were marked for systematic and total annihilation. Jews were singled out for "Special Treatment" (*Sonderbehandlung*), which meant that Jewish men, women and children were to be methodically killed with poisonous gas. In the exacting records kept at the Auschwitz death camp, the cause of death of Jews who had been gassed was indicated by "SB," the first letters of the two words that form the German term for "Special Treatment."

By the spring of 1942, the Nazis had established six killing centers (death camps) in Poland: Chelmno (Kulmhof), Belzec, Sobibor, Treblinka, Maidanek and Auschwitz. All were located near railway lines so that Jews could be easily transported daily. A vast system of camps (called *Lagersystem*) supported the death camps. The purpose of these camps varied: some were slave labor camps, some transit camps, others concentration camps and their sub-camps, and still others the notorious death camps. Some camps combined all of these functions or a few of them. All the camps were intolerably brutal.

The major concentration camps were Ravensbruck, Neuengamme, Bergen-Belsen, Sachsenhausen, Gross-Rosen, Buchenwald, Theresienstadt, Flossenburg, Natzweiler-Struthof, Dachau, Mauthausen, Stutthof, and Dora/Nordhausen.

In nearly every country overrun by the Nazis, the Jews were forced to wear badges marking them as Jews; they were rounded up into ghettos or concentration camps and then gradually transported to the killing centers. The death camps were essentially factories for murdering Jews. The Germans shipped thousands of Jews to them each day. Within a few hours of their arrival, the Jews had been stripped of their possessions and valuables, gassed to death, and their bodies burned in specially designed crematoriums. Approximately 3.5 million Jews were murdered in these death camps.

Many healthy, young strong Jews were not killed immediately. The Germans' war effort and the "Final Solution" required a great deal of manpower, so the Germans reserved large pools of Jews for slave labor. These people, imprisoned in concentration and labor camps, were forced to work in German munitions and other factories, such as I.G. Farben and Krupps, and wherever the Nazis needed laborers. They were worked from dawn until dark without adequate food and shelter. Thousands perished, literally worked to death by the Germans and their collaborators.

In the last months of Hitler's Reich, as the German armies retreated, the Nazis began marching the prisoners still alive in the concentration camps to the territory they still controlled. The Germans forced the starving and sick Jews to walk hundreds of miles. Most died or were shot along the way. About a quarter of a million Jews died on the death marches.

Jewish Resistance

The Germans' overwhelming repression and the presence of many collaborators in the various local populations severely limited the ability of the Jews to resist. Jewish resistance did occur, however, in several forms. Staying alive, clean, and observing Jewish religious traditions constituted resistance under the dehumanizing conditions imposed by the Nazis. Other forms of resistance involved escape attempts from the ghettos and camps. Many who succeeded in escaping the ghettos lived in the forests and mountains in family camps and in fighting partisan units. Once free, though, the Jews had to contend with local residents and partisan groups who were often openly hostile. Jews also staged armed revolts in the ghettos of Vilna, Bialystok, Bedzin-Sosnowiec, Cracow, and Warsaw.

The Warsaw Ghetto Uprising was the largest ghetto revolt. Massive deportations (or *Aktions*) had been held in the ghetto from July to September 1942, emptying the ghetto of the majority of Jews imprisoned there. When the Germans entered the ghetto again in January 1943 to remove several thousand more, small unorganized groups of Jews attacked them. After four days, the Germans withdrew from the ghetto, having deported far fewer people than they had intended. The Nazis reentered the ghetto on April 19, 1943, the eve of Passover, to evacuate the remaining Jews and close the ghetto. The Jews, using homemade bombs and stolen or bartered weapons, resisted and withstood the Germans for 27 days. They fought from bunkers and sewers and evaded capture until the Germans burned the ghetto building by building. By May 16 the ghetto was in ruins and the uprising crushed.

Jews also revolted in the death camps of Sobibor, Treblinka and Auschwitz. All of these acts of resistance were largely unsuccessful in the face of the superior German forces, but they were very important spiritually, giving the Jews hope that one day the Nazis would be defeated.

Liberation and the End of War

The camps were liberated gradually, as the Allies advanced on the German army. For example, Maidanek (near Lublin, Poland) was liberated by Soviet forces in July 1944, Auschwitz in January 1945 by the Soviets, Bergen-Belsen (near Hanover, Germany) by the British in April 1945, and Dachau by the Americans in April 1945.

At the end of the war, between 50,000 and 100,000 Jewish survivors were living in three zones of occupation: American, British and Soviet. Within a year, that figure grew to about 200,000. The American zone of occupation contained more than 90 percent of the Jewish displaced persons (DPs). The Jewish DPs would not and could not return to their homes, which brought back such horrible memories and still held the threat of danger from anti-Semitic neighbors. Thus, they languished in DP camps until emigration could be arranged to Palestine, and later Israel, the United States, South America and other countries. The last DP camp closed in 1957.

Below are figures for the number of Jews murdered in each country that came under German domination. They are estimates, as are all figures relating to Holocaust victims. The numbers given here for Czechoslovakia, Hungary and Romania are based on their territorial borders before the 1938 Munich agreement. The total number of six million Jews murdered during the Holocaust, which emerged from the Nuremberg trials, is also an estimate. Numbers have ranged between five and seven million killed.

Africa	526
Albania	200
Austria	65,000
Belgium	24,387
Czechoslovakia	277,000
Denmark	77
Estonia	4,000
France	83,000
Germany	160,000
Greece	71,301
Hungary	305,000
Italy	8,000
Latvia	85,000
Lithuania	135,000
Luxembourg	700
Netherlands	106,000
Norway	728
Poland	3,001,000
Romania	364,632
Soviet Union	1,500,000
Yugoslavia	67,122

The Nuremberg Laws

Lucy S. Dawidowicz

Looking back on World War II, it is typical to think of
Hitler as a dictator who seized power and ruthlessly murdered the Jews. It is important, however, to remember
that Hitler was democratically elected. The Nazi Party
was supported by a significant proportion of the German
people. Moreover, Hitler used legal means to concentrate
power in his hands (of course, he also used terror to eliminate his opponents). In January 1933 Hitler became
chancellor. When a Dutch Communist set fire to the Reichstag, the German parliament building, Hitler blamed
the fire on the Communists, outlawed their party, and arrested their leaders. The following month Germany held
its last free election. The Nazis won only 43 percent of the
vote; nevertheless, the *Reichstag* passed the Enabling Act,
which gave Hitler dictatorial powers. He used them to
abolish trade unions, dismantle all competing parties, and
eliminate his political opponents. Though terror was also
used against the Jews, persecution in the early years was
done primarily through increasingly restrictive legislation
that prevented them from working, attending school, or
functioning as normal members of German society. This
excerpt discusses the anti-Jewish legislation adopted by
the Nazis, which foreshadowed the extralegal measures
taken later. The late Lucy S. Dawidowicz was one of the
leading Holocaust authors. She taught modern Jewish history at Yeshiva University, Stanford, and the State University of New York at Albany. She wrote several books on
the Holocaust, including the seminal work from which
this excerpt is taken.

Excerpted from Lucy S. Dawidowicz, *The War Against the Jews, 1933–1945.* Copyright © 1975 by Lucy S. Dawidowicz. Reprinted with permission from Henry Holt
and Company, LLC.

The legislation that Hitler's government began to enact sanctioned what violence had already accomplished to a considerable extent—the elimination of Jews from government service and public life. On April 7, two days after Hitler's letter to [President Paul von] Hindenburg promising a "legal" solution to the "Jewish problem," the first anti-Jewish law in the Third Reich was promulgated. Eventually, some four hundred laws and decrees were enacted, inexorably leading to the destruction of the European Jews. The first decree, entitled "Law for the Restoration of the Professional Civil Service," authorized the elimination from the civil service of Jews and political opponents of the Nazi regime. "Civil servants of non-Aryan descent must retire," and honorary officials "must be discharged." Hindenburg's objections were met in a paragraph exempting "officials who were already employed as civil servants on or before August 1, 1914, or who, during the World War, fought at the front for Germany or her allies, or whose fathers or sons were killed in action in the World War."

A companion law, promulgated at the same time, canceled the admission to the bar of lawyers of "non-Aryan" descent and denied permission to those already admitted to practice law, with the Hindenburg exemptions. In rapid succession came similar laws excluding Jews from posts as lay assessors, jurors, and commercial judges (April 7), patent lawyers (April 22), panel physicians in state social-insurance institutions (April 22), dentists and dental technicians associated with those institutions (June 2). On April 25 the Law Against the Overcrowding of German Schools and Institutions of Higher Learning was promulgated, limiting the attendance of "non-Aryan" Germans to a proportion to be "determined uniformly for the entire Reich territory." An accompanying executive decree set that ratio for the admission of new pupils at 1.5 percent until the proportion of "non-Aryans" would be reduced to a maximum of 5 percent. On May 6 the Law for the Restoration of the Professional Civil Service was extended to affect honorary professors, university lecturers, and notaries. With the promulgation of three more laws— the first forbidding the employment by government authorities of "non-Aryans" or of persons married to them (September 28, 1933); the second establishing a Reich Chamber of Culture (September 29, 1933), which saw to the exclusion of Jews from cultural and entertainment enterprises (art, literature, theater, motion pictures); and the third, the National Press Law (October 4, 1933), placing political newspapers under state supervision and applying the so-called Aryan paragraph to newspapermen—the Nazi regime had accomplished a cardinal objective toward which German professionals and academicians had striven as far back as 1847: the exclusion of Jews from public life, government, culture, and the professions.

To simplify and clarify this procedure, a decree defining a "non-Aryan" promulgated on April 11. A "non-Aryan" was anyone "descended from non-Aryan, especially Jewish, parents or grandparents." Descent was "non-Aryan" even if only one parent or grandparent was "non-Aryan": "This is to be assumed especially if one parent or grandparent was of Jewish faith." Thus, in cases of "racial" ambiguity, the religious affiliation would be decisive. Every civil servant had to prove "Aryan" descent, through submission of the appropriate documents—birth certificates and parents' marriage certificate. (Eventually, elaborate genealogical questionnaires had to be answered.) Finally, to deal with ambiguous or exceptional cases, the decree provided that "if Aryan descent is doubtful, an opinion must be obtained from the expert on racial research attached by the Reich Minister of the Interior."

What Is a Jew?

The Nazi definition was simple: a Jew is a Jew is a Jew—that is, down to the third generation. The files of the Ministry of the Interior probably bulged with legal formulas defining who was a Jew. . . .

Three other laws were promulgated in 1933. . . . On April 21, a law was promulgated banning *shehitah*, Jewish ritual slaughtering animals for food. . . .

The Law on the Revocation of Naturalization and Annulment of German Citizenship, promulgated July 14, canceled . . . naturalization of "undesirables," which had been granted during the lifetime of the Weimar Republic. The law's executive order (July 26) specified East European Jews as political undesirables, even if they had committed no offense. On September 29 the Hereditary Farm Law was issued, stipulating that only those farmers could inherit farm property who could prove that their ancestors had no Jewish blood as far back as 1800. . . .

With German thoroughness, the laws had seen to it that the Jews were dismissed from all positions in public life—government, professions, and all of Germany's social, educational, and cultural institutions. Both instrumental and affective purposes were served by the enactment of this legislation. For one thing, thousands of jobs became available. Furthermore, the ouster of the Jews brought high elation, solidified party loyalty, and augmented party strength. What had begun as popular anti-Semitism, when the taste of victory had stimulated the taste for blood, now received complete legal sanction. . . .

More Terror

At the end of March 1935 acts of terror and boycotts of Jewish businesses were renewed. All local and national NSDAP [Nazi] party organizations and their associated institutions joined in a massive discharge of hate and violence. During the summer of 1935 Jews were prevented from going into cinemas, theaters, swimming pools, resorts. Small businesses were paralyzed by boycott and by violence, particularly in Berlin's main shopping street. Jewish newspapers were forced to suspend publication for periods of two to three months. . . .

As once before in 1933, so now in 1935, the violence of anti-Semitism was channeled into law. On the occasion of the annual NSDAP congress in Nuremberg, new anti-Jewish laws, the so-called "Nuremberg Laws," were adopted unanimously by the Reichstag, on September 15, 1935. These laws legitimated racist anti-Semitism and turned the "purity of German blood" into a legal category. They forbade marriage and extramarital relations between Germans and Jews and disenfranchised those "subjects" or "nationals" of Germany who were not of German blood. . . .

Anti-Jewish Legislation

Before long the Law for the Protection of German Blood and German Honor . . . was completed. Its preamble declared:

Imbued with the insight that the purity of German blood is prerequisite for the continued existence of the German people, and inspired by the inflexible will to ensure the existence of the German nation for all times, the Reichstag has unanimously adopted the following law, which is hereby promulgated.

The provisions were simplicity itself: marriage between Jews and "nationals of German kindred blood" was forbidden; extramarital relations between the two groups were forbidden. Jews were forbidden to employ female domestic help under forty-five years of age who were of "German or kindred blood." Finally, Jews were forbidden to fly the German national colors, but could display "Jewish" colors.

Then Hitler asked them to prepare a basic Reich citizenship law. . . . This law gave the Jews a special status as subjects in Germany. . . . The Reich Citizenship Law distinguished between a subject *(Staatsangehörige)* and a citizen of the Reich *(Reichsbürger)*. A subject was anyone who enjoyed the protection of the Reich and was therefore obligated to it. A Reich citizen was a subject with "German or cognate blood" and acquired a "Reich certificate of citizenship," a reward that Hitler had already conceived in *Mein Kampf.* . . .

The Reich Citizenship Law perpetrated a fantastic hoax upon the Germans. The Reich citizen was declared to be the "sole bearer of full political rights." But rights no longer existed in Germany. There were no political parties, no elections, no freedoms, no protection. The only right a citizen had was to give his assent—by shouting himself hoarse at mass rallies or by voting *"Ja"* in one of the five plebiscites that Hitler had substituted for political democracy. For unless the Reich citizen was *kadavergehorsam* [slavishly obedient], he would more likely be cadaver than citizen.

The Jews, however, were not hoaxed. The law and its thirteen supplementary decrees (the last published July 1, 1943) set the Jews apart from the Germans legally, politically, socially. Henceforth, they would be outside the protection of the state. Eventually, they would be completely at the mercy of the secret police, without access to law or courts. Indeed, the *Sachsenspiegel* [a thirteenth-century authoritative legal code in northern Germany] had been far more humane in the protection it afforded the Jew as alien.

The centrality of "blood and race" that obsessed National Socialism was transformed with bureaucratic fastidiousness into legal racial categories. While drafting the Law for the Protection of German Blood and German Honor, the legal experts proposed certain distinctions among different categories of *Mischlinge*, the "mixed" offspring of Germans and Jews. Hitler had rejected these at the time, but left their legal clarification for supplementary decrees. After week-long conferences of legal and racial experts (Hitler had himself called a meeting on this subject), the Ministry of the Interior finally arrived at a set of definitions of the different categories of *Mischlinge*. The basic definition of a Jew, supplanting the definition of April 11, 1933, was published November 14, 1935, in the first supplementary decree to the Reich Citizenship Law. Later regulations defined categories of *Mischlinge* that did not come under the rubric of "Jew."

Briefly, the categories were: (1) Jew, (2) *Mischling*, first degree, and (3) *Mischling*, second degree. A Jew was anyone with at least three full Jewish grandparents. Also legally to be regarded as a Jew was someone who had two full Jewish grandparents and who belonged to the Jewish religious community when the law was promulgated September 15, 1935, or who joined later, or who was married to a Jew then or later, or (looking to the future) who was the offspring of a marriage contracted with a Jew after September 15, 1935, or who was born out of wedlock after July 31, 1936, the offspring of extramarital relations with a Jew. Anyone who was one-eighth or one-sixteenth Jewish—with one Jewish great-grand-parent or great-great-grandparent—would be considered as of German blood.

More complicated was the status of the "part-Jews." A person with two Jewish grandparents, who did not otherwise fit into the group defined as Jews, that is, who was not affiliated with the Jewish religious community, who was not married to a Jew, etc., was designated as "*Mischling*, first degree." A person with only one Jewish grandparent was designated as "*Mischling*, second degree." For the time being, these distinctions affected marriage and offspring of that marriage. Within a few short years they were to decide between life or death.

The Nuremberg Laws completed the disenfranchisement of the Jews of Germany. The first stage of the National Socialist program had been achieved. Hitler himself, in introducing the laws to the Reichstag assembled at Nuremberg, hinted at a forthcoming change in anti-Jewish policy. The Law for the Protection of German Blood and German Honor, he said, was "an attempt to regulate by law a problem that, in the event of repeated failure, would have to be transferred by law to the National Socialist Party for final solution."

Jews in Germany: From Citizens to Outcasts

Saul Friedländer

Adolf Hitler never hid his attitude toward the Jews or his intention to exterminate them. One of the incredible aspects of the Holocaust is how he put his goal into practice in a country considered the most sophisticated and civilized in Europe, and where Jews played such a prominent role in virtually every part of society. Whatever his desires, Hitler could not immediately begin the "Final Solution" after coming to power in 1933. A slow, methodical process was required to make respectable German Jews outcasts and to dehumanize them to the point where they could be murdered with impunity. This excerpt describes how the persecution of the Jews escalated from banning Jewish musicians from performing to taking away their citizenship and ultimately their lives. Saul Friedländer grew up in Nazi-occupied France. Considered one of the leading authorities on the Holocaust, he teaches at the University of California at Los Angeles and at Tel Aviv University.

The exodus from Germany of Jewish and left-wing artists and intellectuals began during the early months of 1933, almost immediately after Adolf Hitler's accession to power on January 30. The philosopher and literary critic Walter Benjamin left Berlin for Paris on March 18. Two days later he wrote to his colleague and friend, Gershom Scholem, who lived in Palestine: "I can at least be certain that I did not act on impulse. . . . Nobody among those who are close to me judges the matter differently." The novelist Lion Feuchtwanger, who had reached the safety of Switzerland, confided in his fellow writer Arnold Zweig: "It was too late for me to save anything. . . . All that was there is lost."

The conductors Otto Klemperer and Bruno Walter were compelled to flee. Walter was forbidden access to his Leipzig orchestra, and, as he was about to conduct a special concert of the Berlin Philharmonic, he was informed that, according to rumors circulated by the Propaganda Ministry, the hall of the Philharmonic would be burned down if he did not withdraw. Walter left the country. Hans Hinkel, the new president of the Prussian Theater Commission and also responsible for the "de-Judaization" of cultural life in Prussia, explained in the April 6 *Frankfurter Zeitung* that Klemperer and Walter had disappeared from the musical scene because there was no way to protect them against the "mood" of a German public long provoked by "Jewish artistic bankrupters.". . .

Albert Einstein was visiting the United States on January 30, 1933. It did not take him long to react. Describing what was happening in Germany as a "psychic illness of the masses," he ended his return journey in Ostend (Belgium) and never again set foot on German soil. The Kaiser Wilhelm Society dismissed him from his position; the Prussian Academy of Sciences expelled him; his citizenship was rescinded. Einstein was no longer a German. . . .

As peripheral as it may seem in hindsight, the cultural domain was the first from which Jews (and "leftists") were massively expelled. . . . Thus, even before launching their first systematic anti-Jewish measures of exclusion, the new rulers of Germany had turned against the most visible representative of the "Jewish spirit" that henceforth was to be eradicated. In general the major anti-Jewish measures the Nazis would take from then on in the various domains were not only acts of terror but also symbolic statements. . . . The regime's initiatives engendered a kind of split consciousness in a great part of the population: For instance, people might not agree with the brutality of the dismissals of Jewish intellectuals from their positions, but they welcomed the cleansing of the "excessive influence" of Jews from German cultural life. . . .

Jews Stay Calm

A benefit for Jewish handicrafts had taken place at Berlin's Café Leon on January 30, 1933. The news of Hitler's accession to the chancellorship became known shortly before the event began. Among the attending representatives of Jewish organizations and political movements, only the Zionist rabbi Hans Tramer referred to the news and spoke of it as a major change; all the other speakers kept to their announced subjects. Tramer's speech "made no impression. The entire audience considered it panic-mongering. There was no response." The board of the Central Association of German Citizens of the Jewish Faith (*Zentralverein deutscher Staatsbürger jüdischen Glaubens*) on the same day concluded a public declaration in the same spirit: "In general, today more than ever we must follow the directive: wait calmly." An editorial in the association's newspaper for January 30, written by the organization's chairman, Ludwig Hollander, was slightly more worried in tone, but showed basically the same stance: "The German Jews will not lose the calm they derive from their tie to all that is truly German. Less than ever will they allow external attacks, which they consider unjustified, to influence their inner attitude toward Germany."

By and large there was no apparent sense of panic or even of urgency among the great majority of the approximately 525,000 Jews living in Germany in January 1933. As the weeks went by, Max Naumann's Association of National German Jews and the Reich Association of Jewish War Veterans hoped for no less than integration into the new order of things. On April 4, the veterans' association chairman, Leo Löwenstein, addressed a petition to Hitler including a list of nationalistically oriented suggestions regarding the Jews of Germany, as well as a copy of the memorial book containing the names of the twelve thousand German soldiers of Jewish origin who had died for Germany during the World War. Ministerial Councillor Wienstein answered on April 14 that the chancellor acknowledged receipt of the letter and the book with "sincerest feelings." The head of the Chancellery, Hans Heinrich Lammers, received a delegation of the veterans on the twenty-eighth, but with that the contacts ceased. Soon Hitler's office stopped acknowledging petitions from the Jewish organization. Like the Central Association, the Zionists continued to believe that the initial upheavals could be overcome by a reassertion of Jewish identity or simply by patience; the Jews reasoned that the responsibilities of power, the influence of conservative members of the government, and a watchful outside world would exercise a moderating influence on any Nazi tendency to excess.

Even after the April 1 Nazi boycott of Jewish businesses, some well-known German-Jewish figures, such as Rabbi Joachim Prinz, declared that it was unreasonable to take an anti-Nazi position. For Prinz, arguing against Germany's "reorganization," whose aim was "to give people bread and work. . .was neither intended nor possible." The declaration may have been merely tactical, and it must be kept in mind that many Jews were at a loss how to react. . . .

For some Jews the continuing presence of the old, respected President Paul von Hindenburg as head of state was a source of confidence; they occasionally wrote to him about their distress. "I was engaged to be married in 1914," Frieda Friedmann, a Berlin woman, wrote to Hindenburg on February 23: "My fiancé was killed in action in 1914. My brothers Max and Julius Cohn were killed in 1916 and 1918. My remaining brother, Willy, came back blind. . . . All three received the Iron Cross for their service to the country. But now it has gone so far that in our country pamphlets saying, 'Jews, get out!' are being distributed on the streets, and there are open calls for pogroms and acts of violence against Jews. . . . Is incitement against Jews a sign of courage or one of cowardice when Jews comprise only one percent of the German people?" Hindenburg's office promptly acknowledged receipt of the letter, and the president let Frieda Friedmann know that he was decidedly opposed to excesses perpetrated against Jews. The letter was transmitted to Hitler, who wrote in the margin: "This lady's claims are a swindle! Obviously there has been no incitement to a pogrom!"

The Jews finally, like a considerable part of German society as a whole, were not sure—particularly before the March 5, 1933, Reichstag elections—whether the Nazis were in power to stay or whether a conservative military coup against them was still possible. . . .

Hitler Becomes Dictator

The primary political targets of the new regime and of its terror system, at least during the first months after the Nazi accession to power, were not Jews but Communists. After the Reichstag fire of February 27, the anti-Communist hunt led to the arrest of almost ten thousand party members and sympathizers and to their imprisonment in newly created concentration camps. Dachau had been established on March 20 and was officially inaugurated by SS chief Heinrich Himmler on April 1. In June, SS Group Leader Theodor Eicke became the camp's commander, and a year later he was appointed "inspector of concentration camps": Under Himmler's aegis he had become the architect of the life-and-death routine of the camp inmates in Hitler's new Germany.

After the mass arrests that followed the Reichstag fire, it was clear that the "Communist threat" no longer existed. But the new regime's frenzy of repression—and innovation—did not slacken; quite the contrary. A presidential decree of February 28 had already given Hitler emergency powers. Although the Nazis failed to gain an absolute majority in the March 5 elections, their coalition with the ultraconservative German National People's Party (*Deutschnationale Volkspartei*, or DNVP) obtained it. A few days later, on March 23, the Reichstag divested itself of its functions by passing the Enabling Act, which gave full legislative and executive powers to the chancellor (at the outset new legislation was discussed with the cabinet ministers, but the final decision was Hitler's). The rapidity of changes that followed was stunning: The states were brought into line; in May the trade unions were abolished and replaced by the German Labor Front; in July all political parties were dissolved with the sole exception of the National Socialist German Workers Party (*Nationalsozialistische Deutsche Arbeiterpartei*, or NSDAP). Popular support for this torrential activity and constant demonstration of power snowballed. In the eyes of a rapidly growing number of Germans, a "national revival" was under way. . . .

Anti-Jewish violence spread after the March elections. On the ninth, Storm Troopers (*Sturmabteilung*, or SA) seized dozens of East European Jews in the *Scheunenviertel*, one of Berlin's Jewish quarters. Traditionally the first targets of German Jew-hatred, these *Ostjuden* were also the first Jews as Jews to be sent off to concentration camps. On March 13 forcible closing of Jewish shops was imposed by the local SA in Mannheim; in Breslau, Jewish lawyers and judges were assaulted in the court building; and in Gedern, in Hesse, the SA broke into Jewish homes and beat up the inhabitants "with the acclamation of a rapidly growing crowd." The list of similar incidents is a long one. There were also killings. . . .

Much of the foreign press gave wide coverage to the Nazi violence. The *Christian Science Monitor*, however, expressed doubts about the accuracy of the reports of Nazi atrocities, and later justified retaliation against "those who spread lies against Germany." And Walter Lippmann, the most prominent American political commentator of the day and himself a Jew, found words of praise for Hitler and could not resist a sideswipe at the Jews. These notable exceptions notwithstanding, most American newspapers did not mince words about the anti-Jewish persecution. Jewish and non-Jewish protests grew. These very protests became the Nazis' pretext for the notorious April 1, 1933, boycott of Jewish businesses. Although the anti-Nazi campaign in the United States was discussed at some length during a cabinet meeting on March 24, the final decision in favor of the boycott was probably made during a March 26 meeting of Hitler and Goebbels in Berchtesgaden. But in mid-March, Hitler had already allowed a committee headed by Julius Streicher, party chief of Franconia and editor of the party's most vicious anti-Jewish newspaper, *Der Stürmer*, to proceed with preparatory work for it.

Jews Are Boycotted

In fact, the boycott had been predictable from the very moment the Nazis acceded to power. The possibility had often been mentioned during the two preceding years, when Jewish small businesses had been increasingly harassed and Jewish employees increasingly discriminated against in the job market. . . .

Hitler informed the cabinet of the planned boycott of Jewish-owned businesses on March 29, telling the ministers that he himself had called for it. He described the alternative as spontaneous popular violence. An approved boycott, he added, would avoid dangerous unrest. The German National ministers objected, and President Hindenburg tried to intervene. Hitler rejected any possible cancellation, but two days later (the day before the scheduled boycott) he suggested the possibility of postponing it until April 4—if the British and American governments were to declare immediately their opposition to the anti-German agitation in their countries; if not, the action would take place on April 1, to be followed by a waiting period until April 4.

On the evening of the thirty-first, the British and American government, declared their readiness to make the necessary declaration. . . .

In the meantime Jewish leaders, mainly in the United States and Palestine, were in a quandary: Should they support mass protests and a counterboycott of German goods, or should confrontation be avoided for fear of further "reprisals" against the Jews of Germany? [Nazi minister Hermann] Göring had summoned several leaders of German Jewry and sent them to London to intervene against planned anti-German demonstrations and initiatives. Simultaneously, on March 26, Kurt Blumenfeld, president of the Zionist Federation for Germany, and Julius Brodnitz, president of the Central Association, cabled the American Jewish Committee in New York: WE PROTEST CATEGORICALLY AGAINST HOLDING MONDAY MEETING, RADIO AND OTHER DEMONSTRATIONS. WE UNEQUIVOCALLY DEMAND ENERGETIC EFFORTS TO OBTAIN AN END TO DEMONSTRATIONS HOSTILE TO GERMANY. By appeasing the Nazis the fearful German-Jewish leaders were hoping to avoid the boycott.

The leaders of the Jewish community in Palestine also opted for caution, the pressure of public opinion notwithstanding. They sent a telegram to the Reich Chancellery "offering assurances that no authorized body in Palestine had declared or intended to declare a trade boycott of Germany." American Jewish leaders were divided; most of the Jewish organizations in the United States were opposed to mass demonstrations and economic action, mainly for fear of embarrassing the president and the State Department. Reluctantly, and under pressure from such groups as the Jewish War Veterans, the American Jewish Congress finally decided otherwise. On March 27 protest meetings took place in several American cities, with the participation of church and labor leaders. As for the boycott of German goods, it spread as an emotional grass-roots movement that, over the months, received an increasing measure of institutional support, at least outside Palestine. . . .

In principle the boycott could have caused serious economic damage to the Jewish population as, according to [historian] Avraham Barkai, "more than sixty percent of all gainfully employed Jews were concentrated in the commercial sector, the overwhelming majority of these in the retail trade. . . . Similarly, Jews in the industrial and crafts sectors were active largely as proprietors of small businesses and shops or as artisans." In reality, however, the Nazi action ran into immediate problems.

The population proved rather indifferent to the boycott and sometimes even intent on buying in "Jewish" stores. . . .

The lack of popular enthusiasm was compounded by a host of unforeseen questions. How was a "Jewish" enterprise to be defined? By its name, by the Jewishness of its directors, or by Jewish control of all or part of its capital? If the enterprise were hurt, what, in a time of economic crisis, would happen to its Aryan employees? What would be the overall consequences, in terms of possible foreign retaliation, of the action on the German economy? . . .

The possibility of further boycotts remained open. . . .

At the same time it was nonetheless becoming increasingly clear to Hitler himself that Jewish economic life was not to be openly interfered with, at least as long as the German economy was still in a precarious situation. A fear of foreign economic retaliation, whether orchestrated by the Jews or as an expression of genuine outrage at Nazi persecutions, was shared by Nazis and their conservative allies alike and dictated temporary moderation. . . .

According to the German Communist periodical *Rundschau*, by then published in Switzerland, only the smaller Jewish businesses—that is, the poorer Jews—were harmed by the Nazi boycott. Large enterprises such as the Berlin-based Ullstein publishing empire or Jewish-owned banks—Jewish big business—did not suffer at all. What looks like merely an expression of Marxist orthodoxy was in part true, because harming a Jewish department-store chain such as Tietz could have put its fourteen thousand employees out of work. For that very reason Hitler personally approved the granting of a loan to Tietz to ease its immediate financial difficulties. . . .

In March 1933, when Hans Luther was replaced by [Hjalmar] Schacht as president of the Reichsbank, three Jewish bankers still remained on the bank's eight-member council and signed the authorization of his appointment. This situation did not last much longer. As a result of Schacht's proddings and the party's steady pressure, the country's banks banished Jewish directors from their boards. . . .

During the first years of the regime, however, there are indications of a somewhat unexpected moderation and even helpfulness on the part of big business in its dealing with non-Aryan firms. Pressure for business takeovers and other ruthless exploitation of the weakened status of Jews came mainly from smaller, midsized enterprises, and much less so, at least until the fall of 1937, from the higher reaches of the economy. Some major corporations even retained the services of Jewish executives for years. But some precautions were taken. Thus, although most Jewish board members of the chemical industry giant I.G. Farben stayed on for a while, the closest Jewish associates of its president, Carl Bosch, such as Ernst Schwarz and Edmund Pietrowski, were reassigned to positions outside the Reich, the former in New York, the latter in Switzerland.

Highly visible Jews had to go, of course. Within a few months, the banker Max Warburg was excluded from one corporate board after another. . . .

Aryanization

When the Nazis acceded to power, they could in principle refer to the goals of their anti-Jewish policy as set down in the twenty-five-point party program of February 24, 1920. Points 4, 5, 6, and 8 dealt with concrete aspects of the "Jewish question." Point 4: "Only members of the nation may be citizens of the State. Only those of German blood, whatever their creed, may be members of the nation. Accordingly no Jew may be a member of the nation." Point 5: "Non-citizens may live in Germany only as guests and must be subject to laws for aliens." Point 6: "The right to vote on the state's government and legislation shall be enjoyed by the citizens of the state alone." Point 8: "All non-German immigration must be prevented. We demand that all non-Germans who entered Germany after 2 August 1914 shall be required to leave the Reich forthwith." Point 23 demanded that control of the German press be solely in the hands of Germans.

Nothing in the program indicated ways of achieving these goals, and the failure of the April 1933 boycott is a good example of the total lack of preparation for their tasks among Germany's new masters. But, at least in their anti-Jewish policy, the Nazis soon became masters of improvisation; adopting the main points of their 1920 program as short-term goals, they learned how to pursue them ever more systematically.

On March 9 State Secretary Heinrich Lammers conveyed a request from the Reich chancellor to Minister of the Interior Frick. He was asked by Hitler to take into consideration the suggestion of State Secretary Paul Bang of the Ministry of the Economy about the application of "a racial [*völkisch*] policy" toward East European Jews: prohibition of further immigration, cancellation of name changes made after 1918, and expulsion of a certain number of those who had not yet been naturalized. Within a week Frick responded by sending instructions to all states (*Länder*):

In order to introduce a racial policy (*völkische Politik*), it is necessary to:

1. Oppose the immigration of Eastern Jews.

2. Expel Eastern Jews living in Germany without a residence permit.
3. Stop the naturalization of Eastern Jews. . . .

The measures taken against the so-called Eastern Jews were overshadowed by the laws of April 1933. The first of them—the most fundamental one because of its definition of the Jew—was the April 7 Law for the Restoration of the Professional Civil Service. In its most general intent, the law aimed at reshaping the entire government bureaucracy in order to ensure its loyalty to the new regime. Applying to more than two million state and municipal employees, its exclusionary measures were directed against the politically unreliable, mainly Communists and other opponents of the Nazis, and against Jews. Paragraph 3, which came to be called the "Aryan paragraph," reads: "1. Civil servants not of Aryan origin are to retire. . . ." (Section 2 listed exceptions, which will be examined later.) On April 11 the law's first supplementary decree defined "non-Aryan" as "anyone descended from non-Aryan, particularly Jewish, parents of grandparents. It suffices if one parent or grandparent is non-Aryan.". . .

For the first time since completion of the emancipation of the German Jews in 1871, a government, by law, had reintroduced discrimination against the Jews. Up to this point the Nazis had unleashed the most extreme anti-Jewish propaganda and brutalized, boycotted, or killed Jews on the assumption that they could somehow be identified as Jews, but no formal disenfranchisement based on an exclusionary definition had yet been initiated. The definition as such—whatever its precise terms were to be in the future—was the necessary initial basis of all the persecutions that were to follow. . . .

In 1933 the number of Jews in the civil service was small. As a result of Hindenburg's intervention (following a petition by the Association of Jewish War Veterans that was also supported by the elderly Field Marshal August von Mackensen), combat veterans and civil servants whose fathers or sons had been killed in action in World War I were exempted from the law. Civil servants, moreover, who had been in state service by August 1, 1914, were also exempt. All others were forced into retirement. . . .

By the end of March, physical molestation of Jewish jurists had spread throughout the Reich. In Dresden, Jewish judges and lawyers were dragged out of their offices and even out of courtrooms during proceedings, and, more often than not, beaten up. . . . At the same time local Nazi leaders such as the Bavarian justice minister, Hans Frank, and the Prussian justice minister, Harms Kerrl, on their own initiative announced measures for the immediate dismissal of all Jewish lawyers and civil servants. . . .

The Justice Ministry had prepared a decree excluding Jewish lawyers from the bar on the same basis—but also with the same exemptions regarding combat veterans and their relatives, and longevity in practice, as under the Civil Service Law. . . . .

Because of the exemptions, the initial application of the law was relatively mild. Of the 4,585 Jewish lawyers practicing in Germany, 3,167 (or almost 70 percent) were allowed to continue their work; 336 Jewish judges and state prosecutors, out of a total of 717, were also kept in office. In June 1933 Jews still made up more than 16 percent of all practicing lawyers in Germany. These statistics should, however, not be misinterpreted. Though still allowed to practice, Jewish lawyers were excluded from the national association of lawyers and listed not in its annual directory but in a separate guide; all in all, notwithstanding the support of some Aryan institutions and individuals, they worked under a "boycott of fear."

Nazi rank-and-file agitation against Jewish physicians did not lag far behind the attacks on Jewish jurists. . . .

Hitler was even more careful with physicians than with lawyers. . . . He suggested that measures against them be postponed until an adequate information campaign could be organized. At this stage, after April 22, Jewish doctors were merely barred de facto from clinics and hospitals run by the national health insurance organization, with some even allowed to continue to practice there. Thus, in mid-1933, nearly 11 percent of all practicing German physicians were Jews. Here is another example of Hitler's pragmatism in action: Thousands of Jewish physicians meant tens of thousands of German patients. Disrupting the ties between these physicians and a vast number of patients could have caused unnecessary discontent. Hitler preferred to wait.

On April 25 the Law Against the Overcrowding of German Schools and Universities was passed. It was aimed exclusively against non-Aryan pupils and students. The law limited the matriculation of new Jewish students in any German school or university to 1.5 percent of the total of new applicants, with the overall number of Jewish pupils or students in any institution not to exceed 5 percent. Children of World War I veterans and those born of mixed marriages contracted before the passage of the law were exempted from the quota. The regime's intention was carefully explained in the press. According to the *Deutsche Allgemeine Zeitung* of April 27: "A self-respecting nation cannot, on a scale accepted up to now, leave its higher activities in the hands of people of racially foreign origin. . . . Allowing the presence of too high a percentage of people of foreign origin in relation to their percentage in the general population could be interpreted as an acceptance of the superiority of other races, something decidedly to be rejected."

The April laws and the supplementary decrees that followed compelled at least two million state employees and tens of thousands of lawyers, physicians, students, and many others to look for adequate proof of Aryan ancestry; the same process turned tens of thousands of priests, pastors, town clerks, and archivists into investigators and suppliers of vital attestations of impeccable blood purity; willingly or not these were becoming part of a racial bureaucratic machine that had begun to search, probe, and exclude. . . .

In September 1933 Jews were forbidden to own farms or engage in agriculture. That month the establishment, under the control of the Propaganda Ministry, of the Reich Chamber of Culture, enabled Goebbels to limit the participation of Jews in the new Germany's cultural life. (Their systematic expulsion, which would include not only writers and artists but also owners of important businesses in the cultural domain, was for that reason delayed until 1935.) Also under the aegis of Goebbels's Propaganda Ministry, Jews were barred from belonging to the Journalists' Association and, on October 4, from being newspaper editors. The German press had been cleansed. (Exactly a year later, Goebbels recognized the right of Jewish editors and journalists to work, but only within the framework of the Jewish press.)

In Nazi racial thinking, the German national community drew its strength from the purity of its blood and from its rootedness in the sacred German earth. Such racial purity was a condition of superior cultural creation and of the construction of a powerful state, the guarantor of victory in the struggle for racial survival and domination. From the outset, therefore, the 1933 laws pointed to the exclusion of the Jews from all key areas of this utopian vision: the state structure itself (the Civil Service Law), the biological health of the national community (the physicians' law), the social fabric of the community (the disbarring of Jewish lawyers), culture (the laws regarding schools, universities, the press, the cultural professions), and, finally, the sacred earth (the farm law). The Civil Service Law was the only one of these to be fully implemented at this early stage, but the symbolic statements they expressed and the ideological message they carried were unmistakable.

Seeing the Future

Very few German Jews sensed the implications of the Nazi laws in terms of sheer long-range terror. One who did was Georg Solmssen, spokesman for the board of directors of the Deutsche Bank and son of an Orthodox Jew. In an April 9, 1933, letter addressed to the bank's board chairman, after pointing out that even the non-Nazi part of the population seemed to consider the new measures "self-evident," Solmssen added: "I am afraid that we are merely at the beginning of a process aiming, purposefully and according to a well-prepared plan, at the economic and moral annihilation of all members, without any distinctions, of the Jewish race living in Germany. The total passivity not only of those classes of the population that belong to the National Socialist Party, the absence of all feelings of solidarity becoming apparent among those who until now worked shoulder to shoulder with Jewish colleagues, the increasingly more obvious desire to take personal advantage of vacated positions, the hushing up of the disgrace and the shame disastrously inflicted upon people who, although innocent, witness the destruction of their honor and their existence from one day to the next—all of this indicates a situation so hopeless that it would be wrong not to face it squarely without any attempt at prettification."

Persecution Spreads

The City of Cologne forbade the use of municipal sports facilities to Jews in March 1933. Beginning April 3 requests by Jews in Prussia for name changes were to be submitted to the Justice Ministry, "to prevent the covering up of origins." On April 4 the German Boxing Association excluded all Jewish boxers. On April 8 all Jewish teaching assistance at universities in the state of Baden were to be expelled immediately. On April 18 the party district chief (Gauleiter) of Westphalia decided that a Jew would be allowed to leave prison only if the two persons who had submitted the request for bail, or the doctor who had signed the medical certificate, were ready to take his place in prison. On April 19 the use of Yiddish was forbidden in cattle markets in Baden. On April 24 the use of Jewish names for spelling purposes in telephone communications was forbidden. On May 8 the mayor of Zweibrücken prohibited Jews from leasing places in the next annual town market. On May 13 the change of Jewish to non-Jewish names was forbidden. On May 24 the full Aryanization of the German gymnastics organization was ordered, with full Aryan descent of all four grandparents stipulated. Whereas in April Jewish doctors had been excluded from state-insured institutions, in May privately insured institutions were ordered to refund medical expenses for treatment by Jewish doctors only when the patients themselves were non-Aryan. Separate lists of Jewish and non-Jewish doctors would be ready by June. . . .

For young Hilma Geffen-Ludomer, the only Jewish child in the Berlin suburb of Rangsdorf, the Law Against the Overcrowding of German Schools meant total change. The "nice, neighborly atmosphere" ended "abruptly. . . . Suddenly, I didn't have any friends. I had no more girlfriends, and many neighbors were afraid to talk to us. Some of the neighbors that we visited told me: 'Don't come anymore because I'm scared. We should not have any contact with Jews.'" Lore Gang-Salheimer, eleven in 1933 and living in Nuremberg, could remain in her school as her father had fought at Verdun. Nonetheless "it began to happen that non-Jewish children would say, 'No I can't walk home from school with you anymore. I can't be seen with you anymore.'" "With every passing day under Nazi rule," wrote Martha Appel, "the chasm between us and our neighbors grew wider. Friends with whom we had had warm relations for years did not know us anymore. Suddenly we discovered that we were different." . . .

The Genetically Inferior Should Die

The Law for the Prevention of Genetically Diseased Offspring (*Gesetz zur Verhütung erbkranken Nachwuchses*) was adopted on July 14, 1933, the day on which all political parties with the exception of the NSDAP were banned and the laws against Eastern Jews (cancellation of citizenship, an end to immigration, and so on) came into effect. The new law allowed for the sterilization of anyone recognized as suffering from supposedly hereditary diseases, such as feeble-mindedness, schizophrenia, manic-depressive insanity, genetic epilepsy, Huntington's chorea, genetic blindness, genetic deafness, and severe alcoholism.

The evolution leading to the July 1933 law was already noticeable during the Weimar period. Among eugenicists, the promoters of "positive eugenics" were losing ground, and "negative eugenics"—with its emphasis on the exclusion, that is, mainly the sterilization, of carriers of incapacitating hereditary diseases—was gaining the upper hand even within official institutions: A trend that had appeared on a wide scale in the West before World War I was increasingly dominating the German scene. As in so many other domains, the war was of decisive importance: Weren't the young and the physically fit being slaughtered on the battlefield while the incapacitated and the unfit were being shielded? Wasn't the reestablishment of genetic equilibrium a major national-racial imperative? Economic thinking added its own logic: The social cost of maintaining mentally and physically handicapped individuals whose reproduction would only increase the burden was considered prohibitive. . . . Although the draft of a sterilization law submitted to the Prussian government in July 1932 still emphasized *voluntary* sterilization in case of hereditary defects, the ideas of *compulsory* sterilization seems to have been spreading. It was nonetheless with the Nazi accession to power that the decisive change took place. . . .

Paragraph 12, section 1, of the new law stated that once sterilization had been decided upon, it could be implemented "against the will of the person to be sterilized.". . . It seems, though, that even before 1933, patients in some psychiatric institutions were being sterilized without their own or their families' consent. About two hundred thousand people were sterilized between mid–1933 and the end of 1937. By the end of the war, the number had reached four hundred thousand.

From the outset of the sterilization policies to the apparent ending of euthanasia in August 1941—and to the beginning of the "Final Solution" close to that same date—policies regarding the handicapped and the mentally ill on the one hand and those regarding the Jews on the other followed a simultaneous and parallel development. These two policies, however, had different origins and different aims. Whereas sterilization and euthanasia were exclusively aimed at enhancing the purity of the *Volksgemeinschaft* [community of people united by German blood], and were bolstered by cost-benefit computations, the segregation and the extermination of the Jews—though also a racial purification process—was mainly a struggle against an active, formidable enemy that was perceived endangering the very survival of Germany and of the Aryan world. Thus, in addition to the goal of racial cleansing, identical to that pursued in the sterilization and euthanasia campaign and in contrast to it, the struggle against the Jews was seen as a confrontation of apocalyptic dimensions.

Kristallnacht

Ben Austin

When Hitler assumed power, the measures he took against the Jews were primarily administrative and legislative, denying them various rights enjoyed by other Germans. Some Jews recognized that their future in Germany was no longer secure, but few could foresee that the Nazis would escalate their campaign from persecution to extermination. It was not until late 1938 that Jews were given a reason to worry about their safety. The organized attacks that were mounted against Jews on November 9 and 10— *Kristallnacht*—were a warning that the situation was going to get much worse before it got better. Of course, it is much easier to see this with the gift of hindsight; many Jews still did not realize that the night of murder and vandalism was only the prelude to a campaign of genocide. Ben Austin, a sociology professor at Middle Tennessee State University, describes in this article what happened on *Kristallnacht* and what that event meant.

Almost immediately upon assuming the Chancellorship of Germany, Hitler began promulgating legal actions against Germany's Jews. In 1933, he proclaimed a one-day boycott against Jewish shops, a law was passed against kosher butchering and Jewish children began experiencing restrictions in public schools. By 1935, the Nuremberg Laws deprived Jews of German citizenship. By 1936, Jews were prohibited from participation in parliamentary elections and signs reading "Jews Not Welcome" appeared in many German cities. . . .

In the first half of 1938, numerous laws were passed restricting Jewish economic activity and occupational oppor-

Excerpted from Ben Austin, "Kristallnacht," a 1999 online article found at www.us-israel.org/jsource/Holocaust/kristallnacht.html. Reprinted with permission from the author.

tunities. In July, 1938, a law was passed (effective January 1, 1939) requiring all Jews to carry identification cards. On October 28, 17,000 Jews of Polish citizenship, many of whom had been living in Germany for decades, were arrested and relocated across the Polish border. The Polish government refused to admit them so they were interned in "relocation camps" on the Polish frontier.

Among the deportees was Zindel Grynszpan, who had been born in western Poland and had moved to Hanover, where he established a small store, in 1911. On the night of October 27, Zindel Grynszpan and his family were forced out of their home by German police. His store and the family's possessions were confiscated and they were forced to move over the Polish border.

Zindel Grynszpan's seventeen-year-old son, Herschel, was living with an uncle in Paris. When he received news of his family's expulsion, he went to the German embassy in Paris on November 7, intending to assassinate the German Ambassador to France. Upon discovering that the Ambassador was not in the embassy, he settled for a lesser official, Third Secretary Ernst vom Rath. Rath, was critically wounded and died two days later, on November 9.

The assassination provided Joseph Goebbels, Hitler's Chief of Propaganda, with the excuse he needed to launch a pogrom against German Jews. Grynszpan's attack was interpreted by Goebbels as a conspiratorial attack by "International Jewry" against the Reich and, symbolically, against the Fuehrer himself. This pogrom has come to be called *Kristallnacht*, "the Night of Broken Glass."

Violence Begins

On the nights of November 9 and 10, rampaging mobs throughout Germany and the newly acquired territories of Austria and Sudetenland freely attacked Jews in the street, in their homes and at their places of work and worship. At least 96 Jews were killed and hundreds more injured, more than 1,000 synagogues were burned (and possibly as many as 2,000), almost 7,500 Jewish businesses were destroyed, cemeteries and schools were vandalized, and 30,000 Jews were arrested and sent to concentration camps. . . .

The official German position on these events, which were clearly orchestrated by Goebbels, was that they were spontaneous outbursts. The Fuehrer, Goebbels reported to Party officials in Munich, "has decided that such demonstrations are not to be prepared or organized by the party, but so far as they originate spontaneously, they are not to be discouraged either."

Three days later, on November 12, Hermann Goering called a meeting of the top Nazi leadership to assess the damage done during the night and place responsibility for it. Present at the meeting were Goering, Goebbels, Reinhard Heydrich, Walter Funk and other ranking Nazi officials. The intent of this meeting was two-fold: to make the Jews responsible for *Kristallnacht* and to use the events of the preceding days as a rationale for promulgating a series of antisemitic laws which would, in effect, remove Jews from the German economy. An interpretive transcript of this meeting is provided by Robert Conot, *Justice at Nuremberg*, New York: Harper and Row, 1983:164–172:

> "Gentlemen! Today's meeting is of a decisive nature," Goering announced. "I have received a letter written on the Fuehrer's orders requesting that the Jewish question be now, once and for all, coordinated and solved one way or another.

> "Since the problem is mainly an economic one, it is from the economic angle it shall have to be tackled. Because, gentlemen, I have had enough of these demonstrations! They don't harm the Jew but me, who is the final authority for coordinating the German economy. If today a Jewish shop is destroyed, if goods are thrown into the street, the insurance companies will pay for the damages; and, furthermore, consumer goods belonging to the people are destroyed. If in the future, demonstrations which are necessary occur, then, I pray, that they be directed so as not to hurt us.

> "Because it's insane to clean out and burn a Jewish warehouse, then have a German insurance company make good the loss. And the goods which I need desperately, whole bales of cloth-

ing and whatnot, are being burned. And I miss them everywhere. I may as well burn the raw materials before they arrive.

"I should not want to leave any doubt, gentlemen, as to the aim of today's meeting. We have not come together merely to talk again, but to make decisions, and I implore competent agencies to take all measures for the elimination of the Jew from the German economy, and to submit them to me."

It was decided at the meeting that, since Jews were to blame for these events, they be held legally and financially responsible for the damages incurred by the pogrom. Accordingly, a "fine of 1 billion marks was levied for the slaying of Vom Rath, and 6 million marks paid by insurance companies for broken windows was to be given to the state coffers."

A Turning Point

Kristallnacht turns out to be a crucial turning point in German policy regarding the Jews and may be considered as the *actual beginning of what is now called the Holocaust.*

1. By now it is clear to Hitler and his top advisors that forced [e]migration of Jews out of the Reich is not a feasible option.
2. Hitler is already considering the invasion of Poland.
3. Numerous concentration camps and forced labor camps are already in operation.
4. The Nuremberg Laws are in place.
5. The doctrine of *lebensraum* [living space] has emerged as a guiding principle of Hitler's ideology. And,
6. The passivity of the German people in the face of the events of *Kristallnacht* made it clear that the Nazis would encounter little opposition—even from the German churches.

Following the meeting, a wide-ranging set of antisemitic laws were passed which had the clear intent, in Goering's words, of "Aryanizing" the German economy. Over the next two or three months, the following measures were put into effect:

1. Jews were required to turn over all precious metals to the government.

2. Pensions for Jews dismissed from civil service jobs were arbitrarily reduced.
3. Jewish-owned bonds, stocks, jewelry and art works can be alienated only to the German state.
4. Jews were physically segregated within German towns.
5. A ban on the Jewish ownership of carrier pigeons.
6. The suspension of Jewish drivers' licenses.
7. The confiscation of Jewish-owned radios.
8. A curfew to keep Jews off the streets between 9:00 P.M. and 5:00 A.M. in the summer and 8:00 P.M. and 6:00 A.M. in the winter.
9. Laws protecting tenants were made non-applicable to Jewish tenants.
10. [Perhaps to help insure the Jews could not fight back in the future, the Minister of the Interior issued regulations against Jews' possession of weapons on November 11. This prohibited Jews from "acquiring, possessing, and carrying firearms and ammunition, as well as truncheons or stabbing weapons. Those now possessing weapons and ammunition are at once to turn them over to the local police authority."]

One final note on the November 12 meeting is of critical importance. In the meeting, Goering announced, "I have received a letter written on the Fuehrer's orders requesting that the Jewish question be now, once and for all, coordinated and solved one way or another." The path to the "Final Solution" has now been chosen. And, all the bureaucratic mechanisms for its implementation were now in place.

It should be noted that there is some controversy among Holocaust scholars as to the origin, intent and appropriateness of the term *Kristallnacht*. The term, after all, was coined by Walter Funk at the November 12 Nazi meeting following the pogrom of November 8–10. The crucial question is whether the term was a Nazi euphemism for an all-out pogrom against German Jews and whether the Nazis used the term in a derisive manner. There is considerable evidence that both of the above questions have an affirmative answer. . . .

What's in a Name?

[Editor] Walter Pehle makes the following observation:

It is clear that the term Crystal Night serves to foster a vicious minimalizing of its memory, a discounting of grave reality: such cynical appellations function to reinterpret manslaughter and murder, arson, robbery, plunder, and massive property damage, transforming these into a glistening event marked by sparkle and gleam. Of course, such terms reveal one thing in stark clarity—the lack of any sense of involvement or feeling of sympathy on the part of those who had stuck their heads in the sand before that violent night.

With good reason, knowledgeable commentators urge people to renounce the continued use of "Kristallnacht" and "Reichskristall-nacht" to refer to these events, even if the expressions have become slick and established usage in our language.

So, it appears, the term "Kristallnacht" or "Crystal Night" was invented by Nazis to mock Jews on that black November night in 1938. It is, therefore, another example of Nazi perversion. There are numerous other examples of this same tendency in the language of the Nazi perpetrators: *Sonderbehandlung* ("special treatment") for gassing victims, Euthanasia for a policy of mass murder of retarded or physically handicapped patients, Arbeit Macht Frei (Work Makes You Free) over the entrance to Auschwitz. When the Nazis launched their plan to annihilate the remaining Jews in Poland in the fall of 1943, they called it "Erntefest," or Harvest Festival. While this may have been a code word, . . . it had the same grim and terrible irony that is reflected in *Kristallnacht* as in so many other instances of the perverted uses of language in the Third Reich. Perhaps most cynical of all is the use of the term, "Endloesung der Judenfrage" (Final Solution of the Jewish Question), for what is now known as the Holocaust. Goebbels frequently used such terminology to amuse his audiences (usually other Nazi officials) and to further demoralize his victims.

On the other side of this controversy are those who argue

that the term should be retained. In the first place, it is the term which has been used now for fifty years and connotes significant meaning to those who study the Holocaust. As [Holocaust scholar] Froma Zeitlin observes:

> But I would like to point out that whether or not the name came into existence as a Nazi euphemism or not, the event itself and what it has come to signify has transformed an "innocent" name into one of unforgettable and dramatic meaning. The term is permanently out of circulation for any other use whatsoever. Can you imagine us now using "Kristallnacht" to refer to some street riot or another, no matter how extensively the streets were littered with broken glass? Certainly not. Moreover, what disturbed the German populace was less the sight of synagogues burning (fires take place all the time, after all—it depends on the scale) than of the savage and wasteful vandalism that confronted bystanders everywhere, disrupting the clean and orderly streets (to say nothing of consumer convenience). What was indeed memorable was the sheer quantity of broken glass. A third point was the economic outcome of this massive breakage. Germany didn't produce enough plate glass to repair the damages (synagogues did not have to be replaced—quite the contrary). The result was twofold: the need to import glass from Belgium (for sorely needed cash) and the outrage of indemnifying the Jewish community to pay for the damages. So the broken glass came to assume yet another outrageous dimension in the wake of the event.

Confinement in Ghettos

Yehuda Bauer

For most people the first image that comes to mind when the word *Holocaust* is mentioned is a concentration camp; however, tens of thousands of Jews died long before they were sent to camps. Millions of Jews living in Eastern Europe and hundreds of thousands in Poland and parts of the Soviet Union were first herded into ghettos. Some ghettos were closed while others were relatively open—at least for a while. Ghetto life might not seem so bad compared to that of the camps; after all, Jews still had some possessions, could live in houses and sleep in regular beds, work (sometimes for pay), and were not subject to the daily rigors and brutalization of camp life. Ghetto life was nevertheless one of squalor, hunger, disease, and despair that grew worse as time passed. Humiliation and brutality became more common, and the constant fear of deportation to an unknown (but probably worse) fate was ever present. This excerpt describes some of the deprivations that the Jews in ghettos faced and the efforts they made—establishing schools, holding religious services, forming orchestras—to retain a measure of normalcy and dignity. Yehuda Bauer is one of the foremost authorities on the Holocaust and the Jona M. Machover Professor of Holocaust Studies and a permanent academic chair of the Institute of Contemporary Jewry at Hebrew University. He has also served as chair of the Vidal Sassoon International Center for the Study of Anti-Semitism.

The ghettoes provided slave labor for the Nazi war machine. From the first days of German occupation, in addition to slave labor camps, the ghettoes supplied labor for German offices, installations, and workshops. In other instances, Jewish slave labor had no recognizable purpose other than dehumanization. In some locations, wages were not paid; in others a minimal sum of 0.50–0.80 reichsmarks ($1 = 2.50 RM) per day was paid. . . .

In the Warsaw ghetto a new aristocracy arose, an aristocracy of smugglers who frequented expensive cafes and restaurants to obtain food. Ruthless and lacking in social consciousness, the smugglers nevertheless risked their lives to bring in food and other essential products. Without them, the ghettoes would have died out quickly. Formerly wealthy people, in contrast, frequently lost their will to live and joined those begging for food on the streets. . . .

In the Warsaw ghetto, the most serious problem was the tremendous influx of refugees . . . . Of a population of close to 450,000 early in 1941, 150,000 were refugees. Elsewhere in occupied Poland, 470,000 other refugees were crammed into the ghettoes, 230,000 of whom were evicted between April and August 1940 from western and southern Poland.

Driven out of their homes with only small bundles on their backs and thrust into a strange environment, the refugees became dependent on social welfare. The meagre resources of the Judenrat, especially in Warsaw, were incapable of feeding this multitude, and the refugees, consequently, were the first victims of starvation and epidemics. In Warsaw, they lived in cellars, synagogues, former schools and cinemas, often without heat and with many broken windows; sanitary facilities were inadequate or nonexistent. They became candidates for death. When efforts to help themselves failed, thousands of adults and children resorted to the streets to beg for food from Warsaw Jews who were themselves underfed and starving. The typhoid epidemic, which began in late 1940, claimed 43,239 lives in 1941 (out of a population of 420,116 in August 1941) and 22,760 in January–May 1942. These deaths reflect the spread of typhoid and other starvation-induced illnesses. Because not all deaths were reported, the actual figures are probably even higher. The 1941–42 deathrate of 10 percent of the ghetto population began to decline in the spring of 1942, as the ty-

A woman hands change to a young beggar in the Warsaw ghetto. Thousands of Jews succumbed to starvation and disease in the ghetto.

phoid epidemic receded. The weakest had died. As time went on, through the efforts of the illicit workshops selling their produce to Poles and also of the smugglers, the situation at least stabilized. A major proportion of the inhabitants of the ghettoes could have survived had the Nazis not decided otherwise. . . .

The Will to Survive

To foil the Nazi goal of breaking their spirit, ghetto inhabitants formed social welfare, religious, educational, cultural. and political (underground) organizations. In some cases, all activities were underground. Membership was usually voluntary. The groups were usually either independent of, or only partially connected with, the Judenrat. . . .

The Judenrat had to acquiesce, in 1941, to the Nazi demand for disinfection actions, supposedly instituted against the spread of epidemics. Polish and Nazi doctors, accompanied by Jewish police, entered apartments and took away warm bedding and clothing to be disinfected. If not stolen, these items were returned, often ruined and torn. People were marched off to baths where they had to stand naked in the bitter cold of an unheated building in the Polish winter while their clothes were disinfected. They showered in boiling hot water and then, without benefit of towels, put on their damp and ruined clothes. Many became ill; epidemics and death were spread rather than averted by these practices. Disinfection squads operated throughout 1941. . . .

Religious Life

The Nazis forbade all public religious practices, despite their claim that their antisemitism was racial, not religious. Jews dressed in traditional garb, especially bearded Jews and others recognizable as believers, were singled out for especially brutal treatment.

Towards the end of 1939 all male Jews of Rawa were forced to assemble in the town square to cut their beards. Among them was Rabbi Rappaport, the rabbi of Rawa, an old man with a white beard. The rabbi had always been on good terms with the local priest, a German, ever since the German occupation during World War I, and also under Polish rule. The daughter of the rabbi went to the priest and asked him to prevent the cutting of her father's beard. The priest went to the town square to intervene on the rabbi's behalf. After the officer in charge had heard the priest's request, he upbraided him for intervening in favor of a Jew. But as he did not dare to ignore the priest's request, he declared—either the beard will be cut off, or one hundred lashes will be administered. The rabbi preferred the lashes. After a number of strokes, the rabbi fainted, covered in blood. He was brought to a hospital where he lay for two weeks, but his beard remained intact. . . . When they put fire to the synagogue of Sierpec at the end of September, 1939, all the Jewish inhabitants were ordered to assemble around the burning synagogue. From among the crowd a young, brilliant student of the Jewish law, Moshe was his name, emerged and ran into the burning house of worship, into the blazing fire, and took out of the ark two scrolls of the Torah, one in each hand. When he came out, he was met with a hail of bullets at the hands of the evil ones. He fell with the Torah scrolls in his hands, and was burned to ashes with them and the synagogue. May the Lord revenge his soul.

Diarist Chaim Kaplan, a teacher, noted:

Public prayer in these dangerous times is a forbidden act. Anyone caught in this crime is doomed to severe punishment. If you will, it is even sabotage, and anyone engaging in sabotage is subject to execution. But this does not deter us. Jews come to pray in a group in some inside room facing the courtyard, with drawn blinds on the windows. . . . Even for the high holy days, there was no permission for communal worship. I don't know whether the Judenrat made any attempt to obtain it, but if it didn't try it was only because everyone knew in advance that the request would be turned down. Even in the darkest days of our exile we were not tested with this trial. Never before was there a government so evil that it would forbid an entire people to pray. Everything is forbidden to us. The wonder is that we are still alive, and that we do everything. And this is true of public prayer too. . . . Hundreds throughout Warsaw organize services, and do not skip over even the most difficult hymns in the liturgy. There is not even a shortage of sermons. Everything is in accordance with the ancient customs of Israel. . . .

They pick some inside room whose windows look out onto the courtyard, and pour out their supplications before the

God of Israel in whispers. This time there are no cantors and choirs, only whispered prayers. But the prayers are heartfelt; it is possible to weep in secret, too, and the gates of tears are not locked.

Although prayer was forbidden in some ghettoes. . .at least 600 *minyanim* [congregants worshipped] in Warsaw alone. In Lódź, public prayer was permitted in 1940. In Riga (Latvia), refugee German Jews were allowed to pray, local Jews were not. In Vilna and Kovno (Lithuania), public prayer was not permitted. In March 1941, Hans Frank, the German governor, permitted religious activity in private homes and in synagogues and prayer houses on the sabbath and holidays. For many people, prayer became more meaningful. Additional liturgy was read, such as prayers for deliverance (e.g., Psalms 22 and 23) and the special prayers written during the Crusades and the persecutions of the Middle Ages when the devout "sanctified the Lord's name" (that is, accepted the martyrdom of death rather than deny the Jewish faith).

Observing the Jewish religious commandments (*mitzvot*) under ghetto conditions was difficult. Keeping the sabbath was impossible because people were forced to labor on that day as well as on festivals and high holy days. Keeping dietary laws (*Kashrut*, the separation of dairy and meat dishes), as well as other commandments, including rules of hygiene, was especially difficult. Starving Jews were prepared to forgo non-kosher meat. In special cases, rabbis permitted the consumption of non-kosher food, because the preservation of life is more important under Jewish law than dietary laws and the sabbath. In Lódź, for instance, rabbis permitted pregnant women to eat non-kosher meat. Jews fasted, especially on the Day of Atonement (Yom Kippur), although their starvation rations forced them to fast on many other days as well. . . .

Education and Cultural Activity

Following the Nazi entry into Poland, and later the USSR, education was forbidden. Newspapers were not permitted and libraries were closed. Under the auspices of Alfred Rosenberg, the official Nazi ideologue, special Nazi units entered the large ghettoes to liquidate Jewish libraries and rob them and other institutions of Jewish cultural treasures. But some treasures were hidden, especially by youth and children, and ghetto libraries were established. Writers continued to write, and painters to paint, and scientists continued their research. The few archives that survive supply ample evidence of a feverish intellectual activity during the ghetto period. The Jewish reverence for education would not be denied.

Orchestras were active in the Vilna and Warsaw ghettoes and elsewhere as well. . . .

Because education was forbidden in Warsaw (in September 1941 the Germans permitted the Judenrat to operate some elementary classes) so-called *complets* sprang up, initiated by teachers or parents for groups of 4 to 8 children. . . . An illegal high school of the Dror Zionist youth movement, which existed between 1940 and the summer of 1942, was supported . . . to prepare youngsters for Polish matriculation exams. Beginning with 3 pupils and 7 teachers, by the spring of 1942 there were 120 pupils and 13 teachers. Scientists and educators earned some slices of bread by teaching math, history, biology, philosophy, and literature to half-starved youngsters. Illicit vocational training courses were offered in pharmacology and technical drawing, as well as university-level courses in education, medicine and technical subjects. The school eventually contained elementary grades 4 to 6, all six high-school grades, and two college-level grades. Most pupils belonged to youth movements and were to participate in the Warsaw ghetto rebellion.

In the Lódź ghetto, education was permitted. During 1940 and 1941, 14,000 students attended 2 kindergartens, 34 secular and 6 religious schools, 2 high schools, 2 college-level schools, and 1 trade school (weaving). In Vilna, 2,700 children, aged 7 to 14, attended school.

Yitzhak Rudashevksy, aged 15, who lived in Vilna, wrote:

A boring day. My mood is just like the weather outside. I think to myself. what would happen if we did not go to school, to the club, and did not read books? We would die of dejection inside the ghetto walls.

Historical Documentation

To document Nazi inhumanity and to preserve the history of life in the ghettoes, various secret archives were established. The most important, the Oneg Shabbat of Warsaw, was founded by . . . historian Dr. Emmanuel Ringelblum, who persuaded writers, journalists, economists, social scientists, and rabbis to contribute to the documentation.

In addition to a number of permanent workers, the archive commissioned others to investigate specific topics. Journalists such as Peretz Opoczynski reported on life in the ghetto. The leader of the health organization TOZ, Dr. Israel Milejkowski, organized a group of doctors to study the effects of hunger on the human body. Discovered after the war, their study was published in Warsaw in 1946. Others reported on education, on cultural life, on slave labor camps. Writers and poets gave their works to Ringelblum for safe-keeping. Others reported on the situation in other ghettoes. . . .

In the summer of 1942, most Oneg Shabbat members were deported to their deaths. Ringelblum managed to hide in the non-Jewish part of Warsaw where he continued to write in his diary. His hideout was discovered in March 1944 and he, his family, and the Polish family with whom they lived were murdered. The archive was buried in the ghetto in three milk pails. Two of these were uncovered after the war; one was never found.

Parts of other archives, collected in Bialystok, by Mordechai Tennenbaum, the commander of the underground, and in Vilna, were discovered after the war. Although many of the diaries written during that period were lost, some survived. . . .

Ghettoes in the USSR

Jews in the USSR were living fairly ordinary lives in 1939–41. But their hope that the Germans would not invade Russia or fail to conquer it if they did was shattered with the outbreak of the German-Soviet war on June 22, 1941. On June 24, 1941, Kovno, Lithuania, was captured. . . .

From the morning of June 23 until the evening of June 24 [1941], Kovno was a no-man's-land. Groups of nationalist Lithuanians and armed criminal elements calling themselves partisans and freedom fighters controlled the city. They seized the opportunity to attack Jews, accusing them of handing over Lithuania to the Soviets. They rioted. They robbed and attacked Jews, killing many during the two days of terror. The atrocities initiated when the German army entered Kovno reached a peak on the night of June 25 when whole families in the poverty-stricken district of Slobodka were killed in a house-to-house murder march.

Throughout the first week of occupation Jews were arrested en masse. First taken to jail, they were then removed to the Seventh Fort, one of a series of nineteenth century fortifications surrounding the city. Ten thousand people were kept without food or drink, some of them in the open, others in the cellars of the old fort. Daily, groups of men were taken out and shot not far from the fort. Women were raped and then shot. On July 7 the surviving women were sent back to the town; 6,000 to 7,000 men were buried in large pits that had been dug by Soviet prisoners of war.

Lithuanian extremists, not Nazis, committed the murders. Here and there some Germans took part, but the authorities described the massacre as a quarrel between Lithuanians and Jews. In actual fact, however, Nazi security police pulled the strings that made the Lithuanians dance. . . .

On August 7 Lithuanian partisans jailed 1,200 men. About 200 were later released; the others were taken outside the town and killed. Kovno Jews were ordered to move into the ghetto on August 15. On August 8, 534 Jewish intellectuals—teachers, lawyers, doctors—were taken, supposedly to do some special intellectual work in the city archives. They were transported not to the archives but to the Fourth Fort where they were shot. . . .

After the ghetto gates were closed, systematic murder actions began. On September 26, Jewish residents of one ghetto area were assembled in the square, where those fit for work were separated from those less fit. After two days, the "fit" ones were released; the others, about 1,000 men, women, and children, were transported to the Ninth Fort and murdered. On October 4 the whole so-called small ghetto was liquidated. Those who were artisans or members of artisans' fam-

ilies were released into the large ghetto, the others—1,500—
were transported to the Ninth Fort. When the hospital in the
small ghetto was burned down, its 60 patients and the doctors
and nurses were burned alive.

Three weeks later, on October 27, the Judenrat received an
order to assemble inhabitants, without exception, in Democracy Square, for "control." It was clear that a "selection"
would be made and that some would die. Some Judenrat
members wanted to refuse to convey the German order. But
an opinion expressed by Rabbi Shapiro was decisive: "If a Jewish community (may God help it) has been condemned to
physical destruction, and there are means of rescuing part of
it, the leaders of the community should have courage and assume the responsibility to act and rescue what is possible.". . .

The "selection" was made. The survivors were permitted
to return to the ghetto; the others, more than 10,000 people,
were escorted under heavy guard to the small ghetto to replace those who had been "selected" in the previous murder
action. Next morning the death march proceeded . . . to the
Ninth Fort, where huge pits had been prepared. The Germans and Lithuanians forced the Jews toward the pits in
small groups and mowed them down with machine guns.
The bodies were covered with lime and earth. This massacre
was termed the "big action" by surviving Jews. Mass murder
then ceased for two and a half years.

The ghetto became a slave labor camp of nearly 17,000 inhabitants, less than half the original number of Kovno Jews.
The labor office of the Judenrat was the most important institution in the ghetto. At first, all men between the ages of
14 and 60 were recruited. Later, women were added. Men
worked six or seven days a week; the women worked three
days at first, then five. By the spring of 1942, most ghetto inhabitants had been assigned specific jobs. Those without a
permanent job were ordered to appear at the gate every
morning to be assigned a temporary job. The foremen of the
ghetto workshops were Jewish, which served as a protection
of sorts. Outside the ghetto, the foremen were Germans or
Lithuanians. Those who worked outside the ghetto were escorted to work by armed Germans or Lithuanian "partisans."

In return for their work, they received as much food as the Nazis decided to provide, but it was not supplied on a regular basis. Often some rations were simply withheld. . . .

A grade school was opened, and a second one followed. . . .

At the end of February 1942, Nazis confiscated all books. Schooling continued, however, until August 1942, when any kind of schooling or instruction was forbidden. Although the two schools were closed, education did not cease. Small groups of children continued to study in various homes. Soon the Judenrat obtained permission to organize a vocational school to train young workers for the workshops. In addition to smithery, carpentry, tinnery, sewing, and so on, basic elementary subjects were taught when the Judenrat extended school hours. A choir, a drama circle, and even a ballet group functioned under the auspices of the vocational school.

In the summer of 1942, the well-known musician Misha Hofmekler asked the Judenrat's permission to form an orchestra. Dr. Elkes was doubtful. An orchestra might be interpreted as an expression of joy, which in the ghetto conditions would be an abomination. Explaining that music satisfied an inner emotional need, Hofmekler got his orchestra. . . . When the chords of the first concert were struck in August 1942, both the performers and the audience cried, tears not only of sorrow but of pride.

Religious observance continued in the Kovno ghetto. Although wearing a beard and sidelocks and showing other outward signs of religious observance were dangerous, many people did so.

A multitude of rabbinical decisions were asked for and given: How should one treat Jews who had been ordered to tear up Torah scrolls and trample on them? Could the clothes of dead Jews be worn? Should those still alive praise God for having been saved?

On August 26, 1941, the Germans closed all prayerhouses. Soon, however, in defiance of the Nazi order, observant Jews reopened illegal prayerhouses to pray and study the Torah.

Life in the Warsaw Ghetto

Mary Berg

The diary of Anne Frank is famous. Anne's story has been made into a successful stage play and movie. Less well known is the story of another teenager who kept a diary during the war. Fortunately, her story has a happier ending. This young woman was an American living in Poland, and she kept a diary chronicling the horrors Jews suffered in the Warsaw ghetto. Her name was Mary Berg. In July 1942 the Bergs were told that all foreigners who had their papers in order would be exchanged for Germans held by the Allies. Mary's family, along with the other foreigners, were then put in Pawiak prison. In January 1943 the Germans decided to release all of the Americans. More than a year later, the Bergs were allowed to go to the United States, nearly three and a half years after being sent to the ghetto. This brief excerpt from Berg's diary covers the summer of 1942, when she was in prison.

President Adam Czerniakow has committed suicide. He did it last night, on July 23. He could not bear his terrible burden. According to the rumors that have reached us here, he took his tragic step when the Germans demanded that the contingents of deportees be increased. He saw no other way out than to leave this horrible world. His closest collaborators, who saw him shortly before his death, say that he displayed great courage and energy until the last moment.

The community has elected a new president to replace Czerniakow. He is old Lichtenbaum, whose son, Engineer Lichtenbaum, is the director of the Construction Office of the community. . . .

August, 1942

Behind the Pawiak [prison] gate we are experiencing all the terror that is abroad in the ghetto. For the last few nights we have been unable to sleep. The noise of the shooting, the cries of despair, are driving us crazy. I have to summon all my strength to write these notes. I have lost count of the days, and I do not know what day it is. But what does it matter? We are here as on a little island amidst an ocean of blood. The whole ghetto is drowning in blood. We literally see fresh human blood, we can smell it. Does the outside world know anything about it? Why does no one come to our aid? I cannot go on living; my strength is exhausted. How long are we going to be kept here to witness all this?

A few days ago, a group of neutrals was taken out of the Pawiak. Apparently the Germans were unable to use them for exchange. I saw from my window several trucks filled with people, and I tried to distinguish familiar faces among them. Some time later, the prison guard came panting to us, and told us that the Jewish citizens of neutral European countries had just been taken to the *Umschlagplatz* [collection point] to be deported. So our turn may come soon, too. I hope it will be very soon. This waiting is worse than death. . . .

Work Means Life?

The Germans have blockaded entire streets in the ghetto. Since the 10,000 people a day they are now demanding have failed to report, the Nazis are using force. Every day they besiege another street, closing all the exits. They enter the apartments, and check the labor cards. Those who do not possess the necessary documents or who, according to the Germans, estimate, are unqualified for work, are taken away at once. Those who try to resist are shot on the spot.

Just now, while I am writing this, such a blockade is taking place on Nowolipie Street, only two blocks from our prison. It has been going on for two days now. The street is completely closed; only the Jewish policemen are allowed to use it.

The wives and children of the men employed in the German factories in the ghetto are officially exempt from deportation, but this exemption is effective only on paper. In actual fact, a husband returning home from work often finds that his whole family has been taken away. He runs in despair to Stawki Street to find his kin, but instead of being able to rescue them he himself is often pushed into one of the cattle cars.

The German factories in the ghetto now work twelve hours a day, with only one hour's rest. The workers receive a quart of watery soup and a quarter of a pound of bread a day. But despite their hunger and slavery, these workers are among the luckiest in the ghetto, for their jobs protect them from deportation. . . .

Good-Bye Children

Dr. Janusz Korczak's children's home is empty now. A few days ago we all stood at the window and watched the Germans surround the houses. Rows of children, holding each other by their little hands, began to walk out of the doorway. There were tiny tots of two or three years among them, while the oldest ones were perhaps thirteen. Each child carried a little bundle in his hand. All of them wore white aprons. They walked in ranks of two, calm, and even smiling. They had not the slightest foreboding of their fate. At the end of the procession marched Dr. Korczak, who saw to it that the children did not walk on the sidewalk. Now and then, with fatherly solicitude, he stroked a child on the head or arm, and straightened out the ranks. . . . They went in the direction of Gesia Street, to the cemetery. At the cemetery all the children were shot. We were also told by our informants that Dr. Korczak was forced to witness the executions, and that he himself was shot afterward.

Thus died one of the purest and noblest men who ever lived. He was the pride of the ghetto. His children's home gave us courage, and all of us gladly gave part of our own scanty means to support the model home organized by this great idealist. He devoted all his life, all his creative work as an educator and writer, to the poor children of Warsaw. Even at the last moment he refused to be separated from them. . . .

The "Lucky" Prisoners

Our family of internees in the Pawiak now numbers sixty-four persons. . . .

We are allowed to go out in the prison yard only once a day. We walk for an hour between the laundry and our building. . . .

Last night was horrible. It was stuffier than ever. We lay naked on our straw bags. The atmosphere was so thick that it could almost be cut with a knife. Through the window a patch of blue sky and a few stars could be seen. Not the slightest noise came from the street. None of us could sleep.

At about eleven o'clock we suddenly heard the heavy screech of a lock opening, and two persons left by one of the prison gates. The heavy steps of soldierly boots could be clearly distinguished from the small steps of a woman. The steps came gradually closer to our windows. Then we heard a woman's tearful voice and several words pronounced in a German-Yiddish accent. . . . But suddenly these words were drowned by the sound of revolver shots. The first shot resounded high in the air near our window, the second was lower, and the third level with the pavement, as though the soldier were firing at the unfortunate woman as she lay on the ground. Then we heard muffled noises, which might have been kicks, and then, finally, there was silence. . . .

The shootings and the cries coming from the streets are slowly driving us mad. The nights are horrible. Last night nearly forty persons were shot under our windows. All of them were men. The slaughter lasted for two hours or more. The murderers finished off their victims with kicks and with blows with the butts of their guns. . . .

Roundups

September 19, 1942

My mother lies on her mattress all day long; she is so starved that she cannot move. Ann [Mary's sister] is like a shadow, and my father is terribly thin, just skin and bones. I seem to bear the hunger better than the others. I just grit my teeth when the gnawing feeling in my stomach begins. At night I begin to wait for the next morning, when we are given our four ounces of bread and the bitter water that is called coffee. Then I wait for lunch at noon, when we are brought our first soup, a dish of hot water with a few grains of kasha. Then again I wait impatiently for the evening, when we get our second dish of hot water with a potato or a beet. The days are endless, and the nights even more so, and full of nightmares The shootings continue, hundreds of people are perishing daily. The ghetto is drenched in blood. People are constantly marching along Dzielna Street toward the *Umschlagplatz* on Stawki Street. No job or occupation is a complete protection any longer. Recently even the families of those employed have been deported, mostly the women and children.

A few weeks ago the Nazis began to round up the wives and children of the men working at Toebens and Schultz. Those who are not working are ruthlessly dragged away. Parents now take their children with them to their work, or hide them in some hole. . . .

September 20, 1942

There have been fewer shootings today. Resistance is subsiding. . . .

Engineer Lichtenbaum asked Mrs. W. whether she had been told by any of the prison officials what the Nazis were planning to do in the Warsaw ghetto. How absurd for him, a high community official, to ask us what is going to happen to the survivors in the ghetto! Is there still any doubt after what has happened before our very eyes? But everyone asks everyone else, hoping to hear a hopeful word.

According to Lichtenbaum and [his friend] First, more than 200,000 Jews have been deported, and more than 10,000 have been killed. Thus nearly 200,000 people still remain.

The underground movement has become more active than ever. Death sentences were carried out not only against the Nazis, Ukrainians, and Lithuanians who murdered the population during the bloody days, but also against the few Jews who allowed themselves to be used as Nazi tools during the massacre. Colonel Szerynski and several community officials are now on the black list. They know it, and dare not appear on the streets without armed bodyguards.

The Germans for their part arc liquidating all the collaborators whom they can no longer use. They shoot them without ceremony, and their bodies are often found on the streets. . . .

The massacres have aroused the underground leaders to

greater resistance. The illegal papers are multiplying and some of them reach us even here in the Pawiak. They are full of good reports from the battle fronts. The Allies are victorious in Egypt, and the Russians are pushing the enemy back at Moscow. The sheets explain the meaning of the deportations and tell of the fate of the deported Jews. The population is summoned to resist with weapons in their hands, and warned against defeatist moods, and against the idea that we are completely helpless before the Nazis. "Let us die like men and not like sheep," ends one proclamation in a paper called *To Arms!*

The situation improved somewhat in the last days of August, and some began to take an optimistic view of the future. But this was only the lull before the storm. On September 3 and 4 the Germans began to blockade the workshops organized by the community. Elite Guards, accompanied by Lithuanians and Ukrainians, entered the shops, and took several dozen people out of each, alleging that they needed skilled workers. These workers, numbering more than a thousand, were led away to Stawki Street and deported to the Treblinki camp.

Now it is generally known that most of the deportees are sent to Treblinki, where they are killed with the help of machines with which the Germans are experimenting for war purposes. But no one knows any details.

Chapter 2

Evil Reaches New Lows: The Final Solution

The Final Solution

John Toland

Hitler had spoken often about his disdain for the Jews.
His views could easily have been discerned long before he
assumed power; yet, even after World War II began, many
people did not take seriously his explicit calls for the extermination of the Jews. Within the Nazi Party itself,
some of the highest-ranking officials were unaware initially that the orders for the killing of Jews were issued directly by Hitler. Though the Jews were persecuted in
Germany before the war and began to be killed from its
outset, the official policy of pursuing a "final solution of
the Jewish problem" was not laid out until the January
1942 Wannsee Conference. From that point on, the campaign to eliminate the Jews became a top priority, at times
seeming to be more important to Hitler than winning the
war. This selection illustrates that Hitler made no effort to
hide his intentions and that his subordinates were happy
to carry out his wishes. John Toland is a Pulitzer
Prize–winning author who has written numerous books.
This biography of Hitler, from which this excerpt is taken,
is considered one of the best.

Two days after the invasion of the Soviet Union the man responsible for the deportation of Jews, Reinhard Heydrich,
complained in writing that this was no answer to the Jewish
problem. . . . It was fitting, therefore, that on the last day of
July Heydrich received a cryptic order (signed by [Her-
mann] Göring upon instructions from the Führer) instruct-
ing him "to make all necessary preparations regarding organizations and financial matters to bring about a complete

Excerpted from John Toland, *Adolf Hitler*. Copyright © 1976 by John Toland.
Reprinted with permission from Random House, Inc.

solution of the Jewish question in the German sphere of influence in Europe."

Behind the innocuous bureaucratic language lay sweeping authority for the SS to organize the extermination of European Jewry. As a preliminary step, [Heinrich] Himmler [the chief of the SS and the director of the extermination campaign] . . . asked the chief physician of the SS what was the best method of mass extermination. The answer was: gas chambers. The next step was to summon Rudolf Höss, the commandant of the largest concentration camp in Poland, and give him secret oral instructions. "He told me," testified Höss, "something to the effect—I do not remember the exact words—that the Führer had given the order for a final solution of the Jewish question. We, the SS, must carry out that order. If it is not carried out now the Jews will later on destroy the German people." Himmler said he had chosen Höss's camp since Auschwitz, strategically located near the border of Germany, afforded space for measures requiring isolation. Höss was warned that this operation was to be treated as a secret Reich matter. He was forbidden to discuss the matter with his immediate superior. And so Höss resumed to Poland and, behind the back of the inspector of concentration camps, quietly began to expand his grounds with intent to turn them into the greatest killing center in man's history. He did not even tell his wife what he was doing.

Hitler's concept of concentration camps as well as the practicality of genocide owed much, so he claimed, to his studies of English and United States history. He admired the camps for Boer prisoners in South Africa and for the Indians in the wild West; and often praised to his inner circle the efficiency of America's extermination—by starvation and uneven combat—of the red savages who could not be tamed by captivity. . . .

In mid-October [1941], after lecturing on the necessity of bringing decency into civil life, he said, "But the first thing, above all, is to get rid of the Jews. Without that, it will be useless to clean the Augean stables." Two days later he was more explicit. "From the rostrum of the Reichstag, I prophesied to Jewry that, in the event of war's proving inevitable, the Jew would disappear from Europe. That race of criminals has on its conscience the two million dead of the First World War, and now already hundreds and thousands more. Let nobody tell me that all the same we can't park them in the marshy parts of Russia! Who's worrying about our troops? It's not a bad idea, by the way, that public rumor attributes to us a plan to exterminate the Jews. Terror is a salutary thing." He predicted that the attempt to create a Jewish state would be a failure. "I have numerous accounts to settle, about which I cannot think today. But that doesn't mean I forget them. I write them down. The time will come to bring out the big book! Even with regard to the Jews, I've found myself remaining inactive. There's no sense in adding uselessly to the difficulties of the moment. One acts shrewdly when one bides one's time."

One reason Hitler had delayed implementing the Final Solution was hope that his implied threat to exterminate the Jews would keep Roosevelt out of the war. But Pearl Harbor ended this faint expectation and Hitler's hope turned into bitterness, with extermination becoming a form of international reprisal.

The decision taken, the Führer made it known to those entrusted with the Final Solution that the killings should be done as humanely as possible. This was in line with his conviction that he was observing God's injunction to cleanse the world of vermin. Still a member in good standing of the Church of Rome despite detestation of its hierarchy ("I am now as before a Catholic and will always remain so"), he carried within him its teaching that the Jew was the killer of God. The extermination, therefore, could be done without a twinge of conscience since he was merely acting as the avenging hand of God—so long as it was done impersonally, without cruelty. Himmler was pleased to murder with mercy. He ordered technical experts to devise gas chambers which would eliminate masses of Jews efficiently and "humanely," then crowded the victims into boxcars and sent them east to stay in ghettos until the killing centers in Poland were completed.

The time had come to establish the bureaucracy of liquidation and the man in charge, Heydrich, sent out invitations to a number of state secretaries and chiefs of the SS main offices for a "Final Solution" Conference, to take place on December 10, 1941. The recipients of his invitation, aware only that Jews were being deported to the East, had little idea of the meaning of "final solution" and awaited the conference with expectation and keen interest. . . .

The Wannsee Conference

At about 11 A.M. [on January 20, 1942] fifteen men gathered in a room at the Reich Security Main Office at number 56-58 Grossen Wannsee. There were representatives from [Alfred] Rosenberg's East Ministry, Göring's Four-Year Plan agency, the Interior Ministry, the Justice Ministry, the Foreign Office and the party chancellery. Once they had seated themselves informally at tables, Chairman Heydrich began to speak. He had been given, he said, "the responsibility for working out the final solution of the Jewish problem regardless of geographical boundaries." This euphemism was followed by a veiled and puzzling remark which involved Hitler himself. "Instead of emigration," he said "there is now a further possible solution to which the Führer has already signified his consent—namely deportation to the East."

At this point Heydrich exhibited a chart indicating which Jewish communities were to be evacuated, and gave a hint as to their fate. Those fit to work would be formed into labor gangs but even those who survived the rigors would not be allowed to go free and so "form a new germ cell from which the Jewish race would again arise. History teaches us that.". . .

Thirty copies of the conference record were distributed to the ministries and SS main offices and the term "Final Solution" became known throughout the Reich bureaucracy yet the true meaning of what Heydrich had said was fathomed only by those privy to the killing operations, and many of this select group, curiously, were convinced that Adolf Hitler himself was not totally aware that mass murder was being plotted. SS Lieutenant Colonel Adolf Eichmann, in charge of the Gestapo's Jewish Evacuation Office, for one knew this was a myth. . . .

A few days later Hitler confirmed, in spite of himself, that he was indeed the architect of the Final Solution. "One must act radically," he said at lunch on January 23, in the presence of Himmler. "When one pulls out a tooth, one does it with a single tug, and the pain quickly goes away. The Jew must clear out of Europe. It's the Jew who prevents everything. When I think about it, I realize that I'm extraordinarily humane. At the time of the rules of the Popes the Jews were mistreated in Rome. Until 1830, eight Jews mounted on donkeys were led once a year through the streets of Rome. For my part, I restrict myself to telling them they must go away. If they break their pipes on the journey, I can't do anything about it. But if they refuse to go voluntarily I see no other solution but extermination." Never before had he talked so openly to his inner circle and he was so absorbed by the subject that on the twenty-seventh he again demanded the disappearance of all Jews from Europe.

His obsession with Jews was publicly expressed a few days later in a speech at the Sportpalast on the ninth anniversary of National Socialism's rise to power. "I do not even want to speak of the Jews," he said, and proceeded to do so at length. "They are simply our old enemies, their plans have suffered shipwreck through us, and they rightly hate us, just as we hate them. We realize that this war can only end either in the wiping out of the Germanic nations, or by the disappearance of Jewry from Europe.". . .

Killing Jews Becomes Paramount

Hitler always took time to oversee the Final Solution. In this matter he neither needed nor took advice. He made this clear in his message on the anniversary of the promulgation of the party program in late February. "My prophecy," he said, "shall be fulfilled that this war will not destroy Aryan humanity but it will exterminate the Jew. Whatever the battle may bring in its course or however long it may last, that will be its final course." The elimination of Jewry overrode victory itself.

Despite such open hints, few had yet been initiated into the secret. [Propaganda minister Joseph] Goebbels himself still did not realize the enormity of the measures being prepared. One of his employees, Hans Fritzsche, did learn about the Einsatzgruppen killings from a letter sent by an SS man in the Ukraine. The writer complained that he had suffered a nervous breakdown after receiving an order to kill Jews and Ukrainian intelligentsia. He could not protest through official channels and asked for help. Fritzsche immediately went to Heydrich and asked point-blank, "Is the SS there for the purpose of committing mass murders?" Heydrich indignantly denied the charge, promising to start an investigation at once. He reported back the next day that the culprit was Gauleiter Koch, who had acted without the Führer's knowledge, then vowed that the killings would cease. "Believe me, Herr Fritzsche," said Heydrich, "anyone who has the reputation of being cruel does not have to be cruel; he can act humanely."

Only that March did Goebbels himself learn the exact meaning of Final Solution. Then Hitler told him flatly that Europe must be cleansed of all Jews, "if necessary by applying the most brutal methods." The Führer was so explicit that Goebbels could now write in his diary:

> A judgment is being visited upon the Jews that, while barbaric, is fully deserved. . . . One must not be sentimental in these matters. If we did not fight the Jew, they would destroy us. It's a life-and-death struggle between the Aryan race and the Jewish bacillus. No other government and no other regime would have the strength for such a global solution of this question.

By spring six killing centers had been set up in Poland. There were four in [Hans] Frank's Generalgouvernement [German-occupied Poland]: Treblinka, Sobibor, Belzec and Lublin; two in the incorporated territories: Kulmhof and Auschwitz. The first four gassed the Jews by engine-exhaust fumes but Rudolf Höss, commandant of the huge complex near Auschwitz, thought this too "inefficient" and introduced to his camp a more lethal gas, hydrogen cyanide, marketed commercially under the name of Zyklon B. . . .

Perhaps the most diabolical innovation of the Final Solution was the establishment of Jewish Councils to administer their own deportation and destruction. This organization, comprising those leaders of the community who believed that co-operation with the Germans was the best policy, discouraged resistance. "I will not be afraid to sacrifice 50,000 of our community," reasoned a typical leader, Moses Merin, "in order to save the other 50,000."

By early summer the mass exterminations began under the authority of a written order from Himmler. Eichmann showed this authorization to one of his assistants, Dieter Wisliceny, with the explanation that Final Solution meant the biological extermination of the Jewish race. "May God forbid," exclaimed the appalled Wisliceny, "that our enemies should ever do anything similar to the German people!"

"Don't be sentimental," said Eichmann. "This is a Führer order." This was corroborated by Himmler in a letter to the chief of the SS Main Office at the end of July: "The occupied Eastern territories will be cleared of Jews. The implementation of this very hard order has been placed on my shoulders by the Führer. No one can release me from this responsibility in any case. So I forbid all interference."

What Kurt Gerstein learned, as head of the Technical Disinfection Service of the Waffen SS, had already driven him to despair. "He was so appalled by the satanic practices of the Nazis," recalled a friend, "that their eventual victory did not seem to him impossible." During a tour that summer of the four extermination camps in the Generalgouvernement, Gerstein saw with his own eyes what he had read about. At the first camp he and two companions—Eichmann's deputy and a professor of hygiene named Pfannenstiel—were informed that Hitler and Himmler had just ordered "all action speeded up." At Belzec, two days later, Gerstein saw these words translated into reality.

"There are not ten people alive," he was told by the man in charge, Kriminalkommissar Christian Wirth, "who have seen or will see as much as you." Gerstein witnessed the entire procedure from the arrival of 6,000 Jews in boxcars, 1,450 of whom were already dead. As the survivors were driven out of the cars with whips, they were ordered over a loudspeaker to remove all clothing, artificial limbs, and spectacles and turn in all valuables and money. Women and young girls were to have their hair cut off. "That's to make something special for U-boat crews," explained an SS man, "nice slippers."

Revolted, Gerstein watched the march to the death chambers. Men, women, children—all stark naked—filed past in ghastly parade as a burly SS man promised in a loud priest-like voice that nothing terrible was going to happen to them. "All you have to do is breathe in deeply. That strengthens the lungs. Inhaling is a means of preventing infectious diseases. It's a good method of disinfection." To those who timorously asked what their fate would be, the SS man gave more reassurance: the men would build roads and houses; the women would do housework or help in the kitchen. But the odor from the death chambers was telltale and those at the head of the column had to be shoved by those behind. Most were silent, but one woman, eyes flashing, cursed her murderers. She was spurred on by whiplashes from Wirth, a former chief of criminal police in Stuttgart. Some prayed, others asked, "Who will give us water to wash the dead?" Gerstein prayed with them.

By now the chambers were jammed with humanity. But the driver of the diesel truck, whose exhaust gases would exterminate the Jews, could not start the engine. Incensed at the delay, Wirth began lashing at the driver with his whip. Two hours and forty-nine minutes later the engine started. After another interminable twenty-five minutes Gerstein peered into one chamber. Most of the occupants were already dead. At the end of thirty-two minutes all were lifeless. They were standing erect, recalled Gerstein, "like pillars of basalt, since there had not been an inch of space for them to fall in or even lean. Families could still be seen holding hands even in death." The horror continued as one group of workers began tearing open the mouths of the dead with iron hooks, while others searched anuses and genital organs for jewelry. Wirth was in his element. "See for yourself," he said, pointing to a large can filled with teeth. "Just look at the amount of gold there is! And we have collected as much only yesterday and the day before. You can't imagine what we find every day—dollars, diamonds, gold! You'll see!"

Gerstein forced himself to watch the final process. The bodies were flung into trenches, each some hundred yards long, conveniently located near the gas chambers. He was told that the bodies would swell from gas after a few days, raising the mound as much as six to ten feet. Once the swelling subsided, the bodies would be piled on railway ties covered with diesel oil and burned to cinders.

The following day the Gerstein party was driven to Treblinka near Warsaw where they saw almost identical installations but on a larger scale: "eight gas chambers and veritable mountains of clothing and underwear, 115 to 130 feet high." In honor of their visit, a banquet was held for employees. "When one sees the bodies of these Jews," Professor Pfannenstiel told them, "one understands the greatness of the work you are doing!" After dinner the guests were offered butter, meat and alcohol as going-away presents. Gerstein lied that he was adequately supplied from his own farm and so Pfannenstiel took the former's share as well as his own.

Upon arrival in Warsaw, Gerstein set off immediately for Berlin, resolved to tell those who would listen of the ghastly sights he had witnessed. A modern Ancient Mariner, he began spreading the truth to incredulous colleagues. As a rock thrown into a pond creates ever widening ripples, so did the tale of Kurt Gerstein.

Human Guinea Pigs

Robert Jay Lifton

One of the distinguishing characteristics of the Holocaust is that people were not just murdered in unprecedented numbers but were also tortured and killed in the most sadistic ways imaginable. Some of the most sickening photographs from the Nazi period are those the Germans took to record their medical experiments. The pseudo-science of the Nazi doctors was aimed at advancing the ideology of the regime in some cases and, in others, advancing a research interest of a particular doctor. Their experiments included the sterilization of men and women, the breaking of bones, and the injection of diseases into healthy people. This excerpt from the most authoritative book on the subject offers an overview of some of the more barbaric experiments conducted by the Nazis and rationale used to justify them. Robert Jay Lifton is a professor of psychiatry and psychology.

Nazi doctors are infamous for their cruel medical experiments. And no wonder: those experiments killed and maimed; as tangible medical crimes, they were given considerable prominence at the Nuremberg Medical Trial. Yet they were no more than a small part of the extensive and systematic medicalized killing. And it is that aspect of the experiments—their relation to the Nazi biomedical vision—that I shall mainly discuss.

Generally speaking, Nazi medical experiments fall into two categories: those sponsored by the regime for a specific ideological and military purpose, and those that were done *ad hoc* out of allegedly scientific interest on the part of an SS doctor.

For example, extensive sterilization and castration experi-

Excerpted from Robert Jay Lifton, *The Nazi Doctors*. Copyright © 1986 by Robert Jay Lifton. Reprinted with permission from Basic Books, a member of Perseus Books, L.L.C.

in Auschwitz, conducted mainly by doctors Carl
Clauberg and Horst Schumann, were encouraged officially as
a direct expression of racial theory and policy; the experiments with typhus contagion (injecting people with blood
from others with active typhus) and with the effectiveness of
various preparations of sera (in treating experimentally induced cases of typhus) were connected with military concerns
about typhus epidemics among German troops and civilian
personnel in the East; while the study of pre-cancerous conditions of the cervix reflected a scientific interest of Dr. Ed-
uard Wirths, the chief SS Auschwitz doctor, and his gynecol-
ogist brother Helmut. But the categories overlapped. . . .
Here we shall focus on the extensive sterilization and castration experiments, in which Auschwitz more less specialized,
and which were a direct extension of the biomedical vision,
but also mention other forms of experimentation and a scientific enterprise, including the establishment of a museum
collection of Jewish skulls provided by Auschwitz.

Block 10

The center for these experimental projects was the notorious Block 10, a place that could be considered to be quin-
tessential Auschwitz. Made up mostly of women prisoners, it
was located in the men's camp, and the windows were kept
closed and shuttered or boarded so that communication with
the outside was totally cut off. . . .

At the same time, inmates on the block were completely
vulnerable to visits and surveillance of various kinds by SS
doctors and, on occasion, by nonmedical officers: "A continuous coming and going of SS . . . [so that] we never felt safe."
For any visit could mean new danger, and inmates therefore
"awaited with impatience . . . the evening when we would be
locked up as animals in a cage but . . . nonetheless felt freer."

Another woman prisoner doctor, Adelaide Hautval, told
of the five hundred women "guinea pigs," all Jewish, from
various countries in Europe, who were usually selected directly from transports, according to the needs of the Nazi
physician experimenters: "Some required married women,
others young girls, a third a mixture of all the categories."

Overall conditions were superior to those in the women's camp, because there the "guinea pigs . . . would have died before the results of the experiments could have been assessed." Inmates suffered from hunger, nonetheless, and from the constant uncertainty about "What will it be this time?" For they had absorbed the Auschwitz principle that *anything is permitted*. At the same time the women deeply feared a transfer to Birkenau, where they knew death was more likely, because in Block 10 there was at least a hope that "maybe they will still let us live after this," though few believed that possible. . . .

Sterilization by Injection: "The Professor"

Block 10 was often known as "Clauberg's block," because it was created for him and his experimental efforts to perfect a cheap and effective method of mass sterilization. He was Block 10's figure of greatest authority, "the main man for sterilization". . . He began his Auschwitz work in December 1942 in Birkenau; but after persuading the authorities that his important research required a special block, he transferred his experiemental setting to Block 10 in Auschwitz in April 1943.

His method was to inject a caustic substance into the cervix in order to obstruct the fallopian tubes. He chose as experimental subjects married between the ages of twenty and forty, preferably those who had borne children. And he first injected them with opaque liquid in order to determine by X ray that there was no prior blockage or impairment. He had experimented with different substances, but was very secretive about the exact nature of the one he used, probably intent upon protecting any "medical discovery" from research competitors. . . .

The injection was done in three stages over a few months, though some women later described four or five injections. The goal of injecting the caustic substance was to create adhesions in the fallopian tubes that would cause them to be obstructed within a period of about six weeks, as would be demonstrated by subsequent X-rays. Clauberg had a prisoner nurse, Sylvia Friedmann, observe the women after the injections for symptoms of any kind.

Despite the terror induced in women victims, Marie L., a French prisoner physician, stressed that many so feared being sent back to Birkenau (where one would be "awaiting death standing in frost, mud, and swamps . . . without water or care") that they could view Block 10 as "a piece of luck and the possibility of survival." Clauberg himself encouraged this hope by his reassurances that he planned not to send them back to Birkenau (meaning the gas chamber) but to take them to his private research clinic at Königshütte, just a few kilometers from Auschwitz. . . .

Clauberg eventually had as many as three hundred women under his control on Block 10. The experiments were supposed to be highly secret, and there was an attempt to isolate women who had been injected from those who had not. Accounts differ about the fate of the women he experimented upon. Those who refused to be experimented upon, or who were considered for one reason or another unsuitable, were sent back to Birkenau and usually gassed—as were those women who became extremely debilitated. Most women experimented upon remained on Block 10, though a considerable number developed fever and various forms of peritoneal infection.

There was the constant fear of being killed because of knowing too much. They also feared both sterilization and artificial insemination. . . .

Descriptions by women experimented upon begin to tell us in human terms what Clauberg was really up to. A Czech Jew named Margita Neumann told of being taken into a dark room with a large X-ray machine:

> Dr. Clauberg ordered me to lie down on the gynecological table and I was able to observe Sylvia Friedmann who was preparing an injection syringe with a long needle. Dr. Clauberg used this needle to give me an injection in my womb. I had the feeling that my stomach would burst with the pain. I began to scream so that I could be heard through the entire block. Dr. Clauberg told me roughly to stop screaming immediately, otherwise I'd be taken back at once to Birkenau concentration camp. . . . After this experiment I had inflammation of the ovaries.

She went on to describe how, whenever Clauberg appeared on the ward, women were "overcome with anxiety and terror," as "they considered what Dr. Clauberg was doing as the actions of a murderer."....

Imprisonment of Clauberg

Clauberg . . . was captured by the Russians on 8 June 1945. Imprisoned in the Soviet Union for three years before being tried, he was then convicted of war crimes and sentenced to twenty-five years' imprisonment. But following Stalin's death (in 1953), and various diplomatic agreements, Clauberg was repatriated with other Germans in October 1955. . . . When interviewed by the press, he spoke proudly of his work at Königshütte and Auschwitz and claimed, "I was able to perfect an absolutely new method of sterilization . . . [which] would be of great use today in certain cases."

After various pressures from survivor groups and others, Clauberg was arrested in November 1955; but for a considerable time, the German Chamber of Medicine, the official body of the profession, resisted action against him that would divest him of his title of doctor of medicine. . . . The German Chamber of Medicine finally did remove Clauberg's license. But when he died, suddenly and mysteriously, in his prison cell on 9 August 1957, the general belief was that he was in the process of naming names at the top of the Nazi medical hierarchy and that, consequently, medical colleagues helped bring about his death. . . .

X-Ray and Surgical Castration

Horst Schumann differed from Clauberg in being not a renowned specialist but a reliable "old Nazi doctor" (he joined the Nazi Party and the SA in 1930) who was available for ruthless medical enterprises. Schumann had been a leading figure in the "euthanasia" program as the director of the killing center at Grafeneck. When that center closed, he took over the one at Sonnenstein. . . .

In this case, [Heinrich] Himmler played an even greater role in formulating the experiments, together with Viktor Brack, the Chancellery official active in both the "euthanasia" project and the establishment of the death camps. In early 1941, Himmler and Brack were already exchanging memos in which they shared a vision of "sterilization or castration . . . by means of X-rays" on a massive scale. Brack later claimed that the idea originated with Himmler for application to Jewish populations, especially in Poland, and also implicated Reinhard Heydrick, the most ruthless voice around Himmler, but at the same time admitted that Himmler's words "made a great impression on me.". . .

By June 1942, at the height of the German military penetration into Russia, Brack became more specific and programmatic. Referring to consultations with his superior and with the head of the area in Poland where the greatest number of Jews was concentrated, he spoke of the necessity of carrying through "the whole Jewish action [the Final Solution]" but estimated that two million to three million of the ten million Jews in Europe were fit enough to work and therefore should be "preserved" but at the same time "rendered incapable of propagating." Ordinary sterilization methods being used for hereditary diseases would take too much time and be too expensive, but "castration by X-ray . . . is not only relatively cheap, but can be performed on many thousands in the shortest time.". . . Himmler, ever the scientist, insisted that "sterilization by X-rays . . . [be] tried out at least once in one camp in a series of experiments." Schumann was chosen for the task and, by late 1942, was at work on X-ray castration on Block 30 in Birkenau. . . .

His experimental policies were brutal and unrestrained. He worked on Block 30, in the women's hospital in Birkenau, in a large room containing two expensive X-ray apparatuses and a small booth for him, which had a window and was, of course, insulated with lead plates to protect him from radiation.

Experimental subjects—relatively healthy young men and women in their late teens or early twenties, who had been obtained by a previous day's order from the camps—were lined up in a waiting room and brought in one by one, often completely ignorant of what was to be done to them. Women were put between plates that pressed against abdomen and back; men placed penis and scrotum on a special plate. Schumann himself turned on the machines, which hummed loudly; and each "treatment" lasted "several minutes" according to Dr. Stanislaw Klociziński, "five to eight minutes" according to Dr. Alina Brenda, another prisoner physician. Many of the women emerged with what Marie L. called "substantial burns," which could become infected and take a long time to heal; and many quickly developed symptoms of peritonitis, including fever and severe pain and vomiting. Not long after the X-rays, the women's ovaries were removed surgically, usually in two separate operations. . . . The ovaries were sent to laboratories to determine whether the X-rays were effective in destroying tissue. . . .

Schumann's experiments with men had a parallel course, as described by Dr. Michael Z. in a written report: First, the rumor that "Jews were being sterilized with X-rays" by "an air-force lieutenant-physician"; then a visit by Schumann to a male medical ward during which he ordered them to prepare for forty inmates on whom they were to keep records of medical observations; the arrival of the experimental victims with burn erythemas [red areas] around the scrotum ("From their description, we recognized the X-ray machine"); the victims' later accounts of their sperm being collected, their prostates brutally massaged with pieces of wood inserted into the rectum; their exposure to an operation removing one or two testicles, and in some cases a second operation removing the remaining testicle (conducted with "noticeable brutality" and limited anesthesia: patients' "screams were frightening to hear"); "disastrous" post-operative developments including hemorrhages, septicemia, absence of muscle tone from wounds, so that "many . . . would die rapidly, weakened morally and physically" and others would be sent to work "which would finish them." But "their deaths mattered little since these guinea pigs have already served the function expected of them."

Dr. Erich G. told of the psychological pain of experimental victims and of their questions to him ("Will I [be able to] be a father? Can I [have relations with] females?") but admitted that at the time that was not the greatest emotional stress ("To survive was more important than to be mutilated or even castrated"); and the fear was that experimental victims would be killed ("It was impossible to believe that they would allow people to live after the war to be a witness"). . . .

Dr. Klociziński writes of as many as 200 men being subjected to X-ray castration, and of about 180 of those to amputation of at least one testicle, 90 of these operations taking place on one day, 16 December 1942. While overall statistics are uncertain, the general estimate is that approximately 1,000 prisoners, male and female, underwent X-ray sterilization or castration, and about 200 of these were subjected to surgical removal of testicles or ovaries. Whatever statistics are available derive from the Auschwitz policy of keeping relatively accurate surgical records of these experiments.

Like Clauberg, Schumann continued his experiments in Ravensbrück, there victimizing thirteen-year-old Gypsy girls.

After the war he managed to live obscurely in Germany— although recognized at Nuremberg as a war criminal—until an application for a license for a hunting gun led to his being identified. He fled Germany precipitately, traveled extensively, and eventually settled in Khartoum in the Sudan as head of a hospital. There for about seven years he apparently became something of a Good Samaritan. . . . He fled to Ghana, from where he was eventually handed over . . . to representatives of West Germany. By then, he had become weakened from chronic malaria and other illnesses. In custody for several years, he was convicted for his involvement in direct medical killing or "euthanasia"; but because of his heart condition and generally deteriorating health, he was released without having stood trial for his sterilization and castration experiments. He died in Frankfurt in 1983.

Specimens for a Museum

Block 10 played an important part in a form of "anthropological research" that was among the most grotesque expressions of the Nazi biomedical vision. Dr. Marie L. tells of its Auschwitz beginnings:

> There appeared [on Block 10] a new protagonist of racial theories. He chose his material by having naked women of all

ages file . . . in front of him. He wanted to do anthropological measurements. . . . He had measurements of all the parts
of the body taken ad infinitum. . . . They were told that they
had the extraordinary good fortune to be selected, that they
would leave Auschwitz to go to an excellent camp, some-
where in Germany . . . [where] they would be very well
treated, where would be happy. . . .

These women were taken to the concentration camp at
Natzweiler, near Strasbourg, which, although not designated as an extermination camp, nonetheless possessed its
own gas chamber with the usual false showerheads as well as
one additional feature: a one-way mirror that allowed those
on the outside of the gas chamber to observe those inside.
This mirror had been installed because the gas chamber itself had been constructed as part of the necessary research
equipment.

A prisoner doctor reported that the group of Auschwitz
women (thirty-nine of them according to other records)
were given a sham physical examination for reassurance,
then gassed, and that the corpses were immediately transported to the anatomy pavilion of the Strasbourg University
Hospital. A French inmate, who had to assist the project's director, SS Captain Dr. August Hirt, told how "preservation
began immediately" with the arrival of bodies that were "still
warm, the eyes . . . wide open and shining." There were two
subsequent shipments of men, from each of whom the left
testicle had been removed and sent to Hirt's anatomy lab. . . .

Toward the end of the war, there was apparently some
confusion about whether and how much to continue with research procedures, and eventually the evidence was ordered
to be destroyed. But that process could not be completed,
and French forces liberating Strasbourg found in Hirt's dissection room "many wholly unprocessed corpses," many
"partly-processed corpses," and a few that had been "de-
fleshed . . . late in 1944," and their heads burned to avoid any
possibility of identification—with "special care taken to remove the number tattooed on the left forearm." Hirt himself disappeared at that time, and is now known to have
killed himself shortly afterward. . . .

The Sick Doctor

Dr. Johann Paul Kremer . . . was fifty-nine years old when he arrived [in Auschwitz] in August 1942. . . .

Kremer had a long-standing research interest in problems of starvation, which he pursued by seeking debilitated inmates selected for death, whom he later termed "the proper specimens." After he had a patient "placed on the dissection table," where he took a history focused on weight and weight loss, an SS orderly injected phenol into the person's heart: "I stood at a distance from the dissection table holding jars, ready for the segments [organs] cut out immediately after death . . . segments of the liver, spleen and pancreas." On some occasions, Kremer arranged to examine these patients or have them photographed prior to their murder. We may say that he made maximally pragmatic use of the death factory for his own scientific aims. Dr. Jan W. told how, if Kremer spotted a prisoner whose cranial shape seemed unusual, or who interested him in any way, he would order that prisoner photographed and injected with phenol for his collection of "fresh corpse samples of liver and other organs," and concluded that "Kremer looked upon the prisoners as so many rabbits."

Dr. Kremer became notorious for a diary he kept (which was eventually discovered and published), with such sequences as:

> September 4, 1942. . . . Present at a special action [selection] in the women's camp. . . . The most horrible of horrors. . . .
>
> September 6. . . . Today, Sunday, an excellent dinner: tomato soup, half a chicken with potatoes and red cabbage (20 g. of fat), sweet pudding and magnificent vanilla ice cream. . . .
>
> October 10. . . . I took and preserved . . . material from quite fresh corpses, namely the liver, spleen, and pancreas. . . .
>
> October 11. . . . Today, Sunday, we got for dinner quite a big piece of roast hare with dumplings and red cabbage for 1.25 RM.

Kremer was imprisoned for ten years in Poland, and again tried back home in Münster, where he was sentenced to another ten years, considered already served. He died in 1965. . . .

Human Guinea Pigs

There is an additional Auschwitz research function: that of the camp as a constant source of victims for research done almost anywhere. Besides the Auschwitz prisoners taken to Strasbourg to be made part of Professor Hirt's skeleton collection, there are many other examples: eight prisoners from Auschwitz sent to Sachsenhausen for experiments with epidemic hepatitis, in which the possible death of the inmates was an accepted part of the arrangement; and the notorious sequence of twenty Jewish children, ages five to twelve, transferred from Auschwitz to Neuengamme in Hamburg, where they were subjected to injections of virulent tubercular serum and to other experiments, until they were removed from Neuengamme and secretly murdered just before the arrival of Allied troops. Auschwitz was not just a medicalized death factory but a source of "raw materials" for everyone's deadly medical experiments

Prisoner physicians could speak with bitter accuracy about the specific way in which their and other inmates' humanity was negated by Nazi experimenters. One observed that "man was the cheapest experimental animal. . . . Cheaper than a rat." Another declared that the experiments "had no scientific basis, and . . . that the main interest they had for those who performed them was to give Berlin, in their detailed reports, the illusion of important and continuous work, so that these brave 'researchers' might be kept far from the front in a position of sinecure."

We know that Nazi doctors partly justified the experiments by their sense that Jews were in any case doomed. While prisoner doctors made no such justification, their emotions were also affected by the Jewish death sentence. Dr. Jacob R. could remember a feeling that "the experiments were of considerably less import than the whole inferno I was viewing there."

The experiments represent, among other things, a removal of medical limits. Ordinary medical behavior is predicated upon maintaining life—and refraining from actual or potential killing or maiming one's patient in the name of enhancing the life of one's own group or people. Paradoxically, that medical vision of social cure contributed directly to using medicine to kill or injure. Hence the array of Auschwitz experiments, and others done elsewhere including artificially inflicted burns with phosphorous incendiary bombs; experiments on the effects of drinking sea water; experiments with various forms of poison, by ingestion as well as in bullets or arrows; widespread experiments on artificially induced typhus, as well as with epidemic hepatitis and with malaria; experiments in cold immersion ("in freezing water") to determine the body's reactions and susceptibilities; experiments with mustard gas in order to study the kinds of wounds it can cause; experiments on the regeneration of bone, muscle, nerve tissue, and on bone transplantation, involving removal of various bones, muscles, and nerves from healthy women. All of the experiments were related to the Nazi biomedical vision, whether they directly contributed to cultural genocide (as in the case of sterilization) or were the work of German physicians taking a leading role in biological and genetic purification.

In experiments in sterilization, of course, the ideological source and goals are clear. But all the other experiments as well reflect the Nazi image of "life unworthy of life," of creatures who, because less than human, can be studied, altered, manipulated, mutilated, or killed—in the service of the Nordic race, and ultimately of remaking humankind. One experiments without limit in order to "gather together the best blood" and "once more breed over the generations the pure type of Nordic German." The task is never accomplished, so one must continue experimenting. All of Auschwitz becomes not only a vast experiment but an unending one.

From Imprisonment to Annihilation

Yitzhak Arad

The Nazis murdered people in many different, often gruesome ways. The way they treated people while they still were alive was also horrible and led to the deaths of tens of thousands of men, women, and children. Try to imagine being confined in a prison with little or nothing to eat. The temperature outside may be freezing and your clothes are little more than rags. You might not have any shoes or a coat. You have to stand outside at attention for hours and perhaps work at a backbreaking task. If you get hurt or sick, you probably will be killed. If you break a rule by, say, trying to get extra food, you can be severely beaten. The guards might beat you for no reason at all. Is it any wonder so few people survived for more than a few months in the camps? The miracle is that anyone survived. This excerpt describes the daily life of prisoners in the camps. Most of the specifics relate to Treblinka, but they apply to most of the other camps as well. Yitzhak Arad is one of the leading experts on the Holocaust and a former chairman of Yad Vashem.

The routine of the prisoner's daily life began early in the morning, usually at four o'clock. In the summer at this time it was already light, but in the winter it was still pitch dark. [Camp survivor] Rudolf Reder described the start of the day in Belzec:

> At 3:30 in the morning the Askar [Ukrainian] who guarded the barrack during the night knocked on the door and shouted: "Get up! Get up!" Before we could even rise, the

bully Schmidt burst in and rushed us out with a whip. We ran out with one shoe in our hand, and sometimes even barefoot. Usually we slept in our clothes and shoes because we had no time to get dressed in the morning. . . . We got up feeling miserable and tired. The same feeling we had gone to sleep with.

As the prisoners got up, the entire area of the Jews' living barracks came alive. The doors of huts were opened from the outside by the Ukrainians and the urination and excrement bowls were taken to the toilets. The huts were cleaned, the blankets were folded, and the prisoners were allowed to leave for their meager breakfast, which was followed by roll call.

During the roll call the prisoners were lined up in several rows in front of the huts. The "barrack elders" reviewed their people and reported the number to the "camp elder." He, in turn, added up the total number of prisoners and submitted his report to the SS man who was reviewing the roll call. These statistics were then reported to the camp commander or his deputy.

After the morning roll call, the prisoners were divided into work groups. The capos [prisoner leaders] escorted the work groups to the work sites and supervised the prisoners throughout the day. Throughout the workday the prisoners were exposed to the harsh treatment of the SS supervisors. Dov Freiberg testified about these cruelties in Sobibor:

> I shall tell the story of one day, an ordinary day, much like any other. That day I worked at cleaning a shed full of belongings and transferring them to the sorting shed. An umbrella had gotten stuck in a roof beam, and the SS man Paul Groth ordered a boy to get it down. The boy climbed up, fell from the roof and was injured. Groth punished him with twenty-five lashes. Groth was pleased with what had happened and called over another German and told him he had found "parachutists" among the Jews. We were ordered to climb up to the roof, one after another. The agile—and I was one of them—succeeded in climbing up without falling. But the majority did not succeed; they fell down, broke legs, were whipped, bitten by [the guard dog] Barry, and shot.

This game was not enough for Groth. There were many

mice around, and each of us was ordered to catch two mice. He selected five prisoners, ordered them to pull down their trousers, and we dropped the mice inside. The people were ordered to remain at attention, but they could not without moving. They were whipped.

But this was not enough for Groth. He called over a Jew, forced him to drink alcohol until he felt dead. When the work was finished, we were ordered to lay the man on a board, pick him up and slowly march while singing a funeral march.

This is the description of one ordinary day. And many of them were even worse. . . .

The Workday

The workday usually lasted from six in the morning until six in the evening, with a short break for lunch. At twelve noon the signal for lunch would be given, and the prisoners, work group by work group, led by the capos, were taken in the direction of the kitchen, where they received their meal. Shortly after, the signal for the end of the lunch break was sounded, and the prisoners were returned to their work sites. On the way to and from work, the prisoners were made to sing, and whoever dared sing without "enthusiasm" was whipped. During periods when there was not much activity going on in the camps, work on Sunday would last only until the afternoon, and the rest of the day would be spent cleaning the living barracks, airing out the blankets, and performing various other cleaning jobs. At six in the evening, the signal for the end of the workday was given, and the prisoners were returned to Roll-Call Square for the evening roll call. This roll call took much longer than the morning roll call and sometimes lasted as much as a few hours. After attendance was taken, the sick or weak-looking prisoners were taken from the ranks, brought to the *Lazarett* [pit], and shot. Reder described a scene of this sort in Belzec:

Usually the doctor prepared the list of the feeble, or the *Oberzugführer* who was in charge of the prisoners prepared the list of the "transgressors" in order to execute thirty to

A prisoner is supported by fellow inmates during roll call. Prisoners who seemed ill or weak were removed from the formation and killed.

forty prisoners. They were taken to the pit and shot. They were replaced by the same number of people, taken from the arriving transport. . . .

Floggings and "Sports"

At the evening roll call, punishment was meted out to those prisoners who had committed some "crime" during the workday. Any small infringement was an excuse for punishing a prisoner: if he did not work fast enough, or energetically enough; if he did not respond properly when an SS man passed him; or if, in a search of his belongings, food, money, a cigarette, or a picture or memento—the only tangible thing left him from his past—was found. Even those prisoners who had already received "treatment" during the workday and who still bore fresh whip lashes on their bodies were given additional "treatment" at the evening roll call.

The punishment at the evening roll call was generally whipping. In Treblinka, at Roll-Call Square, there was a special bench cemented into the ground for this purpose. The prisoner was tied to the bench with straps in a way that his torso rested on the bench while his feet dangled on the floor at a 90-degree angle to his body and his buttocks protruded exactly at the corner of the bench.

In the first months of the camp's existence, they would whip the prisoners while they were dressed. But at one of the whipping sessions it seemed to [SS guard] Kurt Franz, who happened to be present, that there was something suspicious. He ordered the prisoner to take off his pants, and then they saw that the prisoner had stuck a towel in the seat of his pants to soften the blows. From then on the prisoners were ordered to lower their pants before they were strapped to the bench, and the blows were inflicted on the bare skin.

Prisoners were usually given between twenty-five and fifty lashes with a special leather strap. The SS usually did the whipping; sometimes a Ukrainian was given the assignment. Frequently the prisoner had to count the number of lashes out loud, and if he made a mistake, or if he had no more strength to count, they would start over—from the beginning. There were prisoners who, gritting their teeth, took their lashes without a sound; others screamed to high heaven. There were instances of beatings of twelve- or fourteen-year-olds, and their screams shocked and terrified the prisoners standing on the sides. But the SS enjoyed it. As the screams grew louder and louder, Franz and [another guard] Küttner—when they attended the roll call—enjoyed themselves all the more. When the whipping was over, the prisoner's buttocks were a piece of bleeding meat. . . .

Another form of punishment was "sports activities." In Treblinka the prisoners who received punishments of this kind had to run in a circle and alternately drop to the floor and get up, and all the while the SS and the Ukrainians would whip them. The prisoners who had no strength to continue with this "exercise" were taken to the side. The "sports" would continue until all the weak had collapsed and had been removed from the circle of runners. With the completion of the "sports activities," all those who had not been able to go on were taken to the *Lazarett* and put to death. The "activity" itself was a selection in which the strong survived and the weak were finished off. . . .

The whipping, the "sports," and the killing were all part of the routine of the evening roll call. The prisoners had to stand and watch the selections the whipping, and the "sports" until the end. After the orchestra, under the direction of Artur Gold, was established, when the whipping was finished they would play marches and the choir would sing. At the end of the roll call, all the prisoners had to sing the "Treblinka Anthem," and only then was the "Dismissed!" order given. The prisoners finally could return to their quarters. . . .

There was no shower in the area of the living quarters, and the prisoners had no opportunity to wash or shower for months at a time. The limited amount of water that they were rationed was hardly enough to quench their thirst, let alone for washing. . . . Conditions such as these all but invited disease and epidemics.

Food in the Camps

The food that was distributed to the prisoners in the camps was very meager, and it was difficult to live on it for an extended period of time—especially since we are talking about people who were put to work at hard labor for many hours of the day. For breakfast the prisoners received a cup of warm water, which was supposed to be coffee, with 150 to 200 grams of frequency stale bread. For lunch they were given soup with some unpeeled potatoes; sometimes this meal also included horse meat. In the evening they got only coffee.

In Treblinka during the period of almost daily transports, until December 1942, the prisoners were able to help themselves to the food that the transportees had brought with them. In the parcels of those who were taken to the gas chambers were substantial quantities of food, since the deportees thought they were being taken to work camps in the East. The packages usually included bread, potatoes, meat, butter, and other foodstuffs. Although the prisoners were ordered to transfer everything to the camp authorities, the SS became resigned to the fact that some of the large quantity of food that was brought into the camp by the deportees remained for the prisoners. There was therefore never a scarcity of food during the period of the transports, and the prisoners were not hungry. In December, however, as the frequency of the transports subsided, the SS men and Ukrainians took for themselves all the food that was brought into the camp, and the prisoners were forbidden to take any of it. Prisoners caught with a single piece of bread were executed. When the transports for extermination stopped, the Jewish prisoners began starving and had to make do with the meager portions that the Germans distributed. One of the prisoners describes the hunger:

> From day to day our meager rations were reduced. Food was distributed only once a day, in the evening. Every man received six cooked potatoes with the peels still on them. In addition, they distributed a slice of bread which was for the morning and which we were not allowed to eat until then. As we twisted and fumed on the bunks at night, our insides were so empty that we couldn't stop thinking about that slice of bread until we broke off a piece of the bread that tasted like clay and smelled like a sick animal. There were those who gobbled up the entire piece but who were still hungry afterward. What's more, in the morning they could expect harsh punishment as well.

The hunger brought on trade and speculation in food. Money, gold, and other valuables that the prisoners took from the clothes and belongings of the murdered were used to buy food. Trade in food, on a limited scale went on in the camps during the entire time, even when food was relatively plentiful. During those times the prisoners would buy special foods like salami, canned goods, alcoholic drinks, and cigarettes. But when the hunger set in, they bought anything they could get their hands on: bread, potatoes, fat, sugar, and so on. Then the prices soared: they would have to pay gold rubles for a loaf of bread or tens of dollars for a half pint of vodka. The middlemen in the food trade were the Ukrainian guards: the Jewish prisoners paid, and the Ukrainians brought in food from the villages around Treblinka. . . .

A prisoner who was caught with smuggled food, or with money or valuables that he intended to trade for food, paid with his life. The SS men kept a close watch over the buyers and sellers of food. In testimonies about Treblinka, there are even stories of Jews who for the slightest favors or for additional food would be willing to inform on their friends. Informers of this kind were known to all the prisoners. . . .

[Former inmate] Shmuel Wilenberg writes:

> Certain informers were executed by the prisoners. It was
> done at night when the entire camp was deep in sleep. Four
> men would approach the informer, throw a blanket over his
> head, tie a rope to one of the roof beams and hang the ac-
> cused. In the morning, when the SS men would see the
> hanging man, they would not be surprised, for it was a fre-
> quent sight—many people would commit suicide by hanging
> or by swallowing poison.

Other testimonies of prisoners in Treblinka contain no
mention of the killing of informers.

Despite the efforts of the SS personnel and despite the executions that were carried out, the trade in and smuggling of
food in Treblinka never stopped; it continued during the entire period that the camps functioned.

In testimonies from Belzec and Sobibor there is no mention about food smuggling.

Lavatories and *Scheissmeister*

Throughout the day the prisoners were under the careful
watch of the SS, the Ukrainians, and the capos. Theirs was a
day of perpetual work and motion, and woe to anyone who
stopped to rest. Anyone who slowed down would be
whipped on the spot or recorded by the capo or the SS man
in charge for "treatment" at the evening roll call. The only
place the prisoners were able to sit quietly for any amount of
time without being watched was in the lavatories. There
were only a few toilets in the camps, but the prisoners—and
especially the weak and sick among them who continued
working only out of fear that if they stopped working they
faced certain death—found the only place for a short rest
was in the lavatories. In general the Jewish capos were con-
siderate of the sick and looked the other way during their
frequent visits and long stays in the lavatories. During the
winter that the typhus epidemic spread through Treblinka,
the toilets became the main rest area.

In Treblinka, Küttner began noticing the "exaggerated"
use of the toilets by the prisoners and, to put a stop to it, he

appointed a Jewish supervisor over every toilet; these super-visors were given the title *Scheissmeister* ("shit master"). For their entertainment, the Germans dressed the *Scheissmeister* in a special outfit: the clothes of a rabbi and an eight-cornered cantor's turban. He had to wear a large alarm clock around his neck and carry a whip. He was also ordered to grow a Vandyke beard. He would have to make certain that the prisoners did not stay in the toilet for more than two minutes and that there should be no more than five people in the lavatory at a time. It was the duty of the *Scheissmeister* to chase out those who dallied. A prisoner who did not obey the *Scheissmeister* was registered and his number was submit-ted to Küttner.

Thus the lavatories, which had been the only place where the prisoners had found some semblance of peace, turned into yet another place of hardship and torture.

Night in the Camp: A Time of Rest and Reflection

At nine in the evening, the prisoners were locked into their barracks. Shortly thereafter, the lights were turned out and night fell on the camp. In Belzec the lights were turned out half an hour after nightfall, and the prisoners were not even allowed to talk with one another. In Treblinka lights-out was usually at 21:00 and in Sobibor at 22:00.

The night hours in the huts were the only time that the prisoners were able to rest, relax a bit, collect themselves and their thoughts, with no Germans or Ukrainians spying on them. Wilenberg describes night in Treblinka:

> We would welcome the night and the few hours of relative quiet that we had for sleeping. Sleep allowed us to forget the harsh life in the camp, dulled our suffering and sometimes transported us to a dreamland where everything was fantasy. But usually nightmares came to haunt us, actually they were the impressions of what we had seen during the day. Because we were suffering from sickness and weakness from hunger and hard labor, into our sleep came all kinds of weird thoughts, extraordinary notions that, combined with the hal-lucinations that ruled our subconscious, expressed them-selves in nightmares and horrible dreams. Sometimes the

stillness of night was broken by a sigh or scream; sometimes by the muffled cough of someone suffering from tuberculosis, or someone snoring loudly. Here and there someone would wake up, let out a juicy curse, punch his noisy neighbor, and then fall back to sleep—which was more of a snatched nap. But there were also nights with no sleep, full of work, beatings, and endless running.

. . . In spite of the hell they lived in, which became their daily existence, those who survived continued to go through this routine and, to a certain extent, even got used to it. Dov Freiberg says:

> It is difficult for me to explain what happened to us—how we could continue to live. I remember in the beginning when a transport arrived, we wanted to die. But later, after some time, transports arrived, and we were sitting and eating. Even the suicides stopped, and those who did commit suicide were the newcomers who were not yet used to living in this inferno. All this in spite of the fact that we knew that our end would also be cremation in Camp III. If someone among us looked a little better than the others, we used to tell him jokingly, "You'll burn better because of your fat. . . ."

Daily Life

The conditions under which the prisoners were kept in the camps, the daily selections, the torture and punishment, the hunger and disease, all contributed to the fact that the average time that a Jewish prisoner remained alive in the camps was a few months at most. Only a few survived for longer periods. Those who entered the camp around the time of its establishment and lasted until the final stages of the camp's existence can be counted on one hand.

The constant turnover in the prisoner ranks, the daily executions and replacement with new arrivals from transports that came from different cities and countries retarded the growth of personal contact and deeper ties among the prisoners. That hardly anyone knew anyone else was a deterrent to establishing close relationships. It also protected the prisoners from future emotional hurt in the event of a death of a friend.

Auschwitz: The Death Factory

Ota Kraus and Erich Kulka

It is difficult to believe, looking back with the benefit of hindsight and after having read books and seen movies about the Holocaust, that the Jews did not know what was going to happen when they entered the concentration camps. Some people may have heard rumors, but they would not have believed them. The Nazis took elaborate pains to disguise their intentions—from putting signs over the entrance to camps reading "*Arbeit Macht Frei*" ("Work Makes One Free") to putting signs on the gas chambers reading "Delousing" and asking the victims to remember the number of the hook on which they place their clothes so they could collect them when they come out of the "shower." You may recall the powerful scene in *Schindler's List* when a little girl makes a gesture of slashing her throat as a trainload of prisoners goes by. Victims did not get these hints; in fact, the prisoners in the camps were strictly forbidden from saying so much as a word to new arrivals to ensure that there would be no resistance. This excerpt was written by two political prisoners, Ota Kraus and Erich Kulka, each of whom spent virtually the entire war in concentration camps. Both survived Auschwitz.

The first mass destruction by gas in Auschwitz [I] took place in the spring of 1942, at the only crematorium then in existence—in Auschwitz I. Before this, gassing had been carried out on some small group of emaciated prisoners, notably Russian prisoners of war.

The Auschwitz crematorium was small. It had one gas chamber for 600-800 people, and six furnaces.

One of the first experiments in mass execution by gas

Excerpted from Ota Kraus and Erich Kulka, *The Death Factory* (London: Pergamon Press, 1966).

took place when 700 Slovak Jews arrived from Žilina in May, 1942. . . .

In the "confession" which he wrote in Cracow prison in 1947, Rudolf Hoess, former Commandant of Auschwitz, described the first experiments at Auschwitz as follows:

"One day in 1941, when I was on duty, my deputy, Fritsch, carried out a test execution by gas on some prisoners. For this he used hydrocyanic cyclon B which up to then had been used for destroying insects in the camp. The gassing took place in the cells of Block II. I subsequently went to inspect the results wearing a gas mask. The prisoners, packed tight in the cells, had died immediately the crystals of cyclon gas were thrown in. A few stifled cries—and all was over.

"This first attempt at exterminating people with gas did not weigh at all heavily on my conscience—perhaps because I was considerably excited by the efficiency of the experiment. I have a more vivid memory of the gassing of 900 Soviet prisoners of war. This took place shortly afterwards in the old crematorium, since the use of Block II would have caused considerable inconvenience and made it necessary to take elaborate security measures.

"As the Russians were getting out of the train, several holes were drilled in the roof of the mortuary at the crematorium. The Russians undressed in the entrance hall and then filed quietly into the mortuary, having been told that they were to be deloused. Once they were inside the room which they filled completely, the doors were bolted behind them and the gas was turned on through the holes in the roof. I do not know how long they took dying but they made quite a din for some time. As the gas was fed in, some of the prisoners shouted 'gas,' which was followed by prolonged shouting and a furious battering on the door. But the door held. After some hours the mortuary was opened up and aired.

"This was the first time I had seen so large a pile of gassed bodies. I had expected death by gas to be bad enough, but this made me feel ill. I was overcome by a feeling of horror. . . . All the same I have to state quite frankly that I was quite satisfied with the gassing of this convoy because we had soon to begin with the mass extermination of the Jews, and up to that day neither [Final Solution architect Adolf] Eichmann nor I had had any clear idea how to set about the task of mass executions. We knew that some kind of gas had to be used, but we were not sure which gas or how to use it. Thanks to this experiment we had found both the gas and the method of use.". . .

People were brought in lorries [to Birkenau]. As they were unloaded they found themselves surrounded by a close cordon of SS guards, armed with automatic rifles, hand grenades and machine guns. The guards also had trained dogs.

The victims were ordered to enter the undressing-rooms in groups, women and children in one, men in the other. They were told that they were in a work camp and must have a bath and be disinfected as a precaution against infection.

Next they were ordered to undress to the skin and to arrange their clothes and other belongings tidily. They had to hand in their valuables but were promised that they would get them back. After this the SS drove them into the gas chambers. If any of them saw through the trick and offered resistance, the SS beat them with sticks, whips and rifle-butts.

As soon as a gas chamber was full—up to 150 people were crammed into a space of 21 square yards—the SS banged the doors to, screwed up the bars, and fed in the poison through the window in the wall. The window was then hermetically sealed, and for some minutes shouting and groaning could be heard.

After about half an hour the SS opened the rear doors. It was a ghastly sight. Naked women and children were convulsed into the most horrible attitudes, their skin lacerated, their fists clenched and their limbs bleeding from biting each other in their pain. The victims died standing up, for they were so wedged together that they could not fall.

The *Sonderkommando* (special work squad) then set to work throwing the corpses into deep pits prepared in the vicinity. The rooms were quickly cleaned out, whitewashed and sprayed with eau de Cologne (brought in ample quantities by the victims themselves, especially the women). The next convoy must know nothing of the terrible tragedy which had been enacted there but a moment before and now awaited them.

The process of gassing, clearing away the corpses and cleaning the rooms lasted about an hour; a convoy of from two to three thousand people was thus destroyed and cleared away within a few hours.

After a few months, although the corpses were covered with chlorine, lime and earth, an intolerable stench began to hang around the entire neighbourhood. Deadly bacteria were found in springs and wells, and there was a severe danger of epidemics.

To meet this problem, the *Sonderkommando* was increased in size. Day and night, working in two shifts, the prisoners in the squad dug up decaying corpses, took them away on narrow-gauge trucks and burnt them in heaps in the immediate vicinity. The work of exhuming and burning 50,000 corpses lasted almost till December, 1942. After this experience the Nazis stopped burying their victims and cremated them instead.

Such were the emergency methods used for destroying people at Birkenau in the early days. They continued in use

Human remains are visible inside these furnaces, where the bodies of gassed Holocaust victims were burned.

until February, 1943, when the crematoria were completed and brought into use—first Crematorium I, and then the others. . . .

The four cremations together had eight gas chambers with a capacity of 8000 people; there were forty-six furnaces all told, each capable of burning at least three bodies in 20 minutes. . . .

When the furnaces were unable to cope with the number of bodies—a frequent occurrence—the corpses were burnt by the thousand on great heaps. . . .

Direct from Train to Gas Chamber

Until June, 1944, trains to Auschwitz stopped for "classification" at a special ramp, invisible both from the camp itself and the immediate vicinity. A train would consist of from fifty to eighty cattle trucks. As soon as it arrived at the ramp, it was surrounded by a close cordon of SS guards with their dogs. Personnel from the "Canada" Disposal Squad opened up the trucks, and with much yelling and shouting the people were driven out of them in a state of utter confusion.

The first duty of the "Canada" Squad at the station was to unload the newcomers' luggage as quickly as possible and take everything away from them except their handbags. The people were told that their baggage would be returned to them in the camp. If any person tried to object, his luggage was taken off him by force.

The "Canada" Squad were forbidden, under pain of death by shooting, to speak to the new arrivals, and the SS guards watched to see that this order was obeyed.

As the men got out of the trucks, they were separated from the women and children. Then an SS doctor and SS officer, after a superficial examination of each man, would show by a jerk of the thumb whether they were to go to the right or left—life or death.

Children were assigned to death, and women who did not want to be separated from their children went with them. Of the remaining women only those from sixteen to thirty who were young and healthy were selected for the camp; the rest were sent to the gas chambers. Of the men some 15 to 20%

were classified as fit for work.

People destined for the gas chambers were loaded on to waiting lorries. Those classified as fit for work had to walk to the camps on foot, but before they left they were given the option of going on the lorries, if they thought they could not walk—which meant death in the gas chambers. . . .

The Canada Disposal Squad

The "Canada" Disposal Squad consisted exclusively of Jews, both; men and women, though its leaders, also prisoners, were German men and women from the Reich. . . .

Members of the "Canada" squad . . . sabotaged their work wherever possible. The parcels and suitcases brought by the new arrivals were thrown into their blocks in fantastic disarray, and once the blocks were full up the goods were deposited outside. Often the various classified items, such as blankets, underwear, feather-beds, footwear, medicines and other goods, lay about in the rain for weeks on end until they were soaked through and utterly useless. The place was like a huge open-air jumble sale with silk underwear, eau de Cologne, expensive soap, furs, shoes, cigarette lighters, knives, ladies' handbags.

A special detachment from the squad ripped up clothes, tore shoes apart, and searched the various ointments, toothpastes and face-creams for any precious items that might be hidden there, such as gold, diamonds or foreign currency. Some members of the squad deliberately destroyed everything they could lay their hands on, tearing up dollar bills and other bank-notes, breaking watches, and so on. . . .

When they finished work, the "Canadians" were closely searched and often had to strip naked. They were again checked at the entrance to the camp. Nevertheless they still found ways and means of smuggling things into the camp.

"Canada" played an extremely important role in the camp. It was the source from which the prisoners obtained the wherewithal to make their life to some degree bearable. When an escape was being planned, "Canada" supplied money, clothing, compasses, field-glasses, wigs and identity cards. Cameras were also obtained in this way, and some members of a secret organization actually succeeded in taking photos of people being "selected" for the gas chamber. These photos were among the documentary material which we subsequently sent out from the camp through the partisans in the neighbourhood.

On the other hand, many prisoners met their death as a result of their contact with "Canada," for all persons caught carrying forbidden goods, especially valuables, were viciously punished.

Children and the Holocaust

United States Holocaust Memorial Museum

It is not fair to try to distinguish among the victims of the Holocaust, and yet it is impossible not to feel especially sad and angered by the senseless slaughter of children. No one knows how many were killed for sure, but the number is unquestionably in the millions. The horror of what was done to children is too great to go into detail. Why was it necessary to kill infants? What possible threat did they pose to the Third Reich? In Hitler's mind, any Jew was a parasite, the carrier of disease, the source of impurity. To exempt children from the Final Solution would have been to allow Jews to have a future. When Hitler said he planned to exterminate the Jews, he meant every last one. We know that the Jewish people—and the entire world—lost many great musicians, artists, philosophers, and doctors during the Holocaust. How many of the children would have grown up to become Albert Einsteins, Leonard Bernsteins, Henry Kissingers or Marc Chagalls? How many would have married and had children who would have grown up and made the world a better place? How many children would have become loving husbands, wives, fathers and mothers? Many articles in this encyclopedia deal with decisions people made during the Holocaust. Children had no choice. This article from the U.S. Holocaust Memorial Museum briefly describes the fate of Jewish children during World War II.

Full statistics for the tragic fate of children who died during the Holocaust will never be known. Some estimates range as high as 1.5 million murdered children. This figure includes more than 1.2 million Jewish children, tens of thousands of

Reprinted from the United States Holocaust Memorial Museum, "Children and the Holocaust," an online article found at www.ushmm.org. Provided courtesy of the United States Holocaust Memorial Museum, Washington, D.C.

Gypsy children and thousands of institutionalized handicapped children who were murdered under Nazi rule in Germany and occupied Europe.

Although children were seldom the targets of Nazi violence because they were children, they were persecuted along with their families for racial, religious, or political reasons. Children are not a single unified group because of the enormous and complex variations in their situation and ages. It is important to separate the distinct needs of three different age groups: (1) infants and toddlers up to age 6; (2) young children ages 7 to 12; and (3) adolescents from 13 to 18 years old. Their respective chances for survival and their ability to perform physical labor varied enormously by age. Chances of survival were somewhat higher for older children, since they could potentially be assigned to forced labor in concentration camps and ghettos.

The Jews were a special target of Nazi ideology and policies, which ultimately resulted in the Holocaust, the systematic, state sponsored murder of almost 6 million European Jews. From the very first, Jews and their children suffered at the hands of the Nazis, and thus the world of Jewish children was rapidly restricted as soon as the Nazis came to power in Germany in January 1933. Before 1939, German Jewish children were trapped in a no man's land between the alternatives of an increasingly hostile German milieu and the insecure and often unreachable world of potential safety through emigration, the latter was linked to the fate of their families. After 1935, close friends suddenly avoided the company of their Jewish classmates, sometimes becoming hostile, unfriendly, and even spiteful. Letters from German children to the editors of the Nazi tabloid *Der Stürmer* reveal a shameful potpourri of stupidity and fanaticism against their Jewish classmates. There were additional humiliations confronting Jewish and Gypsy children in German classrooms with the oppressive teaching and humiliating tenets of racial biology that humiliated them and designated them as racially inferior. As a result, education as a form of resistance was developed in German Jewish schools after 1933 and provided both background and experience for the later clandestine schools created in the ghettos and concentration camps after 1939.

One of the first laws that affected Jewish students was the "Law against Overcrowding in German schools and universities" of 25 April 1933 that restricted the number of Jewish children in schools, not to exceed 1.5 percent of the total number of students. Jewish children of war veterans and those with a non-Jewish parent were initially exempted. Many schools placed Jewish students on vacation in April 1933, a temporary expedient while awaiting legislative developments. These decrees escalated in intensity and shortly after the November 1938 pogrom ("Kristallnacht"/ Crystal Night). On 15 November 1938, German Jewish children were prohibited from attending German schools. This same measure also excluded Gypsies children from German schools. The segregated Jewish schools existed under steadily deteriorating conditions and increased Nazi pressure until 1942; they were finally closed on 7 July 1942, after the first wave of deportations of German Jews to the East had been completed. After 1938, Gypsy children fell through the social net and their schooling was not of serious concern to Nazi authorities.

First in Germany and later in occupied Europe, the Jewish communal experiences of persecution and pauperization affected children. The world of childhood and adolescence, usually a time of testing and experimentation, became inverted into a world of shrinking horizons and vulnerabilities after 1933. German Jewish children were systematically driven from the wider German milieu, creating a community under beleaguered isolation. They could no longer belong to the same clubs and social organizations as Aryan children, they were banned from using public recreational facilities and playgrounds, and were instead vulnerable to the traumas of loss and separation from their homes and familiar milieus. A few thousand German and Austrian Jewish children were able to escape the Nazi net, since they were sent abroad in "Kindertransports" to the Netherlands, Great Britain, Palestine, and the United States before 1939.

With the onset of war, Jewish children in occupied Poland and later throughout Europe were confined with their families in overcrowded ghettos and transit camps, exposed to malnutrition, disease, exposure, and early death.

Euthanasia

Gypsy and handicapped children were similarly categorized in Nazi Germany and occupied Europe by race and biology. The Nazi quest for a biologically homogeneous society already in July 1933 included the Law to Prevent Offspring with Hereditary Defects. In ever escalating legislation, mentally and physically handicapped children were vulnerable to sterilization prior to 1939 and to murder in the so-called euthanasia program after 1939. Eugenic and racial measures also extended to the small number (ca. 600) of German mulatto children (the offspring of German women and African French colonial troops occupying the Rhineland in the 1920s). These Afro-German children were registered by the Gestapo and Interior Ministry in 1937 and they were all brutally sterilized in German university hospitals that same year.

The methods of children's euthanasia were developed between February and May 1939. First, the physicians and Nazi officials registered their potential victims. Thus, registration forms, called *Meldebogen,* collected data from midwifes and physicians reporting all infants born with specific medical conditions. The first killings of children in special wards by overdoses of poison and medicaments already occurred in October 1939. Recalcitrant parents who attempted to remove their children from the killing wards were rarely able to succeed. With fathers already absent as soldiers, mothers who disagreed were often assigned to contractual labor, thereby necessitating the commitment of handicapped children in state institutions. The killing of disabled children marked the beginning of the euthanasia program and continued throughout the war. Children's euthanasia was central, because children represented posterity and the Nazi physicians considered the elimination of those they considered diseased and deformed as essential to their aim of racial purification. Although it is impossible to calculate the number of children killed in these special children's wards during

World War II, the best estimate is that at least 5,000 German and Austrian children were killed in these programs.

Survivors

Nazi persecution, arrests, and deportations were directed against all members of Jewish families, as well as many Gypsy families, without concern for age. Inevitably the children were among the prisoners at highest risk. Homeless, often orphaned, they had frequently witnessed the murder of parents, siblings, and relatives. They faced starvation, illness, brutal labor, and other indignities until they were consigned to the gas chambers. In relationship to adult prisoners, their chances for survival were usually smaller although their flexibility and adaptability to radically changed circumstances could sometimes increase the odds in their favor. That these Jewish children survived at all and also created diaries, poems, and drawings in virtually all ghettos and concentration camps is truly remarkable.

After 1939, there are four basic patterns that can describe the fate of both Jewish and non-Jewish children in occupied Europe: (1) those killed immediately on arrival in concentration camps and killing centers; (2) those killed shortly after birth (for example, the 870 infants born in the Ravensbrück concentration camp, largely to Jewish and Gypsy women, between 1943 and 1945); (3) those few born in ghettos and camps and surviving, such as the three year old Stefan Georg Zweig born in the Cracow ghetto and carried in a specially prepared rucksack through the concentration camp at Plaszow to Buchenwald in 1944, where he was hidden and protected by German communist prisoners; and (4) those children, usually above the age of 10, utilized as prisoners, laborers, and subjects for Nazi medical experiments. Thus, of the 15,000 children imprisoned in the Theresienstadt ghetto, only about 1,100 survived.

Children sometimes also survived in hiding and also participated in the resistance (as runners, messengers, smugglers). There is no comprehensive study about the fate of children in Nazi Germany and occupied Europe, since the story has been told in an episodic fashion as part of the fate of Jews in each country affected.

Chapter 3

Why Did the Holocaust Happen?

Turning|Points

IN WORLD HISTORY

German Racism

Raul Hilberg

Anti-Semitism did not begin or end with the Nazis. For centuries, Jews have been targets of those who resented Jews' distinct culture, those who were angered by their unwillingness to convert to Christianity, and by those who wanted scapegoats for their own misfortune. Much of the hatred of Jews has been fed by Christian and Protestant theologians whose followers did everything from harass the Jews, to isolate them in ghettos, to expel them from their homelands. The stereotypes attached to Jews through the centuries were handed down from generation to generation and were, therefore, familiar to the German people who heard them repeated by Hitler and his henchmen. The Nazis repeated the anti-Jewish measures of the past and took them to the gravest extreme. This history is described by Raul Hilberg, a retired political science professor, who is considered one of the leading authorities on the Holocaust.

The German destruction of the European Jews was a tour de force: the Jewish collapse under the German assault was a manifestation of failure. Both of these phenomena were the final product of an earlier age.

Anti-Jewish policies and actions did not have their beginning in 1933. For many centuries, and in many countries, the Jews had been victims of destructive action. What was the object of these activities? What were the aims of those who persisted in anti-Jewish deeds? Throughout Western history, three consecutive policies have been applied against Jewry in its dispersion.

The first anti-Jewish policy started in the fourth century

Excerpted from Raul Hilberg, *The Destruction of the European Jews*, the revised and definitive edition. Copyright © 1985 by Raul Hilberg. Reprinted with permission from Holmes and Meier.

after Christ in Rome. Early in the fourth century, during the reign of Constantine, the Christian Church gained power in Rome, and Christianity became the state religion. From this period, the state carried out Church policy. For the next twelve centuries, the Catholic Church prescribed the measures that were to be taken with respect to the Jews. Unlike the pre-Christian Romans, who claimed no monopoly on religion and faith, the Christian Church insisted on acceptance of Christian doctrine.

For an understanding of Christian policy toward Jewry, it is essential to realize that the Church pursued conversion not so much for the sake of aggrandizing its power (the Jews have always been few in number), but because of the conviction that it was the duty of true believers to save unbelievers from the doom of eternal hellfire. Zealousness in the pursuit of conversion was an indication of the depth of faith. The Christian religion was not one of many religions, but the true religion, the only one. Those who were not in its fold were either ignorant or in error. The Jews could not accept Christianity.

In the very early stages of the Christian faith, many Jews regarded Christians as members of a Jewish sect. The first Christians, after all, still observed the Jewish law. They had merely added a few nonessential practices, such as baptism, to their religious life. But their view was changed abruptly when Christ was elevated to Godhood. The Jews have only one God. This God is indivisible. He is a jealous God and admits of no other gods. He is not Christ, and Christ is not He. Christianity and Judaism have since been irreconcilable. An acceptance of Christianity has since signified an abandonment of Judaism.

In antiquity and in the Middle Ages, Jews did not abandon Judaism lightly. With patience and persistence the Church attempted to convert obstinate Jewry and for twelve hundred years the theological argument was fought without interruption. The Jews were not convinced. Gradually the Church began to back its words with force. The Papacy did not permit pressure to be put on individual Jews: Rome prohibited forceful conversions. However, the clergy did use pressure on the whole. Step by step, but with ever widening effect, the Church adopted "defensive" measures against its passive victims. Christians were "protected" from the "harmful" consequences of intercourse with Jews by rigid laws against intermarriage, by prohibitions of discussions about religious issues, by laws against domicile in common abodes. The Church "protected" its Christians from the "harmful" Jewish teachings by burning the Talmud and by barring Jews from public office.

These measures were precedent-making destructive activities. How little success the Church had in accomplishing its aim is revealed by the treatment of the few Jews who succumbed to the Christian religion. The clergy was not sure of its success—hence the widespread practice, in the Middle Ages, of identifying proselytes as former Jews; hence the inquisition of new Christians suspected of heresy; hence the issuance in Spain of certificates of "purity," signifying purely Christian ancestry, and the specification of "half-new Christians," "quarter-new Christians," "one-eighth-new Christians," and so on.

The failure of conversion had far-reaching consequences. The unsuccessful Church began to look on the Jews as a special group of people, different from Christians, deaf to Christianity, and dangerous to the Christian faith. . . .

Jews Get to Choose

From the thirteenth to the sixteenth century, the Jews of England, France, Germany, Spain, Bohemia, and Italy were presented with ultimatums that gave them no choice but one: conversion or expulsion. . . .

The post-ecclesiastic enemies of Jewry also took the idea that the Jews could not be changed, that they could not be converted, that they could not be assimilated, that they were a finished product, inflexible in their ways, set in their notions, fixed in their beliefs.

The expulsion and exclusion policy was adopted by the Nazis and remained the goal of all anti-Jewish activity until 1941. That year marks a turning point in anti-Jewish history. In 1941 the Nazis found themselves in the midst of a total war. Several million Jews were incarcerated in ghettos. Emigration was impossible. A last-minute project to ship the Jews to the African island of Madagascar had fallen through. The "Jewish problem" had to be "solved" in some other way. At this crucial time, the idea of a "territorial solution" emerged in Nazi minds. The "territorial solution," or "the final solution of the Jewish question in Europe," as it became known, envisaged the death of European Jewry. The European Jews were to be killed. This was the third anti-Jewish policy in history. . . .

The destruction of the European Jews between 1933 and 1945 appears to us now as an unprecedented event in history. Indeed, in its dimensions and total configuration, nothing like it had ever happened before. As a result of an organized undertaking, five million people were killed in the short space of a few years. The operation was over before anyone could grasp its enormity, let alone its implications for the future. . . .

German Efficiency

The destruction of the Jews was an administrative process, and the annihilation of Jewry required the implementation of systematic administrative measures in successive steps. There are not many ways in which a modern society can, in short order, kill a large number of people living in its midst. This is an efficiency problem of the greatest dimensions, one which poses uncounted difficulties and innumerable obstacles. Yet, in reviewing the documentary record of the destruction of the Jews, one is almost immediately impressed with the fact that the German administration knew what it was doing. With an unfailing sense of direction and with an uncanny pathfinding ability, the German bureaucracy found the shortest road to the final goal. . . .

Luther and the Jews

The picture of the Jew we encounter in Nazi propaganda and Nazi correspondence had been drawn several hundred years before. Martin Luther had already sketched the main outlines of that portrait, and the Nazis, in their time, had little to add to it. We shall look here at a few excerpts from

Luther's book *About the Jews and Their Lies*. In doing so, let it be stressed that Luther's ideas were shared by others in his century, and that the mode of his expression was the style of his times. His work is cited here only because he was a towering figure in the development of German thought, and the writing of such a man is not to be forgotten in the unearthing of so crucial a conceptualization as this. Luther's treatise about the Jews was addressed to the public directly and, in that pouring recital, sentences descended upon the audience in a veritable cascade. Thus the passage:

> Herewith you can readily see how they understand and obey the fifth commandment of God, namely, that they are thirsty bloodhounds and murderers of all Christendom, with full intent, now for more than fourteen hundred years, and indeed they were often burned to death upon the accusation that they had poisoned water and wells, stolen children, and torn and hacked them apart, in order to cool their temper secretly with Christian blood.

And:

> Now see what a fine, thick, fat lie that is when they complain that they are held captive by us. It is more than fourteen hundred years since Jerusalem was destroyed, and at this time it is almost three hundred years since we Christians have been tortured and persecuted by the Jews all over the world (as pointed out above), so that we might well complain that they had now captured us and killed us—which is the open truth. Moreover, we do not know to this day which devil has brought them here into our country; we did not look for them in Jerusalem.

Even now no one held them here, Luther continued. They might go whenever they wanted to. For they were a heavy burden, "like a plague, pestilence, pure misfortune in our country.". . .

This is Luther's picture of the Jews. First, they want to rule the world. Second. they are archcriminals, killers of Christ and all Christendom. Third. he refers to them as a "plague, pestilence, and pure misfortune." This Lutheran portrait of Jewish world rule, Jewish criminality, and the Jewish plague has often been repudiated. But, in spite of denial and exposure, the charges have survived. In four hundred years the picture has not changed.

German Anti-Semitism

In 1895 the Reichstag was discussing a measure, proposed by the anti-Semitic faction, for the exclusion of foreign Jews. The speaker, Ahlwardt, belonged to that faction. We reproduce here a few excerpts from his speech: . . .

Ahlwardt pointed out that the anti-Semites were fighting the Jews not because of their religion but because of their race. He then continued:

> The Jews accomplished what no other enemy has accomplished: they have driven the people from Frankfurt into the suburbs And that's the way it is wherever Jews congregate in large numbers. Gentlemen, the Jews are indeed beasts of prey. . . .

> Mr. Rickert [another deputy who had opposed the exclusion of the Jews] started by saying that we already had too many laws, and that's why we should not concern ourselves with a new anti-Jewish code. That is really the most interesting reason that has ever been advanced against anti-Semitism. We should leave the Jews alone because we have too many laws?! Well, I think, if we would do away with the Jews, we could do away with half the laws that we have now on the books.

> Then, Deputy Rickert said that it is really a shame—whether he actually said that I don't know because I could not take notes—but the sense of it was that it was a shame that a nation of 50 million people should be afraid of a few Jews. [Rickert had cited statistics to prove that the number of Jews in the country was not excessive.] Yes, gentlemen. Deputy Rickert would be right, if it were a matter of fighting with honest weapons against an honest enemy; then it would be a matter of course that the Germans would not fear a handful of such people. But the Jews, who operate like parasites, are

a different kind of problem. Mr. Rickert, who is not as tall as I am, is afraid of a single cholera germ—and, gentlemen. the Jews are cholera germs. . . .

It is remarkable that two men, separated by a span of 350 years, can still speak the same language. Ahlwardt's picture of the Jews is in its basic features a replica of the Lutheran portrait. The Jew is still (1) an enemy who has accomplished what no external enemy has accomplished: he has driven the people of Frankfurt into the suburbs; (2) a criminal, a thug, a beast of prey who commits so many crimes that his elimination would enable the Reichstag to cut the criminal code in half and (3) a plague or, more precisely, a cholera germ. Under the Nazi regime, these conceptions of the Jew were expounded and repeated in an almost endless flow of speeches, posters, letters, and memoranda. Hitler himself preferred to look upon the Jew as an enemy, a menace, a dangerous cunning foe. This is what he said in a speech delivered in 1940, as he reviewed his "struggle for power":

> It was a battle against a satanical power, which had taken possession of our entire people, which had grasped in its hands all key positions of scientific, intellectual, as well as political and economic life, and which kept watch over the entire nation from the vantage of these key positions. It was a battle against a power which, at the same time, had the influence to combat with the law every man who attempted to take up battle against them and every man who was ready to offer resistance to the spread of this power. At that time, all-powerful Jewry declared war on us. . . .

A number of Nazis, including the chief of the German SS and Police Himmler, the jurist and Generalgouverneur of Poland Hans Frank, and Justice Minister Thierack, inclined to the view that the Jews were a lower species of life, a kind of vermin, which upon contact infected the German people with deadly diseases. Himmler once cautioned his SS generals not to tolerate the stealing of property that had belonged to dead Jews. "Just because we exterminated a bacterium," he said, "we do not want, in the end, to be infected by that bacterium and die of it." Frank frequently referred to the Jews as 'lice.' When the Jews in his Polish domain were killed, he announced that now a sick Europe would become healthy again. . . .

Anti-Jewish racism had its beginning in the second half of the seventeenth century, when the "Jewish caricature" first appeared in cartoons. These caricatures were the first attempt to discover racial characteristics in the Jew. However, racism acquired a "theoretical" basis only in the 1800s. The racists of the nineteenth century stated explicitly that cultural characteristics, good or bad, were the product of physical characteristics. Physical attributes did not change; hence social behavior patterns also had to be immutable. In the eyes of the anti-Semite, the Jews therefore became a "race."

Why Germans Killed Jews

Daniel Jonah Goldhagen

In his controversial and best-selling book based on his doctoral dissertation, Daniel Jonah Goldhagen attempts to explain why the Holocaust happened in Germany and why ordinary German citizens went along with Hitler's orders to murder hundreds of thousands of innocent Jewish men, women and children. Contrary to conventional wisdom, he points out that German soldiers were not killed or punished if they refused to participate in the atrocities. He argues that it was the pervasiveness of anti-Semitism in Germany that prompted Germans to act as they did. Goldhagen is associate professor of Government and Social Studies at Harvard University and an Associate at the university's Minda de Gunzburg Center for European Studies.

Captain Wolfgang Hoffmann was a zealous executioner of Jews. As the commander of one of the three companies of Police Battalion 101, he and his fellow officers led their men, who were not SS men but ordinary Germans, in the deportation and gruesome slaughter in Poland of tens of thousands of Jewish men, women, and children. Yet this same man, in the midst of his genocidal activities, once stridently disobeyed a superior order that he deemed morally objectionable.

The order commanded that members of his company sign a declaration that had been sent to them. Hoffmann began his written refusal by saying that upon reading it, he had thought that an error had been made, "because it appeared to me a piece of impertinence to demand of a decent German soldier to sign a declaration in which he obligates himself not to steal, not to plunder, and not to buy without pay-

Excerpted from Daniel Jonah Goldhagen, *Hitler's Willing Executioners*. Copyright © 1996 by Daniel Jonah Goldhagen. Reprinted with permission from Alfred A. Knopf, a division of Random House, Inc.

ing. . . ." He continued by describing how unnecessary such a demand was, since his men, of proper ideological conviction, were fully aware that such activities were punishable offenses. He also pronounced to his superiors his judgment of his men's character and actions, including, presumably, their slaughtering of Jews. He wrote that his men's adherence to German norms of morality and conduct "derives from their own free will and is not caused by a craving for advantages or fear of punishment." Hoffmann then declared defiantly: "As an officer I regret, however, that I must set my view against that of the battalion commander and am not able to carry out the order, since I feel injured in my sense of honor. I must decline to sign a general declaration."

Hoffmann's letter is astonishing and instructive for a number of reasons. Here is an officer who had already led his men in the genocidal slaughter of tens of thousands of Jews, yet who deemed it an effrontery that anyone might suppose that he and his men would steal food from Poles! The genocidal killer's honor was wounded, and wounded doubly, for he was both a soldier and a German. His conception of the obligations that Germans owed the "subhuman" Poles must have been immeasurably greater than those owed Jews. Hoffmann also understood his parent institution to be so tolerant that he was willing to refuse a direct order and even to record his brazen insubordination in writing. His judgment of his men—a judgment based, no doubt, on the compass of their activities, including their genocidal ones—was that they acted not out of fear of punishment, but with willing assent; they acted from conviction, according to their inner beliefs. . . .

Explaining the Holocaust is the central intellectual problem for understanding Germany during the Nazi period. All the other problems combined are comparatively simple. How the Nazis came to power, how they suppressed the left, how they revived the economy, how the state was structured and functioned, how they made and waged war are all more or less ordinary, "normal" events, easily enough understood. But the Holocaust and the change in sensibilities that it involved "defies" explanation. There is no comparable event in the twentieth century, indeed in modern European history. Whatever the remaining debates, every other major event of nineteenth- and twentieth-century German history and political development is, in comparison to the Holocaust, transparently clear in its genesis. Explaining how the Holocaust happened is a daunting task empirically and even more so theoretically, so much so that some have argued, in my view erroneously, that it is "inexplicable.". . .

Until now the perpetrators, the most important group of people responsible for the slaughter of European Jewry, excepting the Nazi leadership itself, have received little concerted attention in the literature that describes the events and purports to explain them. Surprisingly, the vast literature on the Holocaust contains little on the people who were its executors. Little is known of who the perpetrators were, the details of their actions, the circumstances of many of their deeds, let alone their motivations. A decent estimate of how many people contributed to the genocide, of how many perpetrators there were, has never been made. . .

Perpetrators

The Holocaust was primarily a German undertaking. Non-Germans were not essential to the perpetration of genocide, and they did not supply the drive and initiative that pushed it forward. To be sure, had the Germans not found European (especially, eastern European) helpers, then the Holocaust would have unfolded somewhat differently, and the Germans would likely not have succeeded in killing as many Jews. Still, this was above all a German enterprise; the decisions, plans, organizational resources, and the majority of its executors were German. Comprehension and explanation of the perpetration of the Holocaust therefore requires an explanation of the Germans' drive to kill Jews. Because what can be said about the Germans cannot be said about any other nationality or about all of the other nationalities combined—namely no Germans, no Holocaust—the focus here is appropriately on the German perpetrators. . . .

The Holocaust was the defining aspect of Nazism, but not only of Nazism. It was also the defining feature of German society during its Nazi period. No significant aspect of German society was untouched by anti-Jewish policy; from the economy, to society, to politics, to culture, from cattle farmers, to merchants, to the organization of small towns, to lawyers, doctors, physicists, and professors. No analysis of German society, no understanding or characterization of it, can be made without placing the persecution and extermination of the Jews at its center. The program's first parts, namely the systematic exclusion of Jews from German economic and social life, were carried out in the open, under approving eyes, and with the complicity of virtually all sectors of German society, from the legal, medical, and teaching professions, to the churches, both Catholic and Protestant, to the gamut of economic, social, and cultural groups and associations. Hundreds of thousands of Germans contributed to the genocide and the still larger system of subjugation that was the vast concentration camp system. Despite the regime's half-hearted attempts to keep the genocide beyond the view of most Germans, millions knew of the mass slaughters. Hitler announced many times, emphatically, that the war would end in the extermination of the Jews. The killings met with general understanding, if not approval. No other policy (of similar or greater scope) was carried out with more persistence and zeal, and with fewer difficulties, than the genocide, except perhaps the war itself. The Holocaust defines not only the history of Jews during the middle of the twentieth century but also the history of Germans. While the Holocaust changed Jewry and Jews irrevocably, its commission was possible, I argue, because Germans had *already* been changed. . . .

Germans' antisemitic beliefs about Jews were the central causal agent of the Holocaust. They were the central causal agent not only of Hitler's decision to annihilate European Jewry (which is accepted by many) but also of the perpetrators' willingness to kill and to brutalize Jews. The conclusion of this book is that antisemitism moved many thousands of "ordinary" Germans—and would have moved millions more, had they been appropriately positioned—to slaughter Jews. Not economic hardship, not the coercive means of a totalitarian state, not social psychological pressure, not invariable psychological propensities, but ideas about Jews that were pervasive in Germany, and had been for decades, induced ordinary Germans to kill unarmed, defenseless Jewish men, women, and children by the thousands, systematically and without pity. . . .

For the extermination of the Jews to occur, four principal things were necessary:

1. The Nazis—that is, the leadership, specifically Hitler—had to decide to undertake the extermination.
2. They had to gain control over the Jews, namely over the territory in which they resided.
3. They had to organize the extermination and devote to it sufficient resources.
4. They had to induce a large number of people to carry out the killings. . . .

It is commonly believed that the Germans slaughtered Jews by and large in the gas chambers, and that without gas chambers, modern means of transportation, and efficient bureaucracies, the Germans would have been unable to kill millions of Jews. The belief persists that somehow only technology made horror on this scale possible. "Assembly-line killing" is one of the stock phrases in discussions of the event. It is generally believed that gas chambers, because of their efficiency (which is itself greatly overstated), were a necessary instrument for the genocidal slaughter, and that the Germans chose to construct the gas chambers in the first place because they needed more efficient means of killing the Jews. It has been generally believed by scholars (at least until very recently) and non-scholars alike that the perpetrators were primarily, overwhelmingly SS men, the most devoted and brutal Nazis. It has been a widespread conviction (again until recently) that had a German refused to kill Jews, then he himself would have been killed, sent to a concentration camp, or severely punished. All of these views, views that fundamentally shape people's understanding of the Holocaust, have been held unquestioningly as though they were self-evident truths. They have been virtual articles of faith (derived from sources other than historical inquiry), have substituted for knowledge, and have distorted the way in which this period is understood. . . .

Ordinary Men

One explanation argues for external compulsion: the perpetrators were coerced. They were left, by the threat of punishment, with no choice but to follow orders. After all, they were part of military or police-like institutions, institutions with a strict chain of command, demanding subordinate compliance to orders, which should have punished insubordination severely, perhaps with death. Put a gun to anyone's head, so goes the thinking, and he will shoot others to save himself.

A second explanation conceives of the perpetrators as having been blind followers of orders. A number of proposals have been made for the source or sources of this alleged propensity to obey: Hitler's charisma (the perpetrators were, so to speak, caught in his spell), a general human tendency to obey authority, a peculiarly German reverence for and propensity to obey authority, or a totalitarian society's blunting of the individual's moral sense and its conditioning of him or her to accept all tasks as necessary. So a common proposition exists, namely that people obey authority, with a variety of accounts of why this is so. Obviously, the notion that authority, particularly state authority, tends to elicit obedience merits consideration.

A third explanation holds the perpetrators to have been subject to tremendous social psychological pressure, placed upon each one by his comrades and/or by the expectations that accompany the institutional roles that individuals occupy. It is, so goes the argument, extremely difficult for individuals to resist pressures to conform, pressures which can lead individuals to participate in acts which they on their own would not do, indeed would abhor. . . .

A fourth explanation sees the perpetrators as having been petty bureaucrats, or soulless technocrats, who pursued their self-interest or their technocratic goals and tasks with callous disregard for the victims. . . .

A fifth explanation asserts that because tasks were so fragmented, the perpetrators could not understand what the real nature of their actions was; they could not comprehend that their small assignments were actually part of a global extermination program. . . .

The explanations can be reconceptualized in terms of their accounts of the actors' capacity for volition: The first explanation (namely coercion) says that the killers could not say "no." The second explanation (obedience) and the third (situational pressure) maintain that Germans were psychologically incapable of saying "no." The fourth explanation (self-interest) contends that Germans had sufficient personal incentives to kill in order not to want to say "no." The fifth explanation (bureaucratic myopia) claims that it never even occurred to the perpetrators that they were engaged in an activity that might make them responsible for saying "no."

Each of these conventional explanations may sound plausible, and some of them obviously contain some truth, so what is wrong with them? . . .

The conventional explanations suffer from two major conceptual failings. They do not sufficiently recognize the extraordinary nature of the deed: the mass killing of people. They *assume* and imply that inducing people to kill human beings is fundamentally no different from getting them to do any other unwanted or distasteful task. Also, none of the conventional explanations deems the *identity* of the victims to have mattered. The conventional explanations imply that the perpetrators would have treated any other group of intended victims in exactly the same way. That the victims were Jews—according to the logic of these explanations—is irrelevant.

I maintain that any explanation that fails to acknowledge the actors' capacity to know and to judge, namely to understand and to have views about the significance and the morality of their actions, that fails to hold the actors' beliefs and values as central, that fails to emphasize the autonomous motivating force of Nazi ideology, particularly its central component of antisemitism, cannot possibly succeed in telling us much about why the perpetrators acted as they did. Any explanation that ignores either the particular nature of the perpetrators' actions—the systematic, large-scale killing and brutalizing of people—or the identity of the victims is inadequate for a host of reasons. All explanations that adopt these positions, as do the conventional explanations, suffer a mirrored, double failure of recognition of the human aspect of the Holocaust: the humanity of the perpetrators, namely their capacity to judge and to choose to act inhumanely, and the humanity of the victims, that what the perpetrators did, they did to these people with their specific identities, and not to animals or things.

My explanation—which is new to the scholarly literature on the perpetrators—is that the perpetrators, "ordinary Germans," were animated by antisemitism, by a particular *type* of antisemitism that led them to conclude that the Jews *ought to die*. The perpetrators' beliefs, their particular brand of antisemitism, though obviously not the sole source, was, I maintain, a most significant and indispensable source of the perpetrators' actions and must be at the center of any explanation of them. Simply put, the perpetrators, having consulted their own convictions and morality and having judged the mass annihilation of Jews to be right, did not *want* to say "no.". . .

Interpreters of this period make a grave error by refusing to believe that people could slaughter whole populations—especially populations that are by any objective evaluation not threatening—out of conviction. Why persist in the belief that "ordinary" people could not possibly sanction, let alone partake in wholesale human slaughter? The historical record, from ancient times to the present, amply testifies to the ease with which people can extinguish the lives of others, and even take joy in their deaths.

No reason exists to believe that modern, western, even Christian man is incapable of holding notions which devalue human life, which call for its extinction, notions similar to those held by peoples of many religious, cultural, and political dispensations throughout history, including the crusaders and the inquisitors, to name but two relevant examples from twentieth-century Christian Europe's forebears. Who doubts that the Argentine or Chilean murderers of people who opposed the recent authoritarian regimes thought that their victims deserved to die? Who doubts that the Tutsis who slaughtered Hutus in Burundi or the Hutus who slaughtered Tutsis in Rwanda, that one Lebanese militia which slaughtered the civilian supporters of another, that the Serbs who have killed Croats or Bosnian Muslims, did so out of conviction in the justice of their actions? Why do we not believe the same for the German perpetrators?. . .

The perpetrators were working within institutions that prescribed roles for them and assigned them specific tasks, yet they individually and collectively had latitude to make choices regarding their actions. Adopting a perspective which acknowledges this requires that their choices, especially the patterns of their choices, be discerned, analyzed, and incorporated into any overall explanation or interpretation. Ideal data would answer the following questions:

What did the perpetrators actually do?

What did they do in excess of what was "necessary"?

What did they refuse to do?

What could they have refused to do?

What would they not have done?

What was the manner in which they carried out their tasks?

How smoothly did the overall operations proceed?

In examining the pattern of the perpetrators' actions . . . two directions beyond the simple act of killing must be explored. First, in their treatment of Jews (and other victims), the Germans subjected them to a wide range of acts other than the lethal blow. It is important to understand the *gamut* of their actions towards Jews, . . . Second, the perpetrators' actions when they were *not* engaged in genocidal activities also shed light on the killing. . . .

Breaking Taboos

It is not the only aspect of the Germans' treatment of the Jews that demands systematic scrutiny and explication. Not only the killing but also *how* the Germans killed must be explained. The "how" frequently provides great insight into the "why." A killer can endeavor to render the deaths of others—whether he thinks the killing is just or unjust—more or less painful, both physically and emotionally. The ways in which Germans, collectively and individually, sought in their actions, or merely considered, to alleviate or intensify their victims' suffering must be accounted for in any explanation. An explanation that can seemingly make sense of Germans putting Jews to death, but not of the manner in which they did it, is a faulty explanation. . . .

We must attempt the difficult enterprise of imagining ourselves in their places, performing their deeds, acting as they did, viewing what they beheld. To do so we must always bear in mind the essential nature of their actions as perpetrators: they were killing defenseless men, women, and children, people who were obviously of no martial threat to them, often emaciated and weak, in unmistakable physical and emotional agony, and sometimes begging for their lives or those of their children. Too many interpreters of this period, particularly when they are psychologizing, discuss the Germans' actions as if they were discussing the commission of mundane acts, as if they need explain little more than how a good man might occasionally shoplift. They lose sight of the fundamentally different, extraordinary, and trying character of these acts. The taboo in many societies, including western ones, against killing defenseless people, against killing children, is great. The psychological mechanisms that permit "good" people to commit minor moral transgressions, or to turn a blind eye even to major ones committed by others, particularly if they are far away, cannot be applied to people's perpetration of genocidal killing, to their slaughter of hundreds of others before their own eyes—without careful consideration of such mechanisms' appropriateness for elucidating such actions.

Explaining this genocidal slaughter necessitates, therefore, that we keep two things always in mind. When writing or reading about killing operations, it is too easy to become insensitive to the numbers on the page. Ten thousand dead in one place, four hundred in another, fifteen in a third. Each of us should pause and consider that ten thousand deaths meant that Germans killed ten thousand individuals—unarmed men, women, and children, the old, the young, the healthy, and the sick—that Germans took a human life ten thousand times. Each of us should ponder what that might have meant for the Germans participating in the slaughter. When a person considers his or her own anguish, abhorrence, or revulsion, his or her own moral outrage at the murder of one person, or of a contemporary "mass murder" of, say, twenty people—whether by a serial killer, or by a semi-automatic-toting sociopath in a fast food outlet—that person gains some perspective on the reality that these Germans confronted. The Jewish victims were not the "statistics" that they appear to us on paper. To the killers whom they faced, the Jews were people who were breathing one moment and lying lifeless, often before them, the next. All of this took place independent of military operations.

The second item to bear in mind, always, is the horror of what the Germans were doing. Anyone in a killing detail who himself shot or who witnessed his comrades shoot Jews was immersed in scenes of unspeakable horror. . . . Blood, bone, and brains were flying about, often landing on the killers, smirching their faces and staining their clothes. Cries and wails of people awaiting their imminent slaughter or consumed in death throes reverberated in German ears. Such scenes—not the antiseptic descriptions that mere reportage of a killing operation presents—constituted the reality for many perpetrators.

How Ordinary Men Became Killers

Christopher R. Browning

In this selection Christopher R. Browning tries to explain how ordinary men became killers. Browning looked specifically at one Nazi unit, Reserve Police Battalion 101, a group of policemen, most of whom were recently drafted family men too old for combat, who were sent to Poland and were involved in the murder of Jews. Their most ghastly action was the murder of fifteen hundred men, women, and children in the village of Józefów. These men were not hard-core Nazis, the stereotypical monsters of the SS. In most cases, they were clerks, salesmen, and blue-collar workers drafted into unpleasant service. If such men could commit atrocities, is it possible to say that anyone could resist the kind of pressure they faced to become murderers? Young people in the United States face all sorts of peer pressure to take drugs, drink alcohol, steal, and act in other antisocial or illegal ways. Under the right circumstances, could peer pressure also turn Americans into murderers? Browning is a professor of history at Pacific Lutheran University and a contributor to Yad Vashem's multivolume history of the Holocaust.

Among the perpetrators [of the Holocaust] of course, orders have traditionally been the most frequently cited explanation for their own behavior. The authoritarian political culture of the Nazi dictatorship savagely intolerant of overt dissent, along with the standard military necessity of obedience to orders and ruthless enforcement of discipline, created a situation in which individuals *had no choice*. Orders were orders,

Excerpted from Christopher R. Browning, *Ordinary Men: Reserve Police Battalion 101 and the Final Solution in Poland*. Copyright © 1992, 1998 by Christopher R. Browning. Reprinted with permission from HarperCollins Publishers, Inc.

and no one in such a political climate could be expected to disobey them, they insisted. Disobedience surely meant the concentration camp if not immediate execution, possibly for their families as well. The perpetrators had found themselves in a situation of impossible "duress" and therefore could not be held responsible for their actions. Such, at least, is what defendants said in trial after trial in postwar Germany.

There is a general problem with this explanation, however. Quite simply, in the past forty-five years no defense attorney or defendant in any of the hundreds of postwar trials has been able to document a single case in which refusal to obey an order to kill unarmed civilians resulted in the allegedly inevitable dire punishment. The punishment or censure that occasionally did result from such disobedience was never commensurate with the gravity of the crimes the men had been asked to commit.

A variation on the explanation of inescapable orders is "putative duress." Even if the consequences of disobedience would not have been so dire, the men who complied could not have known that at the time. They sincerely thought that they had had no choice when faced with orders to kill. . . .

For small shooting actions, volunteers were requested or shooters were chosen from among those who were known to be willing to kill or who simply did not make the effort to keep their distance when firing squads were being formed. For large actions, those who would not kill were not compelled. Even officers' attempts to force individual nonshooters to kill could be refused. . . .

The testimonies are filled with stories of men who disobeyed standing orders during the ghetto-clearing operations and did not shoot infants or those attempting to hide or escape. Even men who admitted to having taken part in firing squads claimed not to have shot in the confusion and melee of the ghetto clearings or out on patrol when their behavior could not be closely observed. . . .

Were Nazis Brainwashed?

To what degree, then, did the conscious inculcation of Nazi doctrines shape the behavior of the men of Reserve Police Battalion 101? Were they subjected to such a barrage of clever and insidious propaganda that they lost the capacity for independent thought and responsible action'? Were devaluation of the Jews and exhortations to kill them central to this indoctrination? The popular term for intense indoctrination and psychological manipulation, emerging from the Korean War experience of some captured American soldiers, is "brainwashing." Were these killers in some general sense "brainwashed"?

Unquestionably, [Heinrich] Himmler set a premium on the ideological indoctrination of members of the SS and the police. They were to be not just efficient soldiers and policemen, but ideologically motivated warriors, crusaders against the political and racial enemies of the Third Reich. Indoctrination efforts embraced not only the elite organizations of the SS but also the Order Police, extending even to the lowly reserve police, though the reservists scarcely fit Himmler's notion of the new Nazi racial aristocracy. For instance, membership in the SS required proof of ancestry untainted by Jewish blood through five generations. In contrast, even "first-degree *Mischlinge*" (people with two Jewish grandparents) and their spouses were not banned from service in the reserve police until October 1942; "second-degree *Mischlinge*" (one Jewish grandparent) and their spouses were not banned until April 1943.

In its guidelines for basic training of January 23, 1940, the Order Police Main Office decreed that in addition to physical fitness, use of weapons, and police techniques, all Order Police battalions were to be strengthened in character and ideology. Basic training included a one-month unit on "ideological education." One topic for the first week was "Race as the Basis of Our World View," followed the second week by "Maintaining the Purity of Blood." Beyond basic training, the police battalions, both active and reserve, were to receive continued military and ideological training from their officers. Officers were required to attend one-week workshops that included one hour of ideological instruction for themselves and one hour of practice in the ideological instruction of others. A five-part study plan of January 1941 included the subsections "Understanding of Race as the

Basis of Our World View," "The Jewish Question in Germany," and "Maintaining the Purity of German Blood.". . .

Many of the Nazi perpetrators were very young men. They had been raised in a world in which Nazi values were the only "moral norms" they knew. It could be argued that such young men, schooled and formed solely under the conditions of the Nazi dictatorship, simply did not know any better. Killing Jews did not conflict with the value system they had grown up with, and hence indoctrination was much easier. Whatever the merits of such an argument, it clearly does not hold for the predominantly middle-aged men of Reserve Police Battalion 101. They were educated and spent their formative years in the pre-1933 period. Many came from a social milieu that was relatively unreceptive to National Socialism. They knew perfectly well the moral norms of German society before the Nazis. They had earlier standards by which to judge the Nazi policies they were asked to carry out. . . .

In summary, the men of Reserve Police Battalion 101, like the rest of German society, were immersed in a deluge of racist and anti-Semitic propaganda. Furthermore, the Order Police provided for indoctrination both in basic training and as an ongoing practice within each unit. Such incessant propagandizing must have had a considerable effect in reinforcing general notions of Germanic racial superiority and "a certain aversion" toward the Jews. However, much of the indoctrination material was clearly not targeted at older reservists and in some cases was highly inappropriate or irrelevant to them. And material specifically designed to harden the policemen for the personal task of killing Jews is conspicuously absent from the surviving documentation. One would have to be quite convinced of the manipulative powers of indoctrination to believe that any of this material could have deprived the men of Reserve Police Battalion 101 of the capacity for independent thought. Influenced and conditioned in a general way, imbued in particular with a sense of their own superiority and racial kinship as well as Jewish inferiority and otherness, many of them undoubtedly were; explicitly prepared for the task of killing Jews they most certainly were not.

Going Along to Get Along

A vital factor . . . was conformity to the group. The battalion had orders to kill Jews but each individual did not. Yet 80 to 90 percent of the men proceeded to kill, though almost all of them—at least initially— were horrified and disgusted by what they were doing. To break ranks and step out, to adopt overtly nonconformist behavior, was simply beyond most of the men. It was easier for them to shoot.

Why? First of all, by breaking ranks, nonshooters were leaving the "dirty work" to their comrades. Since the battalion had to shoot even if individuals did not, refusing to shoot constituted refusing one's share of an unpleasant collective obligation. It was in effect an asocial act vis-à-vis one's comrades. Those who did not shoot risked isolation, rejection, and ostracism—a very uncomfortable prospect within the framework of a tight-knit unit stationed abroad among a hostile population, so that the individual had virtually nowhere else to turn for support and social contact.

This threat of isolation was intensified by the fact that stepping out could also have been seen as a form of moral reproach of one's comrades: the nonshooter was potentially indicating that he was "too good" to do such things. Most, though not all, nonshooters intuitively tried to diffuse the criticism of their comrades that was inherent in their actions. They pleaded not that they were "too good" but rather that they were "too weak" to kill.

Such a stance presented no challenge to the esteem of one's comrades, on the contrary, it legitimized and upheld "toughness" as a superior quality. For the anxious individual, it had the added advantage of posing no moral challenge to the murderous policies of the regime, though it did pose another problem, since the difference between being "weak" and being a "coward" was not great. . . .

Insidiously, therefore, most of those who did not shoot only reaffirmed the "macho" values of the majority—according to which it was a positive quality to be "tough" enough to kill unarmed, noncombatant men, women, and children—and tried not to rupture the bonds of comradeship that constituted their social world. Coping with the contradictions imposed by the demands of conscience on the one hand and the norms of the battalion on the other led to many tortured attempts at compromise: not shooting infants on the spot but taking them to the assembly point; not shooting on patrol if no "go-getter" was along who might report such squeamishness; bringing Jews to the shooting site and firing but intentionally missing. Only the very exceptional remained indifferent to taunts of "weakling" from their comrades and could live with the fact that they were considered to be "no man.". . .

The behavior of any human being is, of course, a very complex phenomenon, and the historian who attempts to "explain" it is indulging in a certain arrogance. When nearly 500 men are involved, to undertake any general explanation of their collective behavior is even more hazardous. What, then, is one to conclude? Most of all, one comes away from the story of Reserve Police Battalion 101 with great unease. This story of ordinary men is not the story of all men. The reserve policemen faced choices, and most of them committed terrible deeds. But those who killed cannot be absolved by the notion that anyone in the same situation would have done as they did. For even among them, some refused to kill and others stopped killing. Human responsibility is ultimately an individual matter.

At the same time, however, the collective behavior of Reserve Police Battalion 101 has deeply disturbing implications. There are many societies afflicted by traditions of racism and caught in the siege mentality of war or threat of war. Everywhere society conditions people to respect and defer to authority, and indeed could scarcely function otherwise. Everywhere people seek career advancement. In every modern society, the complexity of life and the resulting bureaucratization and specialization attenuate the sense of personal responsibility of those implementing official policy. Within virtually every social collective, the peer group exerts tremendous pressures on behavior and sets moral norms. If the men of Reserve Police Battalion 101 could become killers under such circumstances, what group of men cannot?

Chapter 4

Could More Jews Have Been Saved?

Turning | Points

IN WORLD HISTORY

Open Immigration Could Have Saved Tens of Thousands

Gary Grobman

It is easy to look back with hindsight and say, Why didn't the Jews leave Germany? Why didn't they flee Europe once the war started? Hundreds of thousands did flee, but even those who tried to escape discovered an often insurmountable hurdle: the unwillingness of any country to take them in. Even the land of immigrants, the great melting pot that is the United States, denied entry to thousands of Jews who sought refuge. In the case of imperial powers such as Britain, governments could block entrance to multiple countries; thus, for example, many Jews who desperately wished to escape to Palestine were prevented from doing so by the British. Why were governments so callous? A number of reasons exist. One is that most countries were just emerging from the Great Depression and did not want to admit mostly penniless refugees who would become welfare cases and compete for scarce jobs. Another reason was a dislike of foreigners in general and an anti-Semitic attitude toward Jews in particular. This article presents a summary of the immigration policies of the United States and several European nations. Gary Grobman is the author or coauthor of seven books. He served as executive director of the Pennsylvania Jewish Coalition and is currently a PhD candidate in Public Administration at Penn State.

Deteriorating economic conditions contributed to the political and social climate which both launched World War II and fueled the anti-Semitism which encouraged the destruc-

Reprinted from Gary Grobman, "Immigration Policies," in *The Holocaust—A Guide for Teachers*. Copyright © 1990 by Gary M. Grobman. Reprinted with permission from the author.

tion of the Jews of Europe. These same economic conditions world-wide resulted in barriers placed against those potential Jewish immigrants who sought refuge from the Nazi terror. Anti-Jewish sentiment in France, England, and even the United States resulted in hundreds of thousands of European Jews being denied a safe haven, which meant virtually certain death. Simple indifference to the plight of Jews, according to many historians, also played a role in the events which led to the Holocaust.

Thousands of Jews in Germany were successful in fleeing before the onset of hostilities in 1939, especially in the early years of the Nazi period. Many of these refugees were able to find their way aboard ships headed for American ports. There are, however, tragic stories of these ships being turned away by immigration officials, and their occupants returned to Europe to face the gas chambers. Each nation had its own story of how its government and citizens responded to the horrors of the Holocaust. The following are capsules of some of these stories.

United States. Despite the fact that the U.S. received early reports about the desperate plight of European Jewry, procrastination and inaction marked its policies toward rescue. Immigration quotas were never increased for the emergency; the existing quotas, in fact, were never filled.

Wagner-Rogers legislation. Legislation was introduced in the United States Congress in 1939 by Rep. Robert Wagner to admit a total of 20,000 Jewish children over a two-year period above the refugee quota applicable at the time. The legislation was inspired by similar efforts by the Dutch and British government to save Jewish children from Nazi terror. The legislation was amended in committee to admit the 20,000 children only if the number of Jewish refugees admitted under the regular quota was reduced by 20,000. The bill died in the House after the sponsor withdrew his support for the bill in frustration.

Bermuda Conference. As the Germans advanced through Europe, more Jews and others who were targets of Nazi racial policies came under Nazi control. By 1943, the war had created millions of refugees in Europe. The Bermuda Conference, jointly sponsored by the United States and Great Britain, was held in Bermuda in April 1943 to discuss solutions to the refugee problem. The conference failed. As Michael Marrus writes in *The Holocaust in History:*

> At the Bermuda Conference in April 1943 . . . the British and Americans proved most adept at postponing serious efforts to change matters. By this point, opinion was mobilized on behalf of several schemes for rescue and refuge. Such views were deflected, however; the press was kept at arm's length and little was achieved.

War Refugee Board. U.S. Secretary of the Treasury, Henry Morgenthau, presented a report to President Roosevelt in 1943 providing details about the Final Solution. It was not until January 1944, however, that the President responded by establishing the War Refugee Board as an independent agency to rescue the civilian victims of the Nazis. By then, most of these civilian victims had already been murdered. The Board joined a plea to the Hungarian Regent, Admiral Miklós Horthy, from Great Britain, Sweden, the Pope, and the International Red Cross to stop the deportations of Hungarian Jews. While Admiral Horthy agreed on July 8, 1944, to discontinue the deportations, fewer than 200,000 Jews of the original number of more than 600,000 remained. Thousands of those permitted this reprieve from the death camps were eventually saved through the efforts of [Swedish diplomat] Raoul Wallenberg and other diplomats.

Spain and Portugal. As many as 40,000 Jews who were able to make their way to Spain and Portugal were saved from the Nazi death camps. More than 20,000 Jews made their way into Switzerland, but many thousands were turned back, according to Michael Marrus' *Holocaust in History.*

Denmark. The rescue of Denmark's 8,000 Jews serves as an example of an entire nation mobilized to rescue humanity from the abyss of German terror. While the story may be apocryphal that King Christian X threatened to abdicate and to wear the Nazi yellow Star of David as a badge of honor, it symbolizes his opposition to all anti-Semitic legislation. Almost all of the Jews of Denmark survived the war, while those in almost every other nation occupied by the Nazis had their ranks decimated.

A September 1943 decision by the Nazi occupiers of Denmark to round up all Danish Jews for shipment to the death camps was thwarted. Courageously acting on a tip from a German shipping official, Danes from all walks of life mobilized whatever would float and ferried 5,900 Jews, 1,300 part-Jews, and 700 Christians married to Jews to safety in Sweden. Of the 500 or so Jews left in Denmark on October 1, 1943, all were deported by the Germans to Theresienstadt. Eighty-five percent survived the war.

Historians have pondered why the citizens of Denmark resisted the war against the Jews, unlike most of their European neighbors. One reason is that Denmark did not have a history of anti-Semitism. Another was that nearby was neutral Sweden, willing to accept the Jews that could be saved.

Bulgaria. Forty-eight thousand Jews in Bulgaria were also spared the horror of the gas chambers as a result of the courage of the Bulgarian people. A public outcry by Bulgarian church officials and others against a deportation order directed at all Jews forced the Bulgarian government to rescind its order. Jews who had been rounded up in Bulgarian-occupied Thrace and Macedonia were not as lucky; virtually all perished in the Holocaust.

Several other governments resisted Nazi deportation orders, including Finland, Hungary, and Italy.

Several embassies in Hungary acted in concert to issue passports to Jews at risk. Yet many other European governments not only complied with the demand of the Germans to deport Jews to the death camps but facilitated the deportations.

France. Pre-war France had a Jewish population of over 300,000, out of a total population of 45 million. Many thousands of these were refugees, and only about 150,000 were native Frenchmen. In May 1940, the German army invaded France and occupied three-fifths of the country in accordance with an armistice signed on June 22nd.

A government was formed in unoccupied France at Vichy. The Vichy government was dominated by advocates for cooperation with the Germans. Many of the decrees of the

Vichy government in 1940–41 paralleled the anti-Jewish edicts of Germany in the mid-1930s. Jewish property was expropriated, and Jews were stripped of their basic civil rights. Non-native French Jews were singled out in October 1940 for internment in labor camps, which resulted in a large number of deaths.

In March 1942, the Germans began deporting Jews from the occupied zones in France to the death camps. In July of that same year, they demanded that all Jews be rounded up in unoccupied France for deportation.

The Vichy government decided to protect French Jews, but handed over 15,000 foreign Jews from the internment camps for deportation to the death camps. Many hundreds of other Jews were executed, as described in Lucy Dawidowicz's *The War Against the Jews* in reprisal for partisan activities. By the time France was liberated, 90,000 of the prewar Jewish population in France had been killed.

More Media Attention Might Have Saved Lives

Deborah E. Lipstadt

It is hard to imagine how the press could have failed to report the Nazi campaign to annihilate the Jews, yet the conventional wisdom is that little was known about Hitler's Final Solution until late in the war or after the concentration camps were liberated. In truth, a great deal was known, from at least 1942 on and the major press did publish stories about the murder of thousands and sometimes millions of people. The problem was these stories were often buried in the paper, suggesting that they were not as important, or credible as those on the front page. Today when a madman goes on a shooting spree and kills nine people it merits banner headlines across the country; yet no such headlines were given to the stories of mass murder during World War II. Why? The answer is not as simple as the absence of a CNN. As Deborah E. Lipstadt found, the problem had a lot to do with the inability of editors to believe what their reporters were telling them. Many people had been conditioned to be skeptical of atrocity stories because World War I propaganda had contained many such stories, which were fabricated purely to provoke sympathy for the war effort. Perhaps in the modern age when "ethnic cleansing" has become common enough that the Holocaust is viewed by many as just one of many examples of genocide, it is difficult to appreciate how shocking it was to discover what humans could do to other humans in World War II. In this excerpt, Lipstadt, the Dorot chair in modern Jewish and Holocaust studies at Emory University, offers an explanation for why the Holocaust was beyond belief.

Excerpted from Deborah E. Lipstadt, *Beyond Belief: The American Press and the Coming of the Holocaust, 1933–1945*. Copyright © 1986 by Deborah E. Lipstadt. Abridged and reprinted with permission from the Free Press, a division of Simon & Schuster, Inc.

Since the onset of Nazi rule Americans had greeted almost all the news of Nazi Germany's persecution of the Jews skeptically. Inevitably, their first reaction was to question whether it was true. Before, during, and even *after* the war many Americans, including those associated with the press, refused to believe the news they heard. . . .

In a January 1943 Gallup poll nearly 30 percent of those asked dismissed the news that 2 million Jews had been killed in Europe as just a rumor. Another 24 percent had no opinion on the question. Informal polls taken by the *Detroit Free Press* and the *New York Post* in 1943 found that a broad range of Americans did not believe the atrocity reports.

Journalists who had been stationed in Germany were among those most distressed by the American refusal to believe that the Germans were engaging in physical persecution. In March 1943 William Shirer, writing in the *Washington Post*, castigated the public for thinking that the stories of the atrocities were untrue or had been magnified for "propaganda purposes." He attributed this attitude to a "silly sort of supercynicism and superskepticism" which persisted despite the fact that there was "no earthly reason" for people not to believe. . . .

In January 1944 Arthur Koestler also expressed his frustration that so many people refused to believe that the "grim stories of Nazi atrocities are true." Writing in the Sunday *New York Times Magazine*, Koestler cited public opinion polls in the United States in which nine out of ten average Americans dismissed the accusations against the Nazis as propaganda lies and flatly stated that they did not believe a word of them. How, he wondered, could Americans be convinced that this "nightmare" was reality? The *Christian Century* responded to Koestler by arguing that there really was no point in "screaming" about the atrocities against the Jews because this would only "emotionally exhaust" those who wanted to devote their energies "*after*" the war to "building peace.". . .

In October 1944 Averell Harriman, American Ambassador to the Soviet Union, felt compelled to reassure the press that the reports of massacres and atrocities committed by the Germans and their supporters in Russian territory "have not been and cannot be exaggerated." Though a December 1944 Gallup poll revealed that 76 percent of those queried now believed that many people had been "murdered" in concentration camps, the estimates they gave of the number who had died indicated that they had not really grasped the scope of the tragedy. Furthermore, while more Americans were now willing to believe that many people had been killed, they generally did not believe in the existence of gas chambers and death camps. . . .

The victims themselves recognized the difficulty they faced in piercing the barriers of incredulity. A Polish underground courier who, in August 1944, reached London with news of the stepped-up pace of the slaughter of Hungarian Jews was shocked to find that despite the fact that he brought news from within Auschwitz itself, "nobody will believe." As late as 1944 eyewitness accounts—particularly those of victims—were not considered irrefutable evidence even if they came from independent sources and corroborated one another. The press often categorized them as prejudiced or exaggerated. At the end of the war Kenneth McCaleb, war editor of the *New York Daily Mirror*, admitted that whenever he had read about German atrocities, he had not taken them seriously because they had always come from "'foreigners' who, many of us felt, had some ax to grind and must be exaggerat[ing]." . . .

Associated Press staff member Daniel De Luce admitted that prior to the visit [to Maidanek] most of the other American and British correspondents in the group "could not even begin to imagine the proportions of its frightfulness." Now they had no doubts.

Edgar Snow of the *Saturday Evening Post*, Richard Lauterbach of *Time* and *Life*, and Maurice Hindus of the *St. Louis Post Dispatch* and the *New York Herald Tribune* all found the storehouse for the personal possessions of the victims more "terrifying" than even the gas chambers and the crematorium. In them they found rooms filled with shoes—one for men's shoes and one for women's—kitchenware, clothes, books, pocketknives, and other items that the unsuspecting victims had brought with them to facilitate their "relocation." Maidanek "suddenly became real" to Lauterbach when he stood on top of a "sea" of 820,000 pairs of shoes which had cascaded out of a warehouse. . . . In the introduction to his detailed description of this camp, Snow explained why he broke with his magazine's norm and wrote about a subject which was fully reported by the daily press. Maidanek was evidence of the way Nazi ideology enabled people to commit "crimes almost too monstrous for the human mind to accept.". . .

Even this news of Maidanek and the eyewitness accounts by reputable American correspondents did not significantly change the way the American press treated this story: momentarily attention was paid, but all too quickly the news was forgotten. . . . After a brief wave of interest, reports once again appeared in short articles on inner pages. But this pattern of deprecating the importance of the news regarding the Final Solution did not originate with the press. In fact the press was faithfully duplicating an Allied policy of obfuscation and camouflage.

Universalizing the Victims

Part of the responsibility for both American skepticism and the press's ambiguous treatment of this news can be traced directly to Allied opposition to publicizing reports of atrocities against Jewish victims. On many occasions when atrocities against Jews were discussed, the identity of the victims was universalized. In other words, Jews became Poles or Russians or innocent civilians. American and British leaders had been intent on avoiding mention of Jews as the specific victims of Nazi hostility as early as 1938 at Evian, and their policy had not substantially changed since. The Allies argued that if they treated Jews as a separate entity, it would validate Nazi ideology. A truer explanation for this behavior was American and British fear that singling out the unique fate of the Jews would strengthen the demands of those who wanted the Allies to undertake specific rescue action on their behalf. The Americans worried that they might be asked to admit more Jewish refugees, and the British were concerned that pressure would be put upon them to open Palestine to Jews.

It therefore became Allied policy to refer to "political refugees" and not Jews, even when these refugees were clearly Jews. Rarely did any reporters or editorial board take note of this policy. . . .

Probably the most outrageous example of this explicit policy of ignoring the Jewish aspect of the tragedy occurred in Moscow in the fall of 1943. There Churchill, Roosevelt, and Stalin met and affixed their signature to what is known as the Moscow Declaration, which warned that

> Germans who take part in the wholesale shooting of *Italian* officers or in the execution of *French, Dutch, Belgian* or *Norwegian* hostages or of *Cretan* peasants, or who have shared in slaughters inflicted on the people of *Poland* or in the territories of the *Soviet Union* . . . will be brought back to the scene of their crimes and judged on the spot by the peoples whom they have outraged.

Nowhere in the declaration were Jews even obliquely mentioned, a phenomenon the press simply ignored. While there were some exceptions to this Allied policy, e.g., the December 1942 statement confirming the Nazi policy of exterminating the Jews, they were few. When declarations did contain references to Jews, as was the case in March 1944 when Roosevelt referred to the Hungarian situation, the President's advisers vigorously worked to ensure that they were not too prominently mentioned. . . .

Deputy Director of the Office of War Information Arthur Sweetser sent a memorandum to Leo Rosten, who was Deputy Director in charge of information on the enemy, on the "impending Nazi extermination of the Jews." In it he argued that the story of atrocities would be "confused and misleading if it appears to be simply affecting the Jewish people," and therefore news of the particular fate of the Jews should be contained and even suppressed. Consequently, when the news of German atrocities was publicized, the Jewish aspect was often eliminated. . . .

Even when war had virtually ended and the camps were being liberated, reporters continued to incorporate the fate of the Jews into that of all other national groups that had been incarcerated and murdered at the camps. For example, Edgar Snow wrote that at Maidanek "Jews, Germans and other Europeans were all robbed in common and were all fed to the same ovens." Other reports described the victims as "men, women and children of 22 nationalities"—some citing Jews as constituting "half" or "most" of the victims, others simply listing them along with Russians, Poles, Frenchmen, Italians, Czechs, Yugoslavs, Greeks, Belgians, Germans, and Dutchmen. *Time* correspondent Sidney Olsen, who accompanied the U.S. Seventh Army as it liberated Dachau, described its inmates as "Russians, French, Yugoslavs, Italians, and Poles." In this camp, Olsen observed, were "the men of all nations whom Hitler's agents had picked out as prime opponents of Nazism; here were the very earliest of Nazi-haters. Here were German social democrats, Spanish survivors of the Spanish Civil War." But nowhere in his article was there a Jew. . . .

The News About Auschwitz: An Eyewitness Account

The extent to which certain American officials were opposed to focusing on the murder of Jews was demonstrated in the fall of 1944 when John Pehle of the War Refugee Board received from American officials in Switzerland a full text of the eyewitness account of Auschwitz. The report contained precise details on the number and national origins of the victims, the process of moving newly arrived victims from the freight trains to the gas chambers, the kinds of work done by the inmates, the physical plant of the camp, the physical dimensions of the barracks, gas chambers, and crematorium, and the way in which the "selections" for the gas chambers were conducted. The escapees who were the eyewitnesses had also witnessed the preparation of the camp for the "handling" of Hungarian Jewry.

When Pehle received the report—he had previously only seen a summary—he did two things. First, he urged John McCloy, Assistant Secretary of War, to "give serious consideration to the possibility of destroying the execution chambers and crematoria in Birkenau through direct bombing action." McCloy rejected Pehle's request with the incorrect but familiar explanation that it would pose too great a risk to American bombers and would divert critically needed air power. Pehle then decided to release the report to the press as a means of awakening public support for action.

Not since *Kristallnacht* had a story been so widely featured or prompted such extensive comment. Many papers carried it on the front page or in a prominent position elsewhere. The headlines alone encapsulated the press's horrified reaction.

New York Herald Tribune:

U.S. CHARGES NAZIS TORTURED MILLIONS TO DEATH IN EUROPE

War Refugee Board Says 1,765,000 Jews Were Killed by Gas in One Camp Alone; Witnesses' Testimony Gives Details of the Atrocities

Louisville Courier Journal:

THE INSIDE STORY OF MASS MURDERING BY NAZIS

Escapees Give Detailed Accounts of the Gassing and Cremating of 1,765,000 Jews at Birkenau

FROM AN OFFICIAL PUBLICATION OF THE WAR REFUGEE BOARD

Philadelphia Inquirer:

1,765,000 JEWS KILLED WITH GAS AT GERMAN CAMP

New York Times:

U.S. BOARD BARES ATROCITY DETAILS TOLD BY WITNESSES AT POLISH CAMPS

Washington Post:

TWO MILLION EXECUTED IN NAZI CAMPS

Gassing, Cremation Assembly-Line Methods Told by War Refugee Boards

The Board appended a one-page preface attesting to its complete faith in the report's reliability. It stressed that all the information—both dates and death tolls—tallied with the "trustworthy yet fragmentary reports" previously received and therefore the eyewitness statements could be considered "entirely credible." The *New York Herald Tribune* described the report as the "most shocking document ever issued by a United States government agency." Virtually every news story on the report emphasized not only that this was an eyewitness report but that it had been released by the War Refugee Board, an official government body, composed of "the three highest ranking Cabinet officials." This was, according to Ted Lewis of the *Washington Times Herald*, "the first American official stamp of truth to the myriad of eyewitness stories of the mass massacres in Poland." The *Louisville Courier Journal*, which devoted an entire page to excerpts from the report, observed in its article that "there is no longer any need to speculate on the mass murdering of millions of civilians.". . .

One of the few papers to inject an explicit note of skepticism into its report was the *Chicago Tribune*, which prefaced its news story with the observation that there have been numerous reports on German atrocities, "some of which have been verified." While previous reports had been accompanied by photographs, "no pictures were released to corroborate the atrocity story released today." The extensive detail was still not enough for the *Tribune*, it wanted pictures. It never mentioned to readers that Auschwitz, the subject of the report, was still in German hands and consequently no pictures were available. . . .

On October 30 *Yank* magazine, published by the armed forces for their members, contacted the War Refugee Board and asked if it "dealt in German atrocity stories." A reporter for the magazine, Sgt. Richard Paul, had been assigned to prepare an article about German atrocities in order to "show our soldiers the nature of their enemy." Paul arranged to meet with Pehle to gather information for the story. At their meeting Pehle gave Paul a copy of the report for use by *Yank*.

A few days later Paul informed the War Refugee Board that the report would appear in the next issue of the magazine. But Paul's superiors intervened, told him that the story was "too Semitic," and instructed him to get a "less Jewish story" from the Board. Pehle's assistant at the War Refugee Board refused to give him one, and in her explanation she explicitly stated something neither the Allied governments nor the Allied press ever really made clear: most of the victims in the German death camps were Jews. . . .

Americans prided themselves on their skepticism. The *Baltimore Sun* tried to explain how, despite so much evidence, Americans had been able to reject the reports as untrue. "Atrocities? Americans, a sophisticated people, smiled at this idea. . . . When it came to atrocities, seeing, and seeing alone, would be believing, with most Americans.". . .

But the press had been shown. It had been shown by reporters who had been stationed in Germany until 1942 and who had heard numerous reports including those of participants in the persecution of Jews. Sigrid Schultz, for example, sat in the train station listening to returning soldiers describe the massacres on the eastern front. In 1942 UP's Glen Stadler, who had just returned from Germany, described what was being done to the Jews as an "open hunt." By 1944 captured soldiers were confessing to atrocities that Harold Denny, the *New York Times* reporter assigned to the American First Army, called "so wantonly cruel that, without such confirmation, they might have been discounted as propagandist inventions." Reporters had seen places such as Babi Yar, where the soil contained human remains, and Maidanek, where mass graves were visible. The American government had released a documented report on Auschwitz. Yet these editors, publishers, and reporters claimed not to believe what they heard.

The truth is that much of the press had not rejected as propaganda all that it heard, but it had erected barriers which enabled it to dismiss parts of it. It accepted a portion, often quite grudgingly, and rejected the rest as exaggeration. It adhered to a pattern which I have chosen to call "Yes but." At first it argued, *Yes*, bad things may be happening *but* not as bad as reported. Subsequently it was willing to acknowledge that *Yes*, many Jews may be victims *but* not as many as claimed. *Yes* many may have died, *but* most probably died as a result of war-related privations and not as a result of having been murdered. *Yes*, many may have been killed *but* not in gas chambers. *Yes*, some Jews may have died in death camps, *but* so did many other people.

As this sequence of events progressed, the press seemed willing to believe a bit more, but rarely was it willing to accept the full magnitude of the atrocities. This was as characteristic of the press's behavior in 1945 as it was in 1933. In 1933 it could not believe that Jews were being indiscriminately beaten up in the streets, and in 1945 it could not believe that they had been singled out to be murdered. When it came to atrocity reports, particularly those concerning the annihilation of the Jewish people, skepticism always tempered belief. By responding in such a fashion, the press obscured the true picture for itself and its readers. . . .

We have seen how the reporters, editors, and publishers who visited the camps generally claimed that until that moment they had simply not believed that the stories were true. After their visits any vestiges of doubt had been eradicated. Now they knew such things could happen, but they could not fathom how. Their amazement had, in fact, only increased. In a front-page story in the *Baltimore Sun* Lee Mc-Cardell, the Sunpapers' war correspondent, voiced his confusion and disorientation after touring a camp.

> You had heard of such things in Nazi Germany. You had heard creditable witnesses describe just such scenes. But now that you were actually confronted with the horror of mass murder, you stared at the bodies and almost doubted your own eyes.
>
> "Good God!" you said aloud, "Good God!"
>
> Then you walked down around the corner of two barren, weatherbeaten, wooden barrack buildings. And there in a wooden shed, piled up like so much cordwood, were the naked bodies of more dead men than you cared to count.
>
> "Good God!" you repeated, "Good God!"

McCardell's reaction to what he found at this camp, Ohrdruf, which was far from the worst scene of German atrocities, was similar to that of the American major who first entered the camp:

> "I couldn't believe it even when I saw it," Major Scotti said, "I couldn't believe that I was there looking at such things.". . .

The magnitude of the horror was unfathomable. The tales of horror beggared the imagination. They were just "too inconceivably terrible." This was certainly a critical factor in allowing the press to suspend belief. There were many failures in America's behavior during this period, and a failure of the imagination was one of them.

But there is a problem with explaining or excusing the press treatment of this news by relying on the fact that this was a story which was "beyond belief." While the unprecedented nature of this news made it easier, particularly at the outset, to discount the news, by the time of the Bermuda conference in 1943 and certainly by the time of the destruction of Hungarian Jewry in 1944 even the most dubious had good reason to know that terrible things were underway. Numerous eyewitness accounts which corroborated one another had been provided by independent sources. Towns, villages, and ghettos which had once housed millions now stood empty. The underground had transmitted documentation regarding the freight trains loaded with human cargo which rolled into the death camps on one day and rolled out shortly thereafter, only to be followed by other trains bearing a similar cargo. Where could these people be going? Where were the inhabitants of the towns and villages? Had they simply disappeared? There was only one possible answer to these questions. And most members of the press—when they stopped to consider the matter—knew it.

Given the amount of information which reached them, no responsible member of the press should have dismissed this news of the annihilation of a people as propaganda, and the fact is that few did. In the preceding pages we have seen numerous examples of papers and journals acknowledging that millions were being killed. By the latter stages of the war virtually every major American daily had acknowledged that many people, Jews in particular, were being murdered. They lamented what was happening, condemned the perpetrators, and then returned to their practice of burying the information.

There was, therefore, something disingenuous about the claims of reporters and editors at the end of the war not to have known until the camps were open. They may not have known just *how* bad things were, but they knew they were quite bad. . . .

There is, of course, no way of knowing whether anything would have been different if the press had actively pursued this story. The press did not have the power to stop the carnage or to rescue the victims. The Allies might have remained just as committed to inaction, even if they had been pressured by the press. But in a certain respect that is not the question one must ask. The question to be asked is did the press behave in a responsible fashion? Did it fulfill its mandate to its readers? . . .

We still cannot answer the question that Malcolm Bingay's colleagues asked one another as they saw the remains of the Nazis' work—"how creatures, shaped like human beings, can do such things." Nor can we explain how the world of bystanders—particularly those with access to the news—were able to treat this information with such apathy. Both the Final Solution and the bystanders' equanimity are beyond belief.

Today we do not doubt that millions of people can be massacred, systematically and methodically, or that millions more can bear witness and do nothing. Over the past forty years we have lost our innocence and have become inured not only to the escalating cycle of human horror but also to the human indifference. Then the news shocked and confounded us. Today similar news, whether it come from Biafra, Cambodia, Uganda, or any one of a number of other places, does not shock us and sometimes it does not even interest us. It has become an "old," all too familiar, and therefore relatively unexciting story.

Our reaction is among the more tragic legacies of the Final Solution. The inability of reports of extreme persecution and even mass murder in foreign lands to prompt us to act almost guarantees that the cycle of horror which was initiated by the Holocaust will continue.

The United States Should Have Done More

David S. Wyman

> The persecution of Jews began in the 1930s, and the killings began before the United States entered the war. It is possible the United States would never have gone to war if Japan had not attacked Pearl Harbor in 1941, and it is clear President Franklin D. Roosevelt was not prepared to go to war to save the Jews. Once in the war, victory became the paramount goal and the rescue of Jews was thought to be a by-product. During the years preceding that victory, however, millions were murdered. Could the United States have done anything to save them? If so, what measures could have been taken? David S. Wyman, a historian at the University of Massachusetts, wrote the seminal work documenting what the U.S. government did and did not do to rescue the Jews. This excerpt highlights some of the Roosevelt administration's failures and ways it could have saved more of Europe's Jews.

America's response to the Holocaust was the result of action and inaction on the part of many people. In the forefront was Franklin D. Roosevelt, whose steps to aid Europe's Jews were very limited. If he had wanted to, he could have aroused substantial public backing for a vital rescue effort by speaking out on the issue. If nothing else, a few forceful statements by the President would have brought the extermination news out of obscurity and into the headlines. But he had little to say about the problem and gave no priority at all to rescue.

In December 1942, the President reluctantly agreed to talk with Jewish leaders about the recently confirmed news

Excerpted from David S. Wyman, *The Abandonment of the Jews: America and the Holocaust, 1941–1945*. Copyright © 1984 by David S. Wyman. Reprinted with permission from the author and the New Press.

of extermination. Thereafter, he refused Jewish requests to discuss the problem. . . .

It appears that Roosevelt's overall response to the Holocaust was deeply affected by political expediency. Most Jews supported him unwaveringly, so an active rescue policy offered little political advantage. A pro-Jewish stance, however, could lose votes. American Jewry's great loyalty to the President thus weakened the leverage it might have exerted on him to save European Jews.

The main justification for Roosevelt's conduct in the face of the Holocaust is that he was absorbed in waging a global war. . . .

Years later, [Congressman] Emanuel Celler charged that Roosevelt, instead of providing even "some spark of courageous leadership," had been "silent, indifferent, and insensitive to the plight of the Jews." In the end, the era's most prominent symbol of humanitarianism turned away from one of history's most compelling moral challenges. . . .

Secretary [of State Cordell] Hull did issue public statements decrying Nazi persecution of Jews. Otherwise he showed minimal interest in the European Jewish tragedy and assigned no priority to it. Ignorant of his department's activities in that area, and even unacquainted with most of the policymakers, he abandoned refugee and rescue matters to his friend Breckinridge Long. Long and his co-workers specialized in obstruction. . . .

The State Department closed the United States as an asylum by tightening immigration procedures, and it influenced Latin American governments to do the same. When calls for a special rescue agency arose in Congress, Long countered them with deceptive secret testimony before a House committee. . . . It is clear that the State Department was not interested in rescuing Jews.

The War Department did next to nothing for rescue. Secretary [of War Henry] Stimson's personal opposition to immigration was no help. Far more important, however, was the War Department's secret decision that the military was to take no part in rescue—a policy that knowingly contradicted the executive order establishing the WRB [War Refugee Board]. . . .

The Office of War Information [OWI], for the most part, also turned away from the Holocaust It evidently considered Jewish problems too controversial to include in its informational campaigns aimed at the American public. Its director, Elmer Davis, stopped at least two plans for the OWI to circulate the extermination news to the American people. . . .

Eleanor Roosevelt cared deeply about the tragedy of Europe's Jews and took some limited steps to help. But she never urged vigorous government action. She saw almost no prospects for rescue and believed that winning the war as quickly as possible was the only answer.

Except for [Secretary of the Treasury Henry] Morgenthau, Jews who were close to the President did very little to encourage rescue action. David Niles, a presidential assistant, briefly intervened in support of free ports. The others attempted less. Bernard Baruch—influential with Roosevelt, Congress, the wartime bureaucracy, and the public—stayed away from the rescue issue. So did Herbert Lehman, director of UNRRA [the United Nations Relief and Rehabilitation Administration]. Supreme Court Justice Felix Frankfurter had regular access to Roosevelt during the war, and he exercised a quiet but powerful influence in many sectors of administration. Although he used his contacts to press numerous policies and plans, rescue was not among them.

As special counsel to the President, Samuel Rosenman had frequent contact with Roosevelt, who relied heavily on him for advice on Jewish matters. But Rosenman considered the rescue issue politically sensitive, so he consistently tried to insulate Roosevelt from it. For instance, when Morgenthau was getting ready to urge the President to form a rescue agency, Rosenman objected. He did not want FDR involved in refugee matters, although he admitted that no one else could deal effectively, with the problem. Rosenman also argued that government aid to European Jews might increase anti-Semitism in the United States.

The President, his administration, and his advisers were not the only ones responsible for America's reaction to the Holocaust. Few in Congress, whether liberals or conservatives, showed much interest in saving European Jews. Beyond that, restrictionism, especially opposition to the entry of Jews, was strong on Capitol Hill.

Congressional attitudes influenced the administration's policies on rescue. One reason the State Department kept the quotas 90 percent unfilled was fear of antagonizing Congress. . . . The State Department was sufficiently worried about this that, when it agreed to the entry of 5,000 Jewish children from France, it forbade all publicity about the plan. . . .

Except for a weak and insignificant resolution condemning Nazi mass murder, Congress took no official action concerning the Holocaust. . . .

Of the seven Jews in Congress, only Emanuel Celler persistently urged government rescue action. Samuel Dickstein joined the struggle from time to time. Four others seldom raised the issue. Sol Bloom sided with the State Department throughout.

One reason for the government's limited action was the indifference of much of the non-Jewish public. It must be recognized, though, that many Christian Americans were deeply concerned about the murder of European Jewry and realized that it was a momentous tragedy for Christians as well as for Jews. In the words of an official of the Federal Council of Churches, "This is not a Jewish affair. It is a colossal, universal degradation in which all humanity shares." The message appeared in secular circles as well. [Newspaper publisher William Randolph] Hearst, for instance, stressed more than once in his newspapers, "This is not a Christian or a Jewish question. It is a human question and concerns men and women of all creeds."

Support for rescue arose in several non-Jewish quarters. And it came from leading public figures such as Wendell Willkie, Alfred E. Smith, Herbert Hoover, Fiorello La Guardia, Harold Ickes, Dean Alfange, and many more. But most non-Jewish Americans were either unaware of the European Jewish catastrophe or did not consider it important.

America's Christian churches were almost inert in the face of the Holocaust and nearly silent too. No major denomination spoke out on the issue. Few of the many Christian publications cried out for aid to the Jews. Few even reported the news of extermination, except infrequently and incidentally. . . .

The Press Buries Holocaust News

Most newspapers printed very little about the Holocaust, even though extensive information on it reached their desks from the news services (AP [Associated Press], UP [United Press], and others) and from their own correspondents. In New York, the Jewish-owned *Post* reported extermination news and rescue matters fairly adequately. *PM's* coverage was also more complete than that of most American papers. The *Times*, Jewish-owned but anxious not to be seen as Jewish-oriented, was the premier American newspaper of the era. It printed a substantial amount of information on Holocaust-related events but almost always buried it on inner pages. The *Herald Tribune* published a moderate amount of news concerning the Holocaust but seldom placed it where it would attract attention. Coverage in other New York City newspapers ranged from poor to almost nonexistent.

The Jewish-owned *Washington Post* printed a few editorials advocating rescue, but only infrequently carried news reports on the European Jewish situation. . . . The other Washington newspapers provided similarly limited information on the mass murder of European Jewry.

Outside New York and Washington, press coverage was even thinner. All major newspapers carried some Holocaust-related news, but it appeared infrequently and almost always in small items located on inside pages.

American mass-circulation magazines all but ignored the Holocaust. Aside from a few paragraphs touching on the subject, silence prevailed in the major news magazines, *Time*, *Newsweek*, and *Life*. The *Reader's Digest*, *American Mercury*, and *Collier's* released a small flurry of information in February 1943, not long after the extermination news was first revealed. From then until late in the war, little more appeared. . . .

American filmmakers avoided the subject of the Jewish catastrophe. During the war, Hollywood released numerous feature films on refugees and on Nazi atrocities. None dealt with the Holocaust. Despite extensive Jewish influence in the movie industry, the American Jewish Congress was unable to persuade anyone to produce even a short film on the mass killing of the Jews. . . .

In August, a month after the Red Army captured the Majdanek killing center, near Lublin, Soviet authorities permitted American reporters to inspect the still-intact murder
camp—gas chambers, crematoria, mounds of ashes, and the
rest. One American voiced the reaction of all who viewed
Majdanek: "I am now prepared to believe any story of German atrocities, no matter how savage, cruel and depraved.". . .

In the last analysis, it is impossible to know how many
Americans were aware of the Holocaust during the war
years. Starting in late 1942, enough information appeared
that careful followers of the daily news, as well as people especially alert to humanitarian issues or to Jewish problems,
understood the situation. Probably millions more had at
least a vague idea that terrible things were happening to the
European Jews. Most likely, though, they were a minority of
the American public. . . .

Throughout the war, most of the mass media, whether
from disbelief or fear of accusations of sensationalism or for
some other reason, played down the information about the
Jewish tragedy. As a result, a large part of the American public remained unaware of the plight of European Jewry. Hes-
itation about giving full credence to reports of the systematic
extermination of an entire people may be understandable.
But those who edited the news surely realized, at the very
least, that European Jews were being murdered in vast numbers. That was important news. But it was not brought
clearly into public view.

Popular concern for Europe's Jews could not develop
without widespread knowledge of what was happening to
them. But the information gap, though extremely important,
was not the only limiting factor. Strong currents of anti-
Semitism and nativism in American society also diminished
the possibilities for a sympathetic response. . . .

American Jewish leaders recognized that the best hope for
rescue lay in a strong effort to induce the U.S. government
to act. The obvious approaches were two: appeals to high
government officials and a national campaign to publicize
the mass killings with a view to directing public pressure on
the Roosevelt administration and Congress. Jewish leaders

made progress in both directions, but their effectiveness was severely limited by their failure to create a united Jewish movement and by their lack of sustained action. . . .

What Might Have Been Done

What could the American government have achieved if it had really committed itself to rescue? The possibilities were narrowed by the Nazis' determination to wipe out the Jews. War conditions themselves also made rescue difficult. And by mid-1942, when clear news of the systematic murder reached the West, two million Jews had already been massacred and the killing was going forward at a rapid rate. Most likely, it would not have been possible to rescue millions. But without impeding the war effort, additional tens of thousands—probably hundreds of thousands—could have been saved. What follows is a selection of twelve programs that could have been tried. All of them, and others, were proposed during the Holocaust.

(1) Most important, the War Refugee Board should have been established in 1942. And it should have received adequate government funding and much broader powers.

(2) The U.S. government, working through neutral governments or the Vatican, could have pressed Germany to release the Jews. If nothing else, this would have demonstrated to the Nazis—and to the world—that America was committed to saving the European Jews. It is worth recalling that until late summer 1944, when the Germans blocked the Horthy offer, it was far from clear to the Allies that Germany would not let the Jews out. On the contrary, until then the State Department and the British Foreign Office feared that Hitler might confront the Allies with an exodus of Jews, a possibility that they assiduously sought to avoid. . . .

(3) The United States could have applied constant pressure on Axis satellites to release their Jews. By spring 1943, the State Department knew that some satellites, convinced that the war was lost, were seeking favorable peace terms. Stern threats of punishment for mistreating Jews or allowing their deportation, coupled with indications that permitting them to leave for safety would earn Allied goodwill, could

have opened the way to the rescue of large numbers from Rumania, Bulgaria, Hungary, and perhaps Slovakia. Before the Germans took control of Italy, in September 1943, similar pressures might have persuaded the Italian government to allow its Jews to flee, as well as those in Italian-occupied areas of Greece, Yugoslavia, and France. . . .

(7) A campaign to stimulate and assist escapes would have led to a sizable outflow of Jews. Once the neutral nations had agreed to open their borders, that information could have been publicized throughout Europe by radio, airdropped leaflets, and underground communications channels. Local currencies could have been purchased in occupied countries, often with blocked foreign accounts. These funds could have financed escape systems, false documentation, and bribery of lower-level officials. Underground movements were willing to cooperate. . . . Even without help, and despite closed borders, tens of thousands of Jews attempted to escape to Switzerland, Spain, Palestine, and other places. Thousands succeeded. With assistance, and assurance of acceptance into neutral nations, those thousands could have been scores of thousands.

(8) Much larger sums of money should have been transferred to Europe. . . . Besides facilitating escapes, money would have helped in hiding Jews, supplying food and other essentials, strengthening Jewish undergrounds, and gaining the assistance of non-Jewish forces. . . .

The measures taken by Raoul Wallenberg in Budapest should have been implemented by all neutral diplomatic missions and repeated in city after city throughout Axis Europe. And they should have begun long before the summer of 1944.

The United States could also have pressed its two great allies to help. The Soviet Union turned away all requests for cooperation. . . . An American government that was serious about rescue might have extracted some assistance from the Russians. . . .

(11) Some military assistance was possible. The Air Force could have eliminated the Auschwitz killing installations. Some bombing of deportation railroads was feasible. The military could have aided in other ways without impeding the war effort. It was, in fact, legally required to do so by the

executive order that established the WRB.

(12) Much more publicity about the extermination of the Jews should have been disseminated through Europe. . . . This might have influenced three groups: the Christian populations, the Nazis, and the Jews. Western leaders and, especially, the Pope [Pius XII] could have appealed to Christians not to cooperate in any way with the anti-Jewish programs, and to hide and to aid Jews whenever possible.

Roosevelt, [Prime Minister Winston] Churchill, and the Pope might have made clear to the Nazis their full awareness of the mass-murder program and their severe condemnation of it. If, in addition, Roosevelt and Churchill had threatened punishment for these crimes and offered asylum to the Jews, the Nazis at least would have ceased to believe that the West did not care what they were doing to the Jews. That might possibly have slowed the killing. And it might have hastened the decision of the SS, ultimately taken in late 1944, to end the extermination. . . .

The European Jews themselves should have been repeatedly warned of what was happening and told what the deportation trains really meant. (With good reason, the Nazis employed numerous precautions and ruses to keep this information from their victims.) Decades later, Rudolf Vrba, one of the escapees who exposed Auschwitz to the outside world, remained angry that the Jews had not been alerted. "Would anybody get me alive to Auschwitz if I had this information?" he demanded. "Would thousands and thousands of able-bodied Jewish men send their children, wives, mothers to Auschwitz from all over Europe, if they knew?" Roosevelt, Churchill, other Western leaders, and major Jewish spokesmen should have warned Jews over and over against the steps that led to deportation and urged them to try to hide or flee or resist. To help implement these actions, the Allies could have smuggled in cadres of specially trained Jewish agents.

None of these proposals guaranteed results. But all deserved serious consideration, and those that offered any chance of success should have been tried. There was a moral imperative to attempt everything possible that would not hurt the war effort. If that had been done, even if few or no lives had been saved, the moral obligation would have been fulfilled. But the outcome would not have been anything like that barren. The War Refugee Board, a very tardy, inadequately supported, partial commitment, saved several tens of thousands. A timely American rescue effort that had the wholehearted support of the government would have achieved much more.

FDR's Excuses

A commitment of that caliber did not materialize. Instead, the Roosevelt administration turned aside most rescue proposals. In the process, government officials developed four main rationalizations for inaction. The most frequent excuse, the unavailability of shipping, was a fraud. When the Allies wanted to find ships for nonmilitary projects, they located them. In 1943, American naval vessels carried 1,400 non-Jewish Polish refugees from India to the American West Coast. The State and War departments arranged to move 2,000 Spanish Loyalist refugees to Mexico using military shipping. In March 1944, blaming the shipping shortage, the British backed out of an agreement to transport 630 Jewish refugees from Spain to the Fedala camp, near Casablanca. Yet at the same time, they were providing troopships to move non-Jewish refugees by the thousands from Yugoslavia to southern Italy and on to camps in Egypt.

When it was a matter of transporting Jews, ships could almost never be found. This was not because shipping was unavailable but because the Allies were unwilling to take the Jews in. . . .

Another stock excuse for inaction was the claim that Axis governments planted agents among the refugees. Although this possibility needed to be watched carefully, the problem was vastly overemphasized and could have been handled through reasonable security screening. It was significant that Army intelligence found not one suspicious person when it checked the 982 refugees who arrived at Fort Ontario. Nevertheless, potential subversion was continually used as a reason for keeping immigration to the United States very tightly restricted. Turkey, Latin American nations, Britain, and other countries used the same exaggerated argument. It played an important part in blocking the channels of rescue.

A third rationalization for failing to aid European Jews took the high ground of nondiscrimination. It asserted that helping Jews would improperly single out one group for assistance when many peoples were suffering under Nazi brutality. Equating the genocide of the Jews with the oppression imposed on other Europeans was, in the words of one of the world's foremost churchmen, Willem Visser 't Hooft, "a dangerous half-truth which could only serve to distract attention from the fact that no other race was faced with the situation of having every one of its members . . . threatened by death in the gas chambers."

The Roosevelt administration, the British government, and the Intergovernmental Committee on Refugees regularly refused to acknowledge that the Jews faced a special situation. One reason for this was to avoid responsibility for taking special steps to save them. Such steps, if successful, would have confronted the Allies with the difficult problem of finding places to put the rescued Jews.

Another reason was the fear that special action for the Jews would stir up anti-Semitism. Some asserted that such action would even invite charges that the war was being fought for the Jews. Emanuel Celler declared years later that Roosevelt did nearly nothing for rescue because he was afraid of the label "Jew Deal"; he feared the political effects of the accusation that he was pro-Jewish. . . .

The fourth well-worn excuse for rejecting rescue proposals was the claim that they would detract from the military effort and thus prolong the war. This argument, entirely valid with regard to projects that actually would have hurt the war effort, was used almost automatically to justify inaction. Virtually none of the rescue proposals involved enough infringement on the war effort to lengthen the conflict at all or to increase the number of casualties, military or civilian.

Actually, the war effort was bent from time to time to meet pressing humanitarian needs. In most of these instances, it was non-Jews who were helped. During 1942, 1943, and 1944, the Allies evacuated large numbers of non-

Jewish Yugoslavs, Poles, and Greeks to safety in the Middle East, Africa, and elsewhere. Difficulties that constantly ruled out the rescue of Jews dissolved. Transportation somehow materialized to move 100,000 people to dozens of refugee camps that sprang into existence. . . . Most of these refugees had been in desperate straits. None, though, were the objects of systematic annihilation. . . .

In all, Britain and the United States rescued 100,000 Yugoslav, Polish, and Greek refugees from disastrous conditions. Most of them traveled by military transport to camps where the Allies maintained them at considerable cost in funds, supplies, and even military staff. In contrast, the United States (with minimal cooperation from the British) evacuated fewer than 2,000 Jews to the three camps open to *them*, the ones at Fedala, Philippeville, and Oswego. . . .

It was not a lack of workable plans that stood in the way of saving many thousands more European Jews. Nor was it insufficient shipping, the threat of infiltration by subversive agents, or the possibility that rescue projects would hamper the war effort. The real obstacle was the absence of a strong desire to rescue Jews. A month before the Bermuda Conference, the Committee for a Jewish Army declared:

> We, on our part, refuse to resign ourselves to the idea that our brains are powerless to find any solution. . . . In order to visualize the possibility of such a solution, imagine that the British people and the American nation had millions of residents in Europe. . . . Let us imagine that Hitler would start a process of annihilation and would slaughter not two million Englishmen or Americans, not hundreds of thousands, but, let us say, only tens of thousands. . . . It is clear that the governments of Great Britain [and] the United States would certainly find ways and means to act instantly and to act effectively.

But the European Jews were not Americans and they were not English. It was their particular misfortune not only to be foreigners but also to be Jews.

Could Auschwitz Have Been Bombed?

Stuart Erdheim

Could the Holocaust have been prevented? Could more people have been saved? These are two of the big questions that will be debated forever. One of the enduring controversies has focused more specifically on the issue of whether the concentration camps could have been bombed to either stop or slow down the killing. As mentioned in this article, Buchenwald *was* bombed, though the damage to the camp was an inadvertent by-product of a raid on an adjacent factory. The Allies also bombed targets near Auschwitz, so the question arises: Why didn't they bomb the death camp? This article offers a response to some of the arguments given for the failure to bomb Auschwitz and suggests that the answer to the question had little or nothing to do with military matters and everything to do with the mindset of the Allied leaders. Stuart Erdheim has both a master's degree in philsophy and a doctorate of divinity from Yeshiva University. He is an independent researcher.

Several works dating from the late 1970s onward have explored the question of whether the Allies had the knowledge and technical capability needed to bomb the killing facilities at Auschwitz-Birkenau. Beginning with a 1978 article in *Commentary* (later incorporated into a 1984 book, *The Abandonment of the Jews*), David Wyman argued that the failure to bomb the death camp did not result from any cogent assessment of military infeasibility, but rather was yet another example of Allied indifference to the ongoing destruction of European Jewry. More recently, two critics have sought to

Excerpted from Stuart Erdheim, "Could the Allies have Bombed Auschwitz-Birkenau?" *Holocaust and Genocide Studies*, Vol. 11, no. 2, Fall 1997. Reprinted with permission from the author.

undermine Wyman's thesis by focusing on the operational obstacles that confronted a potential bombing mission over Auschwitz-Birkenau (hereinafter Birkenau). In separate articles, James H. Kitchens III and Richard H. Levy deflect criticism from the Allies by examining military complexities such as intelligence, target distance and placement, bomber availability and accuracy, and defenses. This article is a direct challenge to their assessment of the military practicality of bombing the death camp. Although the operational issue is clearly a complex one, the research presented below will show that, at least from a military standpoint, bombing Birkenau itself was no more complex than numerous other missions undertaken by the Allied powers during the Second World War. . . .

Photo Reconnaissance and Intelligence

If the Allies had considered Birkenau a potential target, they would have immediately ordered aerial reconnaissance in order to determine the capacity of the air forces to bomb the camp effectively. Photo intelligence was indispensable to the planning of bombing missions, and Birkenau would have been no exception. In order to make any operational assessment, then, we must first apply the same photo reconnaissance techniques to Birkenau that the Allies would have applied to any other target.

Any photo reconnaissance efforts might have been requested on the basis of earlier intelligence about the camp, but certainly by June 1944, when it became available to the Allies, the Vrba-Wetzler report established itself as the most crucial source. The testimony provided by Rudolf Vrba and Alfred Wetzler, who escaped from Auschwitz in April 1944, contained detailed information about the camp, including sketches of its layout. Yet Kitchens dismisses this evidence out of hand, arguing that it "had minimal utility for military intelligence purposes," did not "reliably locate" the gas chambers and crematoria, and that the "maps included with the report contained at least one error which could have puzzled those seeking to correlate the report with aerial photographs.". . .

While Kitchens openly criticizes the Vrba-Wetzler report

for not providing detailed information on the size and design of the crematoria, he fails to discern valuable information that the report did provide. The escapees indicated, for example, that Birkenau prisoners worked outside the camp, thus lowering estimates of potential collateral deaths from a bombing raid. Their report also contained relevant corroborating material for several 1943 reports on gas chambers and crematoria. Finally . . . there was enough intelligence in the report that experts would have had little difficulty locating the extermination facilities, if only they had had aerial imagery with which to correlate it. . . .

"[Prior to 1944] there was enough generally accurate information [obtained through the Polish underground] about Auschwitz-Birkenau to preclude the argument that the Allies did not bomb the camp because they got the necessary information too late." If this information had evoked enough curiosity, if not horror, to have justified just one PR [photo reconnaissance] sortie, Birkenau could have been photographed much sooner. Indeed, as early as October 6, 1942, and August 20, 1943, photo reconnaissance Mosquitos obtained imagery of the oil refinery at Blechhammer, Germany, forty-seven miles from the death camp. When the Joint Chiefs of Staff received reports of crematoria at Oświecim in June 1943 from Polish Military Intelligence, for example, the area could have been included on the August 20 Blechhammer mission. . . .

Allied Intelligence on the Final Solution

Another important issue concerns the level of military intelligence on the Final Solution in general. On this point Kitchens argues that intelligence authorities were not alerted to look for gas chambers and crematoria since genocide was still unknown. Kitchens writes that "before the end of 1944, at least, the Allies lacked enough solid intelligence about the 'Final Solution' to adequately comprehend its hideous import." In support of this, he quotes an October 10, 1944, British War Office Report which, he informs readers, was an attempt to "summarize the concentration camp intelligence then in hand" and indicates that the Allies "had no exact knowledge of the number of camps the Germans were operating, where the camps were located, how many internees there were, or to what overall purpose the detainees were being held.". . .

In the case of the Oct. 10 report, Kitchens completely ignores what it had to say about Auschwitz, which is important not only in an informative sense, but as to the quality of this report itself. First, it provides a great deal of information on the concentration camp system (including identifying and locating all six death camps) and gassing facilities. It correctly locates the Auschwitz camp, states that it had been "mentioned frequently since 1939," and lists the estimated annual population since 1940. The report notes too that the "Birkenau camp is definitely connected, as Auschwitz makes use of Birkenau's gas chambers, though it is said to have ten crematoria and four lethal gas chambers itself." Moreover, the report identifies the leading SS personnel by rank for December 1943 and March 1944 and classifies Birkenau as a "Special KL" (*Konzentrationslager*) and annihilation camp for women, where the inmates are said to be "mostly Hungarian Jews." Under the "remarks" section, it asserts bluntly: "Most likely controlled by AUSCHWITZ, where Jews are sent to keep the four crematoria busy." In short, though they did not get each and every fact exactly right, Allied Intelligence knew the location of an extermination camp that utilized gas chambers and crematoria to murder human beings and efficiently dispose of their remains. . . .

In August 1942, Churchill also learned from decrypts that 8,000 men and women had died in one month at Auschwitz. Although unable to reveal that they were all Jews (that would have exposed the intelligence coup of ULTRA), Churchill nonetheless announced in a radio broadcast to the British people (August 25, 1942) that "whole districts are being exterminated," and that the Germans were perpetrating "the most frightful cruelties." "We are in the presence of a crime without a name," the great wartime leader concluded, leaving no doubt that he understood all too well the "hideous import of the Final Solution."

This "crime without a name" was officially denounced by

the Allied Declaration of December 17, 1942, signed by the United States, Britain, the Soviet Union, and the governments of eight occupied countries. It condemned the German government's "intention to exterminate the Jewish people in Europe," and denounced in the strongest possible terms this bestial policy of cold-blooded extermination." Putting aside its prior hesitations to believe the reports on genocide the Allied governments now publicly confirmed what they had known for over a year.

Why did the Allies wait so long? According to William J. Casey, the former head of the CIA and an OSS agent during the war, the numerous reports on the Jewish genocide "were shunted aside because of the official policy in Washington and London to concentrate exclusively on the defeat of the enemy." Yet many of these reports contained reliable information on the gas chambers and crematoria at Birkenau. One of them, which came from Polish military intelligence in London, reached Washington by diplomatic pouch in May 1943 and the joint Chiefs of Staff by June. Updating information for Auschwitz-Birkenau, the report noted that: "A huge new camp crematorium consumes 3,000 persons daily." A summary of this and similar reports was made public on March 21, 1944, when the Associated Press in London released a report from the Polish Ministry of Information confirming that "more than 500,000 persons, mostly Jews, had been put to death at a concentration camp at Oświecim, southwest of Kracow." The report also stated that "three crematoria had been erected inside the camp to dispose of 10,000 bodies a day." The *Washington Post* published the AP release on the following day on page 2 under the banner, "Poles Report Nazis Slay 10,000 Daily." On March 24, 1944, five days after the Nazis installed a puppet government in Hungary and less than two months before the deportation of Hungarian Jews was to begin, Franklin Delano Roosevelt declared: "In one of the blackest crimes of all history . . . the wholesale systematic murder of the Jews of Europe goes on unabated every hour . . . [the Jews of Hungary] are now threatened with annihilation. . . . All who knowingly take part in the deportation of Jews to their death in Poland

. . . are equally guilty with the executioner.". . .

Based upon the evidence presented above, there no longer can be any question as to what the Allies knew and whether or not they had enough time to act upon it. We must now turn to the question of what they might have done. . . .

Risks to Prisoners

A common argument long marshaled by critics of the notion of bombing Auschwitz is that any concentrated high-altitude air attack on the death camp would have killed many prisoners in the process. We can never know for sure the extent of the prisoner casualties that would have resulted. But by comparing such an attack to raids like that on Buchenwald, we can judge the degree to which this factor should have played a role in any potential bombing decision.

While Kitchens cites the August 24, 1944, raid on Buchenwald as proof that the inaccuracy of heavy bombers would have killed many Birkenau prisoners, the mission itself proves the exact opposite. The Buchenwald raid was, in fact, an extremely accurate one, successfully avoiding the concentration camp during a bombing of the Gustloff Works adjacent to it. According to the *Buchenwald Report*, the attack "completely destroyed the 'industrial development work' of the SS in Buchenwald in one single, well aimed blow." The *Report* further stated that "there were only two large fires caused by incendiary bombs," and an inmate wrote that "no [heavy] bombs struck the camp itself; only one bomb fell adjacent to the crematorium." The 384 prisoners killed were working in the factory areas at the time of the raid and were not allowed to retreat to the camp or to use bomb shelters during an air-raid alarm or attack, prompting another inmate to write: "The sole responsibility for the unfortunate deaths of several hundred prisoners in this attack falls on the SS, which at the time forbade prisoners to evacuate into the camp during an air raid alarm. . . ." The same prisoner also made it a point to note the effort of the Allied pilots to avoid collateral damage: "The Allied pilots in particular did all they could in order not to hit prisoners. The high number of prisoners killed is to be charged exclusively against the debit accounts of the Nazi murderers.". . .

A final aspect of this raid also is useful in conceptualizing what might have happened at Birkenau. The Buchenwald factories were believed by the Allies to be producing V-2 rocket parts and were thus attacked as part of the Crossbow offensive, despite the fact that the Allies knew well of the adjacent concentration camp. Whether they knew too that over 82,000 inmates were there is unclear, though even assuming a far lesser figure the decision to bomb was made with full knowledge that numerous prisoners could be killed if accuracy was below average (and this for a questionable strategic and tactical objective). Indeed, if the accuracy had not been up to standards, it is conceivable that more inmates would have been killed in this one raid than the total number of British civilians killed by all V-2 rocket attacks. To be consistent in their reasoning, then, those opposed to high-altitude bombing of Birkenau because of collateral deaths would have to consider this raid unconscionable. The British government, however, had its own priorities. . . .

Kitchens dismisses any attack by heavy bombers, arguing that their limited accuracy would have killed too many prisoners, thus resulting in unacceptable collateral damage. The problem, in this case, is not so much Kitchens' argument as his reasoning. He ignores, for example, the fact that most of these prisoners would be killed anyway, focusing only on how many Jews might have been killed by the bombing, rather than how many could have been saved. . . .

On July 7, 1944, British Foreign Secretary Anthony Eden wrote to the Secretary of State for Air, Sir Archibald Sinclair, inquiring "if anything could be done by bombing to stop the murder of Jews in Hungary." Sinclair and his staff replied on July 15 that due to various operational problems the RAF could do nothing. And though he did propose bringing the question up with the Americans, Sinclair added: "I am not clear that it would really help the victims." Next to this remark, Eden scribbled: "He wasn't asked his opinion of this; he was asked to act," and then summed up the letter as "characteristically unhelpful.". . .

First, Sinclair argued that bombing the camp was "out of

bounds of possibility for [RAF] Bomber Command, because the distance is too great for the attack to be carried out at night." Levy quotes Air Marshal Harris (a.k.a. "Bomber" Harris) for confirmation that "the extent of darkness" affects range. In other words, the major operational obstacle for the RAF in attacking Birkenau was the inability of British bombers to return to their bases in England under cover of darkness. Yet this same inability of airlift bombers to leave from and return to Italian bases at night did not prevent them from being sent in August and September to Warsaw, 150 miles farther than Birkenau was from Allied bases in Italy. . . .

Conclusion

Both Sinclair and John J. McCloy, the U.S. Assistant Secretary of War, indicated that the target could not be bombed, thus putting an end to any further discussion on the matter. Yet their determination was not based upon standard operational procedure. As we have seen above, neither the British nor the Americans ever deliberately took a single photograph of Birkenau, though it would hardly have stretched their resources to do so. Further, no one ever bothered to make a simple request to the photo library for imagery of the Auschwitz area. The "could not" assessment, in short, appeared the most expedient way to implement the already established policy of not using the military to aid "refugees."

Even if the death camp could have been bombed, as this paper has sought to prove, the next line of argument against doing so was that it would have required, as McCloy indicated the "diversion of considerable air support essential to the success of our forces now engaged in decisive operations." This term "diversion can be applied to those actions which are (1) not directly related to military operations, or (2) not expressly ordered by the proper authority. Thus if Churchill (and the War Cabinet) or Roosevelt or any high-ranking commander had ordered an attack, then that mission would not be considered a diversion. . . .

From a simple comparison with other missions, there can be no question that the Birkenau extermination facilities could have been attacked by P-38 or Mosquito fighters using low-level precision bombing and causing minimal collateral damage. . . .

Also indisputable is the fact that both USAAF and RAF heavy and medium bombers had the range to attack the camp, though the inconsistent bombing accuracy of the heavies made it necessary to consider the cost/benefit ratio in human terms. In other words, how many would have to die to prevent the slaughter of how many others? Such a judgment, of course, was not unique to Birkenau, but constituted a decision taken even for strictly military operations. . . .

Such a cost/benefit analysis was simply never made in the case of Birkenau. The judgment that many inmates may have been killed was decided upon without any feasibility study and in complete ignorance of the location of the extermination facilities in relation to the camp. For all the Allies knew, the crematoria were situated in a field a mile from the camp and could have been destroyed with a few well placed bombs, as Cheshire suggests. In short, moral values and political considerations were tragically neglected in the case of the Holocaust. . . .

Richard Breitman argues that with intelligence reports received in 1943, enough could have been known about Birkenau to plan a raid in early 1944, had there been the will to act. If we consider a scenario in which Roosevelt ordered an attack at the time of his March 24, 1944, speech and it took place sometime in May (just as the Hungarian deportations were beginning), destroying at least Crematoria II and III (which constituted 75% of the capacity), would the killing process have been impeded? First, as Wyman points out, it took eight months to build these complex "industrial structures" at a time when Nazi Germany was at the height of its power. To organize the skilled labor and refashion highly specialized parts in the spring/summer of 1944 would have been difficult, if not impossible.

Kitchens' suggestion that the Jews could have been sent to Mauthausen, Belsen, or Buchenwald, none of which were extermination camps (or capable of accepting a few hundred thousand inmates on short notice), shows a lack of full knowledge of the camp system. Without the extermination facilities, the SS undoubtedly would have been forced to slow or altogether halt the deportations (which in the spring/summer of 1944 amounted to 70–80,000 Hungarian Jews a week) while they resorted to other, less efficient means of killing and body disposal. Cremation ditches, like those used for a short period in 1944 for the overflow of corpses, were hardly a practical alternative due to the problems posed by contamination as well as the threat of disease. It was for these very reasons, in fact, that Himmler had ordered the crematoria built in the first place. . . .

Doris Kearns Goodwin, a noted Roosevelt historian, once said that she thought bombing Auschwitz would have been worthwhile "if it had saved only one Jew. FDR somehow missed seeing how big an issue it was." With the kind of political will and moral courage the Allies exhibited in other missions throughout the war, it is plain that the failure to bomb Birkenau, the site of mankind's greatest abomination, was a missed opportunity of monumental proportions.

Roosevelt Saved the World

Robert Edwin Herzstein

Roosevelt & Hitler, excerpted here, is critical of President Roosevelt and his administration for failing to do enough to save the victims of the Holocaust. Still, even among Jews, Roosevelt is held in high esteem and is regarded as one of the greatest presidents in U.S. history. How can this be explained? In Roosevelt's case, he saved the world, but could not save every life. This brief excerpt, written by Robert Edwin Herzstein, a professor of history at the University of South Carolina, explains how the pursuit of the larger goal of winning the war helped the Jews and insured Roosevelt's high standing in history.

Thanks in large measure to Roosevelt's policies, the United States became involved in a faraway quarrel, among nations viewed with suspicion by a large majority of the citizenry. Roosevelt's mix of economic, ideological, ethical, and political motives led him to pursue a policy representing a violent break with recent American attitudes, including his own.

Roosevelt believed that active intervention by the White House on behalf of Jewish refugees and victims of Hitler would endanger his strategy. By isolating and politically castrating the Jew-haters, through means both fair and foul, Roosevelt helped to rake the United States in an anti-Nazi direction in foreign policy. . . .

The president refused to support changes in the immigrant quota system so as to provide sanctuary for Austrian and German Jewish refugees. He feared congressional reaction, as well as a domestic anti-Semitic backlash. Roosevelt viewed a battle with Congress over the refugee question as a diversion, one that would only give respectability to fringe

Excerpted from Robert Edwin Herzstein, *Roosevelt & Hitler: Prelude to War*. Copyright © 1989 by Robert Edwin Herzstein. Originally published by Paragon House, New York. Reprinted with permission from the author and his literary agent, Susan Ann Protter.

groups and assorted anti-Semites. . . .

Roosevelt was thus too cautious when dealing with the refugee question, and at times betrayed a lack of humanitarian compassion. In making such assertions, his critics have been right. Nevertheless, the prime interest of the Jews, and of all humanity, was to rid the world of Hitlerism. Roosevelt's policy toward the immigration issue must be put in the broader context of his revolutionary foreign policy. This interventionist initiative, developed when the country was economically troubled, isolationist, and at peace, is our best guide to Roosevelt's intentions, and to his greatness or failure. Jewish refugees were tragic pawns, for FDR sacrificed them to a strategy calculated to ensure American global hegemony in a world free of the Nazis. . . .

Franklin D. Roosevelt

Had Roosevelt not discredited the far-right and anti-Semitic movements between 1938 and 1941, would the United States have been willing to accept his forward policy in the North Atlantic after March, 1941? If Roosevelt had not helped to secure an anti-Nazi alliance and begun to prepare the United States for war in 1940 and 1941, would any Jews have been alive west of Moscow in 1945? If Roosevelt had taken the easy way out, there would have been no Grand Alliance, no extermination of Hitler. The most likely outcome would have been a German victory, or a strategic stalemate in Europe. . . .

In 1935, . . . the great German novelist Thomas Mann visited President Roosevelt. He recalled, "When I left the White House after my first visit [on 30 June, 1935], I knew

Hitler was lost." The imagination of the novelist saw more deeply than the observers who accused Roosevelt of timidity or lack of direction. Mann later avowed, "I passionately longed for war against Hitler and 'agitated' for it; and I shall be eternally grateful to Roosevelt, the born and conscious enemy of l'Infame [the infamous one, i.e., Hitler], for having manoevered his all-important country into it with consummate skill." A "born and conscious enemy"—this is what Hitler saw, and why he hated FDR so.

Another observer, who had reason to revile Roosevelt for his inaction during the Holocaust, says something of even greater significance. No one spent more time trying to tell the world about the Holocaust than the Polish resistance courier Jan Karski. He had been inside a Nazi camp and had seen the Warsaw Ghetto. Forty years later, he was still haunted by his inability to awaken the West to the full horror of his story. This Jan Karski visited Roosevelt on 28 July 1943, and spoke with him for eighty minutes. FDR asked a lot of questions about the Jews, "but he didn't tell me anything." Surely Karski would be bitter about this man, who viewed the military destruction of the Reich as the great aim of the Allied cause? No. Karski still views FDR as the embodiment of "[g]reatness. Power. I saw in him the height of humanity. Everyone did—all the people of Europe. Roosevelt was a legend. So much so that when I left his office, I walked out backwards." Karski does not accept nor does he condemn the military explanation for Allied failure to save the Jews. He concludes in sorrow more than anger: Yes, "[s]ix million Jews perished. Six million totally helpless, abandoned by all." But Karski adds, "What do I know about strategy. They won the war, didn't they? They crushed Germany. If it were not for this victory, all of Europe would be enslaved today. That I know."

Chapter 5

The Legacy of the Holocaust

Turning|Points

IN WORLD HISTORY

Bringing Nazis to Justice: The Nuremberg Trials

Robert E. Conot

Though the Allies could be criticized for not doing more to save the Jews, they did not ignore the Germans' actions. In fact, starting at the end of 1942, Roosevelt and Churchill expressed their horror at the behavior of the Nazis and vowed to bring the Nazi criminals to justice. The problem was that these statements seemed like little more than bluster and idle threats since no action was being taken. Slowly the idea evolved to gather evidence of the Nazis' crimes and bring them to justice. The United States led the effort to conduct a trial, in part to serve as a means of documenting everything for posterity. The British, at least initially, were more interested in summarily executing the men responsible for the war. This excerpt traces the development of the concept of holding a war crimes trial in Nuremberg and the process involved in choosing the defendants. The International Military Tribunal finished its work and handed down its verdicts on October 1, 1946. Of the 22 defendants, 11 were given the death penalty, 3 were acquitted, 3 were given life imprisonment and four were given imprisonment ranging from 10 to 20 years.

Nearly two years had passed since President Roosevelt, on October 7, 1942, had first declared: "It is our intention that just and sure punishment shall be meted out to the ringleaders responsible for the organized murder of thousands of innocent persons in the commission of atrocities which have violated every tenet of the Christian faith." Two months

Excerpted from Robert E. Conot, *Justice at Nuremberg*. Copyright © 1983 Robert E. Conot. Reprinted with permission from HarperCollins, Inc.

later, on December 17, British Foreign Secretary Anthony Eden had told the House of Commons: "The German authorities are now carrying into effect Hitler's oft repeated intention to exterminate the Jewish people of Europe. From all the occupied centers of Europe Jews are being transported in conditions of appalling horror and brutality to eastern Europe. In Poland, which has been made the principal Nazi slaughterhouse, the ghettos established by the Nazi invaders are being systematically emptied of all Jews except a few highly skilled workers required for war industries. None of those taken away are ever heard of again. The able-bodied are slowly worked to death in labor camps. The infirm are left to die of exposure and starvation, or are deliberately massacred in mass executions."

The next year, Roosevelt, Churchill, and Stalin formally stated in the Moscow Declaration their determination to bring the guilty to justice. On October 26, 1943, the United Nations War Crimes Commission, composed of fifteen Allied nations (not including the Soviet Union) held its first meeting in London. Again, on March 24, 1944, Roosevelt warned: "None who participate in these acts of savagery shall go unpunished. All who share in the guilt shall share the punishment."

Yet nothing had been done to implement the multitude of declarations. Morgenthau was bitter at the State Department for its bureaucratic bumbling and failure to facilitate the escape of Jews; and President Roosevelt was concerned about the possible loss of the Jewish vote in an election year. In the weeks following the Normandy landing on June 6, Eisenhower became more and more incensed as scores of British, Canadian, and American prisoners of war were shot by the Waffen SS in what seemed like calculated policy. In Washington, G-I, the Office of the Chief of Staff of the Personnel Division, was charged with collecting evidence on crimes committed against American servicemen. In July, the task was delegated to Lieutenant Colonel Murray C. Bernays; and Bernays was to prove the guiding spirit leading the way to the Nuremberg trial. . . .

On July 11, Churchill had written to Foreign Secretary

Anthony Eden: "There is no doubt that this is probably the greatest and most horrible crime ever committed in the whole history of the world, and it has been done by scientific machinery by nominally civilized men in the name of a great State. . . . It is quite clear that all concerned who may fall into our hands, including the people who only obeyed orders by carrying out the butcheries, should be put to death after their association with the murders has been proved."

Morgenthau, who advocated the division and deindustrialization of Germany, concurred with Churchill and the British Lord Chancellor, John Simon, that the principal Nazi leaders should be charged with their crimes, then summarily shot. On the other hand, Colonel Mickey Marcus of the Army Civil Affairs Division, which was charged with formulating postwar policy for Germany, was disturbed by Morgenthau's emotional approach. At a meeting with Bernays, he agreed that retribution must not appear to be a Judaic act of revenge. Summary execution, no matter how justified, could never serve as a substitute for justice.

"Not to try these beasts would be to miss the educational and therapeutic opportunity of our generation," Bernays argued. "They must be tried not alone for their specific aims, but for the bestiality from which these crimes sprang.". . .

Bernays proposed that an international tribunal should be established to condemn violence, terror, racism, totalitarianism, and wanton destruction; the tribunal should arouse the German people to a sense of their guilt and a realization of their responsibility. Otherwise, Germany would simply have lost another war; the German people would not come to understand the barbarism they had supported, nor have any conception of the criminal character of the Nazi regime. The fascist potential would remain undiminished, and the menace remain. Only the staging of a great trial—or, possibly, a number of trials—in which the conspiracy of the Nazi leadership would be proved and the utilization of the Nazi organizations in the furtherance of that conspiracy would be established, could all the objectives be attained, and all criminals, large and small, be caught in the same web. . . .

Churchill and Lord Simon stuck to the proposition that "it

is beyond question that Hitler and a number of arch criminals associated with him [including Mussolini, Himmler, Goering, Ribbentrop, and Goebbels] must, so far as they fall
into Allied hands, suffer the penalty of death for their conduct leading up to the war and for their wickedness in the
conduct of the war. It being conceded that these leaders must
suffer death, the question arises whether they should be tried
by some form of tribunal claiming to exercise judicial functions, or whether the decision taken by the Allies should be
reached and enforced without the machinery of a trial."

After weighing the pros and cons, the British concluded
once more that the dangers of a trial outweighed the advantages and that "execution without trial is the preferable
course.". . .

On April 30, however, Hitler had committed suicide and
been followed by Goebbels. Mussolini was captured and executed by Italian partisans. Two weeks later Himmler bit
into a capsule of cyanide. With these men dead, the British
opposition to a trial softened. . . .

The British suggested that the trial might be held in Munich, the cradle of the Nazi movement; or, alternately, in
Berlin or Leipzig. Jackson replied that he had no objection
to Munich, which was in the American zone, but that the
United States did not want the trial held in either of the
other two cities, which were under Russian occupation. Fyfe
proposed ten top Nazis as defendants: Hermann Goering,
commander of the Luftwaffe, director of the Four Year Plan,
founder of the Gestapo, and onetime heir apparent to Adolf
Hitler; Rudolf Hess, party secretary and Hitler's right-hand
man until 1941, when he had mysteriously parachuted from
a Messerschmitt fighter over Scotland; Joachim van Ribbentrop, the foreign minister; Robert Ley, director of the German Labor Front; Alfred Rosenberg, party theoretician and
minister for the Occupied Eastern Territories; Wilhelm
Frick, interior minister; Field Marshal Wilhelm Keitel, chief
of staff of the Wehrmacht; Julius Streicher, a gauleiter and
notorious Jew baiter; Ernst Kaltenbrunner, head of the Reich
Security Office, the second ranking man in the SS after
Himmler; and Hans Frank, governor of occupied Poland. . . .

The Anglo-American system of trial had little in common with the continental, followed by the French and Russians. Jackson was as ill-informed about continental practices as Major General I.T. Nikitchenko, the forty-five-year-old head of the Soviet delegation, was about American; and repeatedly one was unable to comprehend the other. Furthermore, it quickly became clear that the American and Soviet conceptions of the International Military Tribunal were startlingly at odds.

Nikitchenko maintained: "We are dealing here with the chief war criminals who have already been convicted by both the Moscow and Crimea [Yalta] declarations." The job of the court was merely to decide the degree of guilt of each individual, and to mete out punishment. The essence of the case would be determined before the start of the trial—in the continental system, the prosecutor assembled all evidence both against and in favor of the accused and presented it to an examining judge, who then decided whether the person should be brought to trial. If the judge ruled in the affirmative, he was, in effect, finding the person guilty, so that the burden of proof from then on rested on the defendant.

Unlike procedure in Anglo-American law, where the prosecutor and, defense counsel are adversaries, with the judge acting as arbiter, in continental law prosecutor, defense counsel, and judge are all charged with the task of arriving at the truth. . . .

Nikitchenko's conception of the trial so shocked Jackson that he suggested, on June 29, that the best thing might be for each nation to go ahead and try the Nazis it held in custody according to its own customs.

The following day he recovered sufficiently to reiterate the American position that it was "necessary to authenticate by methods of the highest accuracy the whole history of the Nazi movement, its extermination of minorities, its aggression against neighbors, its treachery and its barbarism. . . . We envision it as a trial of the master planners.". . .

The next day produced new disagreement. SHAEF (Supreme Headquarters Allied Expeditionary Force) had conducted a survey of German cities as possible sites for the trial, Jackson revealed. The only undamaged facilities extensive enough to accommodate the trial were in Nuremberg, so Nuremberg should be selected as the location. . . .

The Nazi leadership was indicted for (1) Crimes Against Peace, including the launching of an aggressive war; (2) War Crimes, that is, acts contrary to acceptable usages and against the provisions of the Hague and Geneva conventions; and (3) Crimes Against Humanity, covering any and all atrocities committed by the regime during its reign. . . .

The most spectacular of the finds were the records of Alfred Rosenberg, providing a detailed description of German operations in the East and of the looting of the various occupied territories. Discovered hidden beneath wet straw behind a wall in a Bavarian barn by an OSS lieutenant seeking photographic material, the forty-seven crates were flown to Paris, where Jackson had set up his continental document-collecting center. Though, by the end of July, the contents. of the crates had been only cursorily examined, one of Bernays's investigators wrote him: "This is an almost unbelievable admission of *systematic* killings, looting, etc.". . .

The Accused

During his stay in London, Bernays had compiled a master list of the major German war criminals; by the time he departed, the number stood at 122. On the first ten of these, Goering, Hess, Ribbentrop, Ley, Rosenberg, Frick, Keitel, Streicher, Kaltenbrunner, and Frank, suggested originally by the British, the Americans immediately agreed. Only Hess, because of his disoriented mental condition, posed a question mark. The Americans proposed five others: Admiral Karl Doenitz, head of the submarine service until his elevation to command of the entire Nazi navy in January 1943; Arthur Seyss-Inquart, an Austrian who had played a pivotal role in Hitler's Anschluss in 1938 and subsequently had been head of the German administration in the occupied Netherlands; Albert Speer, chief of Nazi war production during the last three and one-half years of the war; Hjalmar Schacht, economics minister and head of the Reichsbank during the first five years of the Hitler regime; and Walther Funk, who had replaced Schacht as minister of economics and president of the Reichsbank. The latter three primarily interested the Americans, with their emphasis on the economic aspects of the Nazi aggression; but the British had no objection to them.

Almost everyone on the American and British delegations had his favorite candidate, and lists were compiled periodically. But by August 8, when the charter was signed, only Martin Bormann, who had succeeded Hess as party secretary, had been added. Since all the men were to be charged with a conspiracy, it was thought proper, and perhaps necessary, to list Hitler at the head of the group. The prosecutorial staff, nevertheless, hesitated to include him, for—although there was little doubt that he had killed himself—they feared that to do so might generate rumors of his survival.

No criteria had been established for inclusion in the list of defendants, and additions were arbitrary. The British suggested Baldur von Schirach, organizer and leader of the Hitler Youth, and subsequently gauleiter of Vienna. The Americans, adhering to the concept that each of the individual organizations should be represented by one or more of its leaders, had named Keitel for the armed forces, Doenitz the navy, and Goering the Luftwaffe, but were missing a man for the army. So General Alfred Jodl, the chief of the Wehrmacht operations staff, was included.

The OSS thought that to present a true panorama of Nazi crimes at least thirty defendants, including several industrialists, would have to be selected. The best known was Alfried Krupp, operating head of the world-famous armaments firm. His name was added, as was that of Fritz Sauckel, who had impressed workers from all over Europe into Hitler's labor program. By mid-August, however, no final determination had been made, and Jackson's list of potential defendants still contained seventy-three names.

After thinking the matter over, Jackson decided there was no point in trying a dead man, and dropped Hitler. However, Franz von Papen, who had preceded Hitler as chancellor and briefly been vice-chancellor in Hitler's cabinet, was tacked on.

When the tentative list was shown to the French and Russians in the third week of August, the French were chagrined that it contained no German held by them, and combed their roster for a candidate. They came up with Baron Constantin von Neurath, who had been living in retirement upon his estate in Württemberg, which was part of the French occupation zone. Neurath's tenure as Protector of Bohemia and Moravia and head of a "Secret Cabinet Council" placed him under suspicion. No one on the Allied staffs knew what this cabinet council had consisted of; but it sounded appropriately menacing.

On August 25, Jackson, Fyfe, Gros, and Nikitchenko agreed on a list of twenty-two defendants. Twenty-one were in custody. The twenty-second, Bormann, had, according to rumors, been captured by the Russians. Jackson repeatedly questioned Nikitchenko whether the Russians held Bormann; but Nikitchenko did not know, and apparently could not find out. A press release naming the accused was prepared, and about to be released on August 28, when Nikitchenko rushed in to announce that the Soviets did not hold Bormann, but that they had captured two Germans whom they wanted added to the list.

First was Admiral Erich Raeder, commander of the German navy until January 1943. Raeder had been a marginal candidate for the trial, so far as the British and Americans were concerned, but had gained importance by the discovery of a document indicating he had been a prime instigator of the invasion of Norway.

The other was Hans Fritzsche, a popular newscaster and second-rank official in Goebbels' Propaganda Ministry, who had not been on any of the many lists of top war criminals. Had he been suggested by a member of the American or British prosecutorial staffs, he would have been summarily rejected. But since the Americans were contributing thirteen defendants, the British seven, and the French one, it was a matter of national pride to the Russians that they be permitted at least two.

In the interim, the Americans had second thoughts about naming thirty-eight-year-old Alfried Krupp, who had been active in the company's affairs only since the start of the war, rather than his seventy-five-year-old father, Baron Gustav Krupp von Bohlen und Halbach. At the last moment, Gustav's name was substituted for Alfried's. It turned out to be an incredible error, but one typical of a case in which the charges were prepared and the defendants chosen before the facts had been more than cursorily investigated.

On August 30, the list of Nazi leaders selected for the first trial was released to the press.

Living with the Nightmares

William B. Helmreich

This encyclopedia is filled with horror stories. They are difficult to read and it is impossible to imagine what it must have been like to actually live through the war. How can anyone live with the memories of what happened to them, what they saw in the camps, with the loss of loved ones? The resilience of humans is remarkable and is no more evident than in the lives of Holocaust survivors. Every one was deeply affected by his or her experience, but surprisingly few were incapacitated by it or driven to such despair that they would kill themselves. Most lived and are living what we would consider "normal" lives. Some were driven by their experiences to extraordinary success and wealth. Even these people, however, are different than their peers because of their past. This excerpt examines some of the ways that Holocaust survivors dealt with their experiences and how it affected their lives. William B. Helmreich is a professor of sociology and Judaic studies at City University of New York Graduate Center and City College of New York and the author of several books.

If you've been through Auschwitz and you *don't* have nightmares, then you're not normal," a survivor once remarked to me. Her comment highlighted the importance of evaluating the survivors within the context of their own experience. If by normal we mean a happy, perfectly well-adjusted individual, then many survivors, as well as others who did not go through the Holocaust, could not be so described. But if we are referring to people who get up in the morning, go to work, raise a family, and enjoy a variety of leisure time pursuits, then an overwhelming majority of the survivors would qualify as normal.

Indeed, many survivors did quite well. They achieved financial security, raised families, and were active in community affairs. There is, however, another, more subtle yet crucial, measure of success that has not yet been looked at carefully—how the survivors live with their memories of what happened to them. What do years of incarceration in a world whose very raison d'être was inflicting pain and punishment do to the psyche? What are the long-range psychological effects and how do they influence the individual's outlook on life in general? In short, were the survivors able to resolve the turmoil and conflict that resulted from their ordeals? What insights into life did they gain because of what happened to them? . . .

A Viennese-born child survivor who is today a college professor [explains]:

> Many of us refuse to display symbols that identify us as Jews right off the bat; so that we will not wear a Star of David, for instance. . . . A few years ago my son, who had joined B'nai B'rith Youth Organization [BBYO], was going to have a simple march in support of the State of Israel . . . but that was the year of the massacres in Sabra and Shatila and I had received a nasty anonymous phone call, accusing me of being responsible for Sabra and Shatila. . . . So I called the regional leader for BBYO and asked him to cancel the march, because I was afraid. I told them I was a survivor . . . so yes, there is some fear. When I moved to this town and the Jewish stores were closed for the High Holidays, my thought was: "The next time they want to throw stones, they'll know exactly which ones are Jewish stores."

Nightmares are probably the most common symptom of disturbance among survivors. . . . Their frequency and intensity vary from one individual to the next but they are often accompanied by screaming and feelings of anxiety, as depicted in the well-known film *The Pawnbroker*. Most often the survivors dream about what happened to them during the war, but sometimes these memories intermingle with more current fears, such as running and hiding with their children, who were, in fact, born after their liberation. Some survivors awake, are comforted by their spouses, and go back to sleep; others find it necessary to read, walk around the house, or eat something. Most have learned to cope on their own, but a few require regular medication to help them. One man has been taking tranquilizers for almost forty years. Several survivors attributed an increase in nightmares to having read books and seen films on the Holocaust when the topic became very popular in recent years.

Living with Guilt

Of course, guilt is a normal emotion felt by most people, but, among survivors it takes on special meaning when related to the Holocaust. Most feel guilty about the death of loved ones whom they feel they could have, or should have, saved. Even if they could have done nothing to help their friends or relatives, they find themselves asking over and over: "Why did *I* live and not them?" Some feel guilty about situations in which they behaved selfishly even if there was no other way to survive.

Survivors, particularly males, also blame themselves for not having displayed bravery in the face of oppression. As David Jagoda, a survivor living in Minneapolis, put it:

Sometimes I feel like I am really not a survivor. You know why? A lot of times, it came to my mind, like 100 Germans took 10,000 Jews. We could kill them in no time at all. If every one Jew would kill one German, they would be in trouble.

Jagoda makes no mention of the lack of arms, the physical condition of most Jews, or other factors, saying only, "I sometimes feel guilty because I survived; because I did not survive properly. I didn't do anything." In the following example, a survivor described how such guilt was engendered when individuals were forced to make impossible choices between those dear to them:

I remember a man whose wife and son were at the mercy of the Gestapo, and they told him that if he didn't tell them where his parents were in hiding, they would kill his young family. He went to his parents and asked them what he should do, and they said, "You must give us up"; so he did. And he survived the war, as did his wife and child. I have seen him a few times—he lives in New York now—but I can never meet him without thinking of the permanent agony those sadists condemned him to because of what they made him do.

Such agonizing dilemmas cannot ever be forgotten or ignored. In their happiest moments, the survivors remain aware of how human beings can be made to suffer. Moreover, it is an inner misery that remains with them no matter where they are. It affects their daily functioning and, most certainly, their judgments about people, not to mention their worldview. Even as they grapple with the implications of what they were compelled to do, they wonder whether others would have acted less nobly or more nobly were they in a similar situation. The words of a character in Sheila Levin's novel *Simple Truths* bring into sharp focus the horror of having to make such decisions. A father, he is responding to his daughter's question, "What is worse than death?":

> Erosion. . . . To be nibbled away at, day after day. Not just from the beatings, the starvation, the fear of death. Worse than that is the mutilation of the spirit. The body can endure what the mind cannot. The brutality was unendurable because it was incomprehensible. . . .
>
> The choices that that world allowed were a masterpiece of evil. Civilization was gone. Boundaries, parameters, limits, all canceled. 'Shall we send these hundred-and-fifty boys to the ovens, or these? Tell me, sir, would you prefer us to rape your wife or your daughter? Which twin shall we castrate?' Those were the choices. Madness. Those were the choices. Not once, but every day, every hour, day after day. Every day was the end of the world.

Guilt, depression, intense feelings of loneliness, withdrawal, anxiety, paranoia, all these formed part of the reaction known as Concentration Camp Survivors Syndrome. . . .

Nevertheless, only a minority of survivors found that these problems interfered with their ability to function on a daily basis and that in itself attests to their resiliency as a group. For those unable to cope, the support of friends and family greatly helped to cushion the impact of their suffering and many referred to it as a key factor in their ability to come to terms with what had happened. . . .

It is ultimately impossible to expect people to be like everyone else when the central event of their lives did not happen to anyone else and they know it. This perception of self is clearly and eloquently elucidated in a book by Cecilie Klein, a camp survivor currently living on Long Island.

> A survivor will go to a party and feel alone.
> A survivor appears quiet but is screaming within.
> A survivor will make large weddings, with many guests,
> but the ones she wants most will never arrive.
> A survivor will go to a funeral and cry, not for the
> deceased but for the ones that were never buried.
> A survivor will reach out to you but not let you get
> close, for you remind her of what she could have been,
> but will never be.
> A survivor is at ease only with other survivors.

When Memories Return

. . . In some instances, survivors are presented with an opportunity to respond openly and forcefully to those who participated in the war. Some are afraid to do so, others are not. The following story, told by a woman who survived Auschwitz, demonstrates how deep the scars can be:

> I was shopping in Bloomingdale's and, as I held up a jacket, a man behind me commented that, in his country, the jacket was much more expensive. He kept saying that, so, out of courtesy, I asked: "Where is your country?" "Oh, Germany," he said. "Where are you from?" he asked. "You have an accent." "Hungary," I answered. "I was in Hungary, in 1944," the man said. Then the blood rushed to my head. "In what unit were you, in the Gestapo or the SS?" He said: "No, I wasn't in the Gestapo or the SS. I was in the Wehrmacht." Then I said: "In 1944, in Hungary, there were only SS or Gestapo." And he answered: "No, I wouldn't be ashamed to

tell you if I was in the SS unit or the Wehrmacht. I am proud of my Führer. I always was proud. He was a very good man. I am very, very proud of him. He didn't do anything wrong." I started to shake. I started to scream: "You murderer!" And as I was screaming, two salesmen came over and in the meantime, he ran away down the escalator and disappeared. But in that moment I would have been able to kill him.

Of course, aggressive behavior need not be limited to the physical arena. Another form it took was that of the almost stereotypical, hard-driving survivor who worked long hours and fought tooth and nail to succeed in business. Indeed, many survivors did just that. . . . By succeeding, the survivor acquires the very power by which he feels threatened and gains control over his environment. To better understand the motivation involved, we need only consider the opposite of success. To require and receive assistance from others was often viewed by former camp inmates as a sign of weakness, something they could ill afford to have shown during that time. . . .

Not long after I began this project, I interviewed an elderly lady who had been in both ghettos and concentration camps. Her adaptation to life in America had been fairly smooth. She had raised two children and appeared to be happily married. Her demeanor was calm and she smiled often, especially when she spoke about her children and grandchildren. After I finished, her daughter happened to walk in. We spoke briefly about the study I was conducting. Then she called me aside and said, "I suppose you think my mother is well adjusted." "It would seem that way," I replied. "Well, she is, except for one thing. I live in Brooklyn and she lives in the Bronx. Every day she calls me at 3:30 sharp to ask if my kids came home, and if they haven't she goes crazy. One time, when the kids were twenty minutes late, she got into a cab and came over here, all the way from the Bronx, during the rush hour." "Why does she act this way?" I asked. "Because 3:30 is the exact time she was taken away from her parents in the ghetto in Poland and she never saw them again."

This woman's story made me realize early on that survivors can never really banish what happened to them from their minds. . . .

One general feature is that survivors' homes are very clean and neat. . . . Some researchers have noted that survivor women are compulsive house-cleaners. This seems to be related to life in the camps, where it was extremely difficult to stay clean, both personally and in general. "We had to live with dirt for so long, and every time I see a dirty place I remember those years," observed one former Dachau inmate. . . .

Since food was so basic to survival in the camps, survivors hate to see it wasted. Congressman Tom Lantos elaborated on this to me: "I cannot put food on my plate that I don't finish. In a restaurant I always have trouble ordering anything that is more than a reasonable portion because to send food back is a crime.". . .

Why Me?

The majority of believers did not become atheists, but there was a definite decrease in the number of believers. Moreover, for most the Holocaust created grave doubts about the nature of God and His relationship to human beings even as the survivors continued to believe in Him. . . .

For some survivors simply remaining alive during the Holocaust was enough of a miracle to justify continued faith in God. One man extended this view to the period after the war as well, saying: "I got through Auschwitz and nothing happened to me. I went through the Korean War and nothing happened to me, so somebody must be looking after me." Sam Halpern was more specific: "I escaped from camp and didn't know whether to go right or left. Then I saw a pigeon flying and I said: 'I think I'll follow this pigeon.' Well, the pigeon was going to the front and that was the right direction." The proof is presented here in terms of personal survival. However, whenever I pressed respondents to explain why God had not chosen to save others in a similar manner, the response was invariably: "We can't understand God." No one claimed to have been saved because they were more worthy than someone else who died. Most simply asserted that they did not know why God had chosen to save them or why He had decided not to intervene on behalf of those who perished.

Some survivors justified their having been rescued from certain death conditionally, that is, God now expected certain things from them. One wealthy businessman, William Ungar, posed the dilemma in the following terms:

> Why did I survive and others didn't? Why was I only wounded and others were killed? I survived to be a witness to what took place. And I also think God let me live to see what good I would do. This may be a very primitive way to answer the question but I feel that if I did survive, it was to do some good deeds in my lifetime. Of course, I wouldn't preach about it or advertise it. I'm not trying to elevate myself that I'm the only one who deserved to survive.

This individual clearly understood that he could not explain

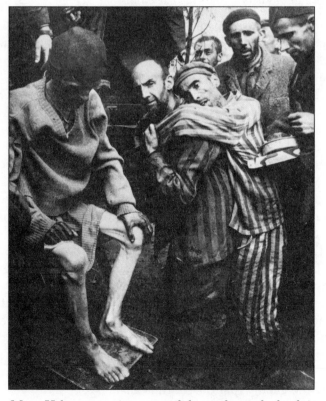

Many Holocaust survivors struggled to understand why their lives were spared when so many millions had perished.

why he was, so to speak, "anointed" by God. He is active in the Jewish community and has given generously to charity. It is perhaps the best way for him to justify God's seeming faith in *him*. . . .

For most survivors, . . . the questions remain and are not so easily resolved. They believe in varying degrees, but they question, and often they are very angry. . . . And sometimes survivors act out their anger directly:

> A good friend of mine was in Bergen-Belsen and the first thing she did when she got out was she got a sandwich with some kind of meat and put cheese on it [a clear violation of the laws of kashruth]. Then she looked up at God and said, "See? Do me something!" Is that somebody who doesn't believe in God? No. She's *mad* at God.

Even those who remain steadfast in their religious observance can engage in behavior of this sort. One woman always places a drop of milk in her chicken soup and says, "This is to punish you, God, for what you have done."

Challenging and questioning God is not an act of heresy according to Jewish law. On the contrary, it is an ancient tradition, one first articulated in the Bible by Abraham when he wondered aloud whether God's desire to destroy Sodom and Gomorrah was just. Jonah defies God when told to go to Nineveh. . . .

For Jews who adhere to the teachings of the faith there is a causal connection between sin and punishment, even if its precise workings are not known. They read in the Bible of God's threats to the Jews of retribution if they forsake His commandments and they inevitably wonder what transgressions brought about the Holocaust. In [another] study 21 percent saw a direct relationship between the death of six million Jews and man's sinfulness. I asked one respondent who felt this way why so many of the Jews who were killed were observant. Her answer: "When it rains, everyone gets wet. On the other hand, the State of Israel was a reward to show the enemy that our Lord is alive.". . .

Some survivors find meaning in the tortures they endured by viewing them as a part of Jewish history, of which the

Holocaust is simply the latest and most systematically brutal instance of cruelty to Jews. Hence they do not see it as a unique tragedy. . . .

For the survivors, ritual observance and cultural involvement became the vehicles for honoring and commemorating those no longer present. Miriam Brach summed it up best in the following words:

> I believe that it was my destiny to survive, to come back from the ashes and to be the link from the past that would begin life again and pass it on to future generations. My goal was to remain faithful to the religion into which I was born and to my upbringing. This upbringing gave me the strength to survive the war. When I live this way, I know I am living the kind of life my departed parents would have wanted me to live.

Non-Believers

. . . When all is said and done, however, there is still a sizable segment of the survivor community whose members have either lost their faith and openly admit it, or who never believed to begin with. One unequivocally asserted: "I don't believe in anything and you wouldn't either if you went through what I went through.". . .

A number of nonbelieving survivors coupled their assertions with a wish that it could be otherwise. One such individual, who lived through Auschwitz, spoke of her doubts with sincere regret:

> It's easier to believe than not to, but I can't believe. I listened as my granddaughter read the story in synagogue of how the whale spit up Jonah after three days, and of course I couldn't say anything to the children about what a stupidity this is after we were in such a fire, in Auschwitz, where the sky was always black from the flesh of people they burned. There were a few Jews who tried to revolt; so they pushed them into the ovens alive. So I ask, couldn't there have been just one little miracle, something to show that there is justice in the world? I saw how the Nazis learned how to shoot by killing children. So that's why I never believed. There were no miracles. There were no miracles.

The Holocaust Deniers

Deborah E. Lipstadt

As the years pass and World War II becomes a distant memory with few living witnesses to the terrible events of that time, it becomes easier for people to challenge the facts associated with the Holocaust. A number of people, some associated with neo-Nazi or other anti-Semitic and racist movements, claim the Holocaust never happened. They offer a variety of theories, some crackpot, others more plausible to the uninformed, to suggest that Jews either made up the whole thing or have greatly exaggerated what happened for their own political purposes. These "revisionists," as they are often called, have had great success in propagating their ideas over the Internet and on college campuses. This article discusses some of the arguments these Holocaust deniers use, the ways in which they try to spread their ideas, and the responses to what Deborah E. Lipstadt calls "the growing assault on truth and memory." Lipstadt holds the Dorot chair in modern Jewish and Holocaust studies at Emory University. Her first book, *Beyond Belief*, examined the press coverage of the Holocaust and offered explanations for why it did not receive the publicity it deserved.

The producer was incredulous. She found it hard to believe that I was turning down an opportunity to appear on her nationally televised show: "But you are writing a book on this topic. It will be great publicity." I explained repeatedly that I would not participate in a debate with a Holocaust denier. The existence of the Holocaust was not a matter of debate. I would analyze and illustrate who they were and what they tried to do, but I would not appear with them. (To do so would give them a legitimacy and a stature they in no way deserve. It would elevate their antisemitic ideology—which is what Holocaust denial is—to the level of responsible historiography—which it is not.) Unwilling to accept my no as final, she vigorously condemned Holocaust denial and all it represented. Then, in one last attempt to get me to change my mind, she asked me a question: "I certainly don't agree with them, but don't you think our viewers should hear the *other side?*". . .

The attempt to deny the Holocaust enlists a basic strategy of distortion. Truth is mixed with absolute lies, confusing readers who are unfamiliar with the tactics of the deniers. Half-truths and story segments, which conveniently avoid critical information, leave the listener with a distorted impression of what really happened. The abundance of documents and testimonies that confirm the Holocaust are dismissed as contrived, coerced, or forgeries and falsehoods. . . .

Deniers have found a ready acceptance among increasingly radical elements, including neo-Nazis and skinheads, in both North America and Europe. Holocaust denial has become part of a mélange of extremist, racist, and nativist sentiments. Neo-Nazis who once argued that the Holocaust, however horrible, was justified now contend that it was a hoax. As long as extremists espouse Holocaust denial, the danger is a limited one. But that danger increases when the proponents of these views clean up their act and gain entry into legitimate circles. . . .

Denial and Free Speech

In response to student and faculty protests about the decision of the *Duke Chronicle* to run an ad denying the Holocaust, the president of Duke University, Keith Brodie, said that to have done otherwise would have "violated our commitment to free speech and contradicted Duke's long tradition of supporting First Amendment rights." Brodie failed to note that the paper had recently rejected an ad it deemed offensive to women. No one had complained about possible violations of the First Amendment.

Let this point not be misunderstood. The deniers have

the absolute right to stand on any street corner and spread their calumnies. They have the right to publish their articles and books and hold their gatherings. But free speech does not guarantee them the right to be treated as the "other" side of a legitimate debate. Nor does it guarantee them space on op-ed pages or time on television and radio shows. . . .

Why Denial Has Grown

While Holocaust denial is not a new phenomenon, it has increased in scope and intensity since the mid-1970s. It is important to understand that the deniers do not work in a vacuum. Part of their success can be traced to an intellectual climate that has made its mark in the scholarly world during the past two decades. The deniers are plying their trade at a time when much of history seems to be up for grabs and attacks on the Western rationalist tradition have become commonplace.

This tendency can be traced, at least in part, to intellectual currents that began to emerge in the late 1960s. Various scholars began to argue that texts had no fixed meaning. The reader's interpretation, not the author's intention, determined meaning. . . . It became more difficult to talk about the objective truth of a text, legal concept, or even an event. In academic circles some scholars spoke of relative truths, rejecting the notion that there was one version of the world that was necessarily right while another was wrong. Proponents of this methodology, such as the prominent and widely read philosopher Richard Rorty, denied the allegation that they believed that two incompatible views on a significant issue were of equal worth. But others disagreed. Hilary Putnam, one of the most influential contemporary academic philosophers, thought it particularly dangerous because it seemed to suggest that every conceptual system was "just as good as the other." Still others rightfully worried that it opened the doors of the academy, and of society at large, to an array of farfetched notions that could no longer be dismissed out of hand simply because they were absurd. . . .

Holocaust denial is part of this phenomenon. It is not an assault on the history of one particular group. Though denial of the Holocaust may be an attack on the history of the annihilation of the Jews, at its core it poses a threat to all who believe that knowledge and memory are among the keystones of our civilization. Just as the Holocaust was not a tragedy of the Jews but a tragedy of civilization in which the victims were Jews, so too denial of the Holocaust is not a threat just to Jewish history but a threat to all who believe in the ultimate power of reason. It repudiates reasoned discussion the way the Holocaust repudiated civilized values. It is undeniably a form of antisemitism, and as such it constitutes an attack on the most basic values of a reasoned society. Like any form of prejudice, it is an irrational animus that cannot be countered with the normal forces of investigation, argument, and debate. The deniers' arguments are at their roots not only antisemitic and anti-intellectual but, in the words of historian Charles Maier, "blatantly racist anthropology.". . .

Casting Doubt on the Truth

What claims do the deniers make? The Holocaust—the attempt to annihilate the Jewish people—never happened. Typical of the deniers' attempt to obfuscate is their claim that they do not deny that there was a Holocaust, only that there was a plan or an attempt to annihilate the Jewish people. . . . They begin with a relatively innocuous supposition: War is evil. Assigning blame to one side is ultimately a meaningless enterprise. Since the central crime of which the Nazis are accused never happened, there really is no difference in this war, as in any other, between victor and vanquished. Still, they assert, if guilt is to be assigned, it is not the Germans who were guilty of aggression and atrocities during the war. The real crimes against civilization were committed by the Americans, Russians, Britons, and French against the Germans. The atrocities inflicted on the Germans by the Allies were—in the words of Harry Elmer Barnes, a once-prominent historian and one of the seminal figures in the history of North American Holocaust denial— "more brutal and painful than the alleged exterminations in the gas chambers." Once we recognize that the Allies were the aggressors, we must turn to the Germans and, in the words of Austin App, a professor of English literature who became one of the major "theoreticians" of Holocaust denial, implore them "to forgive us the awful atrocities our policy caused to be inflicted upon them."

For some deniers Hitler was a man of peace, pushed into war by the aggressive Allies. According to them, the Germans suffered the bombing of Dresden, wartime starvation, invasions, postwar population transfers from areas of Germany incorporated into post-war Poland, victors' vengeance at Nuremberg, and brutal mistreatment by Soviet and Allied occupiers. Portrayed as a criminal nation that had committed outrageous atrocities, Germany became and remains a victim of the world's emotional and scholarly aggression.

But it is showing the Holocaust to have been a myth that is the deniers' real agenda. They contend that the ultimate injustice is the false accusation that Germans committed the most henious crime in human history. The postwar venom toward Germany has been so extreme that Germans have found it impossible to defend themselves. Consequently, rather than fight this ignominious accusation, they decided to acknowledge their complicity. This seeming contradiction—namely that the perpetrators admit they committed a crime while those who were not present exonerate them—presents a potential problem for the deniers. How can a group that did not witness what happened claim that the perpetrators are innocent while the perpetrators acknowledge their guilt? The deniers explain this problem away by arguing that in the aftermath of World War II the Germans faced a strategic conflict. In order to be readmitted to the "family of nations," they had to confess their wrongdoing, even though they knew that these charges were false. They were in the same situation as a defendant who has been falsely convicted of committing horrendous crimes. He knows he will be more likely to receive a lenient sentence if he admits his guilt, shows contrition, and makes amends. So too the innocent Germans admitted their guilt and made (and continue to make) financial amends.

The defendants at the war crimes trials adopted a similar strategy. They admitted that the Holocaust happened but tried to vindicate themselves by claiming they were not *personally* guilty. . . .

Deniers acknowledge that some Jews were incarcerated in places such as Auschwitz, but, they maintain, as they did at the trial of a Holocaust denier in Canada, it was equipped with "all the luxuries of a country club," including a swimming pool, dance hall, and recreational facilities. Some Jews may have died, they said, but this was the natural consequence of wartime deprivations.

The central assertion for the deniers is that Jews are not victims but victimizers. They "stole" billions in reparations, destroyed Germany's good name by spreading the "myth" of the Holocaust, and won international sympathy because of what they claimed had been done to them. In the paramount miscarriage of injustice, they used the world's sympathy to "displace" another people so that the state of Israel could be established. This contention relating to the establishment of Israel is a linchpin of their argument. It constitutes a motive for the creation of the Holocaust "legend" by the Jews. Once the deniers add this to the equation, the essential elements of their argument are in place.

Some have a distinct political objective: If there was no Holocaust, what is so wrong with national socialism? It is the Holocaust that gives fascism a bad name. Extremist groups know that every time they extol the virtues of national socialism they must contend with the question: If it was so benign, how was the Holocaust possible? Before fascism can be resurrected, this blot must be removed. At first they attempted to justify it; now they deny it. This is the means by which those who still advocate the principles of fascism attempt to reintroduce it as a viable political system. For many falsifiers this, not antisemitism, is their primary agenda. It is certainly a central theme for the European deniers on the emerging far right.

When one first encounters them it is easy to wonder who could or would take them seriously. Given the preponderance of evidence from victims, bystanders, and perpetrators, and given the fact that the deniers' arguments lie so far beyond the pale of scholarly argument, it appears to be ludicrous to devote much, if any, mental energy to them. They are a group motivated by a strange conglomeration of conspiracy theories, delusions, and neo-Nazi tendencies. The natural inclination of many rational people, including historians and social scientists, is to dismiss them as an irrelevant fringe group. Some have equated them with the flat-earth theorists, worthy at best of bemused attention but not of serious analysis or concern. They regard Holocaust denial as quirky and malicious but do not believe it poses a clear and present danger.

There are a number of compelling reasons not to dismiss the deniers and their beliefs so lightly. First, their methodology has changed in the past decade. Initially Holocaust denial was an enterprise engaged in by a small group of political extremists. Their arguments tended to appear in poorly printed pamphlets and in right-wing newspapers such as the *Spotlight, Thunderbolt,* or the Ku Klux Klan's *Crusader.* In recent years, however, their productivity has increased, their style has changed, and, consequently, their impact has been enhanced. They disguise their political and ideological agendas. Their subterfuge enhances the danger they pose. Their publications, including the *Journal of Historical Review*—the leading denial journal—mimic legitimate scholarly works, generating confusion among those who . . . do not immediately recognize the *Journal's* intention. Their books and journals have been given an academic format, and they have worked hard to find ways to insinuate themselves into the arena of historical deliberation. One of the primary loci of their activities is the college campus, where they have tried to stimulate a debate on the existence of the Holocaust. It is here that they may find their most fertile field, as is evident from the success they have had in placing advertisements that deny the Holocaust in college newspapers. . . . They have also begun to make active use of computer bulletin boards, where they post their familiar arguments. Certain computer networks have been flooded with their materials. Their objective is to plant seeds of doubt that will bear fruit in coming years, when there are no more survivors or eyewitnesses alive to attest to the truth.

There is an obvious danger in assuming that because Holocaust denial is so outlandish it can be ignored. The deniers' worldview is no more bizarre than that enshrined in the *Protocols of the Elders of Zion*, a report purporting to be the text of a secret plan to establish Jewish world supremacy. The deniers draw inspiration from the *Protocols*, which has enjoyed a sustained and vibrant life despite the fact it has long been proved a forgery. . . .

Reason Versus Myth

The vast majority of intellectuals in the Western world have not fallen prey to these falsehoods. But some have succumbed in another fashion, supporting Holocaust denial in the name of free speech, free inquiry, or intellectual freedom. An absolutist commitment to the liberal idea of dialogue may cause its proponents to fail to recognize that there is a significant difference between reasoned dialogue and anti-intellectual pseudoscientific arguments. They have failed to make the critical distinction between a conclusion, however outrageous it may be, that has been reached through reasonable inquiry and the use of standards of evidence, on the one hand, and ideological extremism that rejects anything that contradicts its preset conclusions, on the other. Thomas Jefferson long ago argued that in a setting committed to the pursuit of truth all ideas and opinions must be tolerated. But he added a caveat that is particularly applicable to this investigation: Reason must be left free to combat error. One of the ways of combating errors is by making the distinctions between scholarship and myth. In the case of Holocaust denial, we are dealing with people who consciously confuse these categories. As a result reason becomes hostage to a particularly odious ideology.

Reasoned dialogue, particularly as it applies to the understanding of history, is rooted in the notion that there exists a historical reality that—though it may be subjected by the historian to a multiplicity of interpretations—is ultimately found and not made. The historian does not create, the historian uncovers. The validity of a historical interpretation is determined by how well it accounts for the facts. Though the historian's role is to act as a neutral observer trying to follow the facts, there is increasing recognition that the historian brings to this enterprise his or her own values and biases. Consequently there is no such thing as value-free history. However, even the historian with a particular bias is dramatically different from the proponents of these pseudoreasoned ideologies. The latter freely shape or create information to buttress their convictions and reject as implausible any evidence that counters them. They use the language of scientific inquiry, but theirs is a purely ideological enterprise. . . .

History matters. Whether the focus be the Middle East, Vietnam, the Balkans, the Cold War, or slavery in this country, the public's perception of past events and their meaning has a tremendous influence on how it views and responds to the present. Adolf Hitler's rise to power was facilitated by the artful way in which he advanced views of recent German history that appealed to the masses. It did not matter if his was a distorted version—it appealed to the German people because it laid the blame for their current problems elsewhere. Although history will always be at a disadvantage when contending with the mythic power of irrational prejudices, it must contend nonetheless. . . .

And if history matters, its practitioners matter even more. The historian's role has been compared to that of the canary in the coal mine whose death warned the miners that dangerous fumes were in the air—"any poisonous nonsense and the canary expires." There is much poisonous nonsense in the atmosphere these days. The deniers hope to achieve their goals by winning recognition as a legitimate scholarly cadre and by planting seeds of doubt in the younger generation. Only by recognizing the threat denial poses to both the past and the future will we ultimately thwart their efforts.

The Creation of a Jewish Homeland

Michael Berenbaum

The Jews who survived the Holocaust needed to first be rehabilitated from their weak and sickly condition and then required new homes. Some hoped to return to the homes they'd left behind, but, in most cases, those no longer existed or had been taken over by non-Jews after they left. No one was welcoming the Jews back to their old homes. On the contrary, the anti-Semitic attitudes that had allowed the Nazis to persecute the Jews remained strong. In Kielce, Poland, for example, returning Jews were massacred by the inhabitants. With no place to go, hundreds of thousands of Jews found themselves back in camps. The conditions were completely different and they were now supervised by Allied forces, but the survivors were still fenced in. Reluctantly, western nations, including the United States, began to allow some of them to immigrate, but the numbers were relatively small, and the quotas tended to still favor non-Jews. Many of the survivors hoped to go to Palestine where Jews were fighting to create a new independent Jewish state. The British controlled Palestine, however, and did not want thousands of Jews streaming into the country and complicating their relations with the Arabs. Consequently, clandestine efforts were required to bring the Jews to Palestine. This article, by Michael Berenbaum, the former project director of the U.S. Holocaust Memorial Museum, describes what happened to many of the Jews who survived the Holocaust.

As the Allied armies swept through Europe in 1944 and 1945, they found seven to nine million displaced people living in countries not their own. More than six million returned to their native lands. But more than one million refused repatriation. Most of them were Poles, Estonians, Latvians, Lithuanians, Ukrainians, and Yugoslavs. Some had collaborated with the Nazis and were afraid of retaliation should they return home. Others feared persecution by the new Communist regimes in Eastern Europe.

Jewish survivors could not return home. Their communities were shattered, their homes destroyed or occupied by strangers. In the east, they were not welcome in the land of their birth. With nowhere to go, they were forced to live in camps set up on the sites where they had been imprisoned. For most of them, this meant a prolonged stay in Germany living in the midst of those who had sought to impose the Final Solution.

The beleaguered American army was hard pressed to juggle the multiple assignment of serving as both an occupation force and a counterforce in the new Cold War, and of dealing with the problems of the survivors. Short-term problems—housing, medical treatment, food, attempting to reunite families—were acute and demanding. The army had no long-range strategy for resettling those who could not or would not return home.

Most Jewish displaced persons wanted to begin a new life in Palestine. Although many would have preferred to emigrate to the United States, they were not willing to wait for years to qualify for admission. In 1945, most Jewish DPs were survivors of the concentration camps, partisans, or those who had spent the war in hiding. Life in the concentration camps had taken a hard toll. The survivors were destitute, and often sick. . . . They were haunted by nightmares and mistrusted authority—even the American authorities who were trying to help them.

Living conditions in the camps were unpleasant. Camps were overcrowded, and although the DPs were not starved, there was never enough food. Coping again with life, with the prospect of living after everything that had been endured, was the greatest difficulty. Major Irving Heymont who directed the Landsberg displaced persons camp wrote to his wife:

The camp is filthy beyond description. Sanitation is virtually unknown. . . . The Army units we relieved obviously did nothing more than insure that rations were delivered to the camp. With few exceptions the people of the camp themselves appear demoralized beyond hope of rehabilitation. They appear to be beaten both spiritually and physically.

Britain was unwilling to permit Jewish emigration to Palestine. Trying to preserve the remnants of its empire, it was reticent to alienate the Arab world hostile to a potential Jewish state. The United States was not ready to receive an influx of refugees. Soldiers were coming home from the war. It was a time of transition from war production to a civilian economy, and there was a fear that refugees would consume scarce resources and take jobs away from Americans. Nativistic thinking did not end with World War II, even if the isolationists were silenced. Within a few weeks of taking office as president, Harry Truman dispatched Earl Harrison, the dean of the University of Pennsylvania Law School, to report on the displaced-persons camps. The report was a bombshell. Harrison concluded that:

We (the United States] appear to be treating the Jews as the Nazis treated them, except that we do not exterminate them. They are in concentration camps in large numbers under our military guard instead of SS troops. One is led to wonder whether the German people seeing this are not supposing that we are following or at least condoning Nazi policy.

His recommendations were sweeping: the special status of Jews must be recognized; they should be evacuated from Germany swiftly; and 100,000 Jews should be admitted to Palestine. Truman, who was later to become a hero to the Jews for recognizing Israel as a state, followed his humanitarian impulses. He endorsed the report, rebuked the army, and intensified the pressure on Britain to allow Jews to immigrate to Palestine. He also opened the United States to limited immigration. His personal sentiments were clear: "It is unthinkable that they should be left indefinitely in camps in Europe.". . .

On July 4, 1946, a mob of Poles attacked the one hundred and fifty Jews who had returned to the town of Kielce. Forty-two were killed and fifty wounded. Before the war, twenty-four thousand Jews had lived in Kielce; the one hundred and fifty who were targets of the pogrom were survivors who had come home looking for their families and their homes. The Kielce pogrom was inspired by the age-old blood libel that was part of the classic pattern of anti-Jewish violence: the mob believed that Jews were killing Christian children and drinking their blood, or using the blood to bake Passover wafers. In Kielce, the Poles were also stirred up by fear that the Jews would reclaim their lost property. . . .

The news of the Kielce pogrom spread like wildfire throughout the remnant of the Jewish community in Eastern Europe. It was as though nothing had changed. Jews throughout Poland understood that it was not safe to return home; the future lay elsewhere.

On December 22, 1945, President Truman granted preferential treatment to displaced persons who wanted to immigrate to the United States. Within the next eighteen months, 22,950 DPs were admitted, 15,478 of them Jews. But the problem of what to do with the displaced persons could not be solved merely by a minor adjustment of the quotas. . . . In the summer of 1946, with the American zone of occupied Germany flooded by the 100,000 Polish Jews newly released by the Soviet Union and by Jews fleeing Eastern Europe after the Kielce pogrom, congressional action could no longer be avoided. . . .

In 1948, Congress passed a bill providing for the admission of 200,000 over four years. Truman called it "flagrantly discriminatory against Jews." In 1950, the act was amended to make it slightly less discriminatory. The change was too late: in 1949, most of the Jewish DPs had gone to the newly established state of Israel. . . .

During the three years after the war, only 41,000 DPs were admitted to the United States. Two-thirds of them were Jews. In the four years following the passage of the immigration law of 1948, 365,223 displaced persons were brought to American shores. Half the immigrants were

Roman Catholic and only 16 percent Jews. Some of the DPs openly admitted to having collaborated with the Nazis. All in all, fewer than 100,000 Jews were able to reach the United States in the years between the end of the war and the closing of the last DP camp seven years later. . . .

Between 1944 and 1948, more than 200,000 Jews fled from Eastern and Central Europe to Palestine, crossing borders legally, semilegally, or illegally. The means did not seem to matter: the borders were crossed somehow.

The movement began spontaneously and in a small way. In the summer of 1944, three partisans, Abba Kovner of Vilna, Vitka Kempner, and Ruzhka Korczak, a former subordinate commander in Vilna, met in the Rudninkai Forest to discuss their future. They decided that every effort must be made to get to Palestine. At the same time, a survivor in Rovno, Eliezer Lidovsky, organized the first group to leave Poland, first to Romania and then to Palestine via the Black Sea. . . .

The pogrom in Kielce and other manifestations of continuing antisemitism, coming after the devastation of Jewish towns and villages in Eastern Europe, sent a clear message. Those who returned were convinced there was no future in what had been home. Poland was a vast Jewish graveyard, a place of bitter memories. Jewish life still seemed to hang by a thread.

Soon the inchoate movement was organized and given a name—Bricha, the Hebrew word for escape. Bricha facilitated the border crossings, but it did not initiate the migration. Operatives were brought in from the Jewish Brigade and the Hagana, the defense forces of Jews in Palestine. Two major routes were established. One went west from Lódź to Poznan and Szczecin, and then to the British or American zone in Germany. The other went south from Lódź to Katowice or Krakow, then through Czechoslovakia, Hungary, or Austria to Italy or Yugoslavia.

The borders were crossed by day and at night, on foot and by train. Some border guards had to be bribed. Others simply turned aside and pretended not to notice. Czechoslovakia cooperated with the refugees; at times Poland did as well. Most countries were quite pleased to be rid of the Jews and gladly helped them on their way. Much to the chagrin of the British, the Americans allowed Jews into their sector of Germany.

In the summer of 1945, when Earl Harrison wrote his report. there were about 50,000 Jews in Germany and Austria. At that moment, the Jewish DP problem could easily have been solved by the issuance of 100,000 entry permits to Palestine. In the next year and a half, the number of Jews in the American sector increased fourfold, creating political pressure on both the British and the Americans that led to the establishment of a Jewish state.

Meanwhile, Jews were not content to wait while the politicians decided their fate. They set out for Palestine on their own, assisted by a Zionist underground network composed of Palestinian soldiers from the Jewish Brigade and Jews serving in Allied armies or working in Europe as civilians. Between 1945 and May 1948, 69,000 Jews made the journey by sea illegally on sixty-five boats. Only a few of the ships that ran the British blockade succeeded in reaching the coast of Palestine. Most were stopped by the British Royal Navy. The passengers were then sent to detention camps in Cyprus.

The movement of Jews to Palestine was known by several names. According to the British, it was illegal immigration. Palestinian Jews referred to it as Aliya Bet. (In Hebrew, *aliya* means a going up to the land, and *bet* is the second letter of the alphabet; hence, a second means of ascent to the land)

Clandestine intelligence networks of Mossad (Mossad L'Aliya Bet, the agency for the Aliya Bet, which later evolved into the famed Israeli intelligence agency) operated most of the ships. The sailings, however, were anything but secret. Journalists were notified in advance. Pictures of the British forcibly removing Holocaust survivors from ships and imprisoning them yet again were sent to newspapers throughout the world as part of a campaign to discredit the British mandate over Palestine.

The most famous event in Aliya Bet was the journey of the *Exodus*, a ship that set sail from Marseilles in July 1947 carrying forty-five hundred passengers. After a brief fight, the ship was captured. Instead of sending the passengers to Cyprus, the British took a "get tough" policy and forced the ship back to Marseilles. The passengers refused to disembark in Europe. They went on a hunger strike, which captured international attention.

The British cabinet would not relent in a struggle they saw as a test of wills with the Jews. They feared losing control of the situation and did not understand the special sensitivity for Holocaust survivors that would galvanize world public opinion. The passengers would be taken to Germany and there returned to Bergen-Belsen against their will. It took tear gas to force the concentration camp survivors off the ship. For two months the *Exodus* claimed the sympathy and attention of the world. The decision to send survivors back to a concentration camp caused international revulsion.

Aliya Bet dramatized the indomitable will of survivors to reach the land of Israel and broke the back of the British mandate over Palestine. Four months later, the United Nations voted for the establishment of an independent Jewish state in Palestine. Aliya Bet provided the means of migration to Palestine. The will to go to the Jewish homeland was pervasive among the survivors. I.F. Stone reported on the simple yearnings of the survivors: "I am a Jew," he was told. "That's enough. We have wandered enough. We have worked and struggled too long on the lands of other peoples. We must build a land of our own.". . .

On May 14, 1948, David Ben-Gurion proclaimed the state of Israel. That evening, the last British troops departed as the Union Jack was lowered. In its place rose the blue and white Star of David. That evening, Israel was also attacked by five Arab countries. A Jewish army was in place to defend its country.

In its Declaration of Independence, the provisional government of the new state ended all restriction on Jewish immigrants. In a few days, two ships, the *State of Israel* and *To Victory*, arrived with displaced persons now coming home. In the first days of independence, the Israeli government began the evacuation of the camps in Cyprus and the DP camps in Europe. It also began an intensive recruitment effort for the Israel Defense Forces among the young and able-bodied survivors, some of whom had fought in the Allied armies or as partisans. Resistance fighters from Warsaw and Vilna soon fought in Jerusalem and the Negev.

By the autumn of 1949, Jews were leaving the DP camps of Europe at a rate of ten thousand a month. On December 17, 1950, the Central Committee of Jewish Displaced Persons was disbanded. All those who wanted to settle in Israel had arrived. In 1950, Israel passed the Law of Return, granting Jews immediate citizenship upon their arrival. Once unwanted everywhere, Jews now had a country willing to open its borders to them. Israel offered itself as a haven to Jews fleeing persecution anywhere. Under the Law of Return, Jews fleeing Khomeini's Iran, segregated South Africa, starvation in Ethiopia, and persecution in the Soviet Union have found freedom in Israel.

Jewish survivors of the Holocaust finally found a place they could call home, a country that wanted them and that they wanted. The task of state-building was challenging and looked to the future. There were wars to be fought, cities and villages to be built, crops to be planted. These activities did not allow much time to dwell on the past. It would take a long time for the survivors to rebuild their lives from the ashes, and even more time to face the haunting memories of a painful past. . . .

The birth of the state of Israel was the most significant positive consequence of the Holocaust. The independent Jewish state might have come into being because of the impetus of Jewish nationalism and the Zionist movement of return to the land of Israel. But the presence of survivors in displaced-persons camps after the war increased worldwide support and sympathy for the Jewish state and hastened its formation. Yet Israel is not an answer to the Holocaust. Its formation could not undo the horror of the death camps. . . .

Appendix of Documents

Document 1: Who Will Speak?

Martin Niemöeller was a Protestant pastor who supported the Nazis until the church was made subordinate to state authority. In 1934 he started the Pastors' Emergency League to defend the church. Hitler became angered by Niemöeller's rebellious sermons and popularity and had him arrested. He spent the next seven years in concentration camps in "protective custody." He was liberated in 1945. Niemöeller is best known for his powerful statement about the failure of Germans to speak out against the Nazis, which is excerpted from Lionel Kochan's Encyclopedia of the Holocaust.

In Germany they came first for the communists, and I didn't speak up because I wasn't a communist. Then they came for the Jews, and I didn't speak up because I wasn't a Jew. Then they came for the trade unionists, and I didn't speak up because I wasn't a trade unionist. Then they came for the Catholics, and I didn't speak up because I was a protestant. Then they came for me, and by that time no one was left to speak up.

Document 2: A Directory of Major Concentration Camps

Concentration Camp	Location	Type of Camp	Operation	Closure	Present Status
Auschwitz-Birkenau	Poland	annihilation; forced labor	April 1940–January 1945	liberated by USSR	camp preserved
Belzec	Poland	annihilation	March 1942–June 1943	liquidated by Germany	monument
Bergen-Belsen	Germany	holding center	April 1943–April 1945	liberated by UK	graveyard
Buchenwald	Germany	forced labor	July 1937–April 1945	liberated by USA	camp preserved; museum
Chelmno	Poland	annihilation	December 1942–March 1943; June 1944–January 1945	liquidated by Germany	monument
Dachau	Germany	forced labor	March 1933–April 1945	liberated by USA	camp preserved; museum
Dora/Mittelbau	Germany	forced labor	September 1943–April 1945	liberated by USA	memorial sculpture plaza
Flossenbürg	Germany	forced labor	May 1938–April 1945	liberated by USA	buildings; monument

Gross-Rosen	Poland	forced labor	August 1940–February 1945	liberated by USSR	camp preserved; museum
Jan Wska	Ukraine	forced labor; annihilation	September 1941–November 1943	liquidated by Germany	not maintained
Kaiserwald	Latvia	forced labor	March 1943–September 1944	liquidated by Germany	not maintained
Majdanek	Poland	annihilation	July 1941–July 1944	liberated by USSR	camp preserved; monument
Mauthausen	Austria	forced labor	August 1938–May 1945	liberated by USA	buildings; monument
Natzweiler/Struthof	France	forced labor	May 1941–September 1944	liquidated by Germany	camp preserved
Neuengamme	Germany	forced labor	June 1940–May 1945	liberated by UK	used as prison; monument
Oranienburg	Germany	holding center	March 1933–March 1935	liquidated by Germany	not maintained
Plaszow	Poland	forced labor	December 1942–January 1945	liquidated by Germany	not maintained
Ravensbrück	Germany	forced labor	May 1939–April 1945	liberated by by USSR	buildings; monument
Sachsenhausen	Germany	forced labor	July 1936–April 1945	liberated by USSR	museum; buildings
Sobibor	Poland	annihilation	May 1942–October 1943	liquidated by Germany	monument
Stutthof	Poland	forced labor	September 1939–May 1945	liberated by USSR	buildings; museum
Terezin (Theresienstadt)	Czech Republic	holding center; transit ghetto	November 1941–May 1945	liberated by USSR	buildings; monument
Treblinka	Poland	annihilation	July 1942–November 1943	liquidated by Germany	monument
Westerbork	Netherlands	transit camp	October 1939–April 1945	liberated by Canada	monument

The Simon Wiesenthal Center

Document 3: The Liberation of Buchenwald

In his April 16, 1945, article "They Died 900 a Day in 'the Best' Nazi Death Camp," legendary CBS reporter Edward R. Murrow describes the scene at Buchenwald when he entered the camp after liberation.

There surged around me an evil-smelling stink, men and boys reached out to touch me. They were in rags and the remnants of uniforms. Death already had marked many of them, but they were smiling with their eyes. I looked out over the mass of men to the green fields beyond, where well-fed Germans were ploughing. . . .

[I] asked to see one of the barracks. It happened to be occupied by Czechoslovaks. When I entered, men crowded around, tried to lift me to their shoulders. They were too weak. Many of them could not get out of bed. I was told that this building had once stabled 80 horses. There were 1,200 men in it, five to a bunk. The stink was beyond all description.

They called the doctor. We inspected his records. There were only names in the little black book—nothing more—nothing about who had been where, what he had done or hoped. Behind the names of those who had died, there was a cross. I counted them. They totaled 242—242 out of 1,200, in one month.

As we walked out into the courtyard, a man fell dead. Two others, they must have been over 60, were crawling toward the latrine. I saw it, but will not describe it.

In another part of the camp they showed me the children, hundreds of them. Some were only 6 years old. One rolled up his sleeves, showed me his number. It was tattooed on his arm. B-6030, it was. The others showed me their numbers. They will carry them till they die. An elderly man standing beside me said: "The children—enemies of the state!" I could see their ribs through their thin shirts. . . .

We went to the hospital. It was full. The doctor told me that 200 had died the day before. I asked the cause of death. He shrugged and said: "tuberculosis, starvation, fatigue and there are many who have no desire to live. It is very difficult." He pulled back the blanket from a man's feet to show me how swollen they were. The man was dead. Most of the patients could not move.

I asked to see the kitchen. It was clean. The German in charge . . . showed me the daily ration. One piece of brown bread about as thick as your thumb, on top of it a piece of margarine as big as three sticks of chewing gum. That, and a little stew, was what they received every 24 hours. He had a chart on the wall. Very complicated it was. There were little red tabs scattered through it. He said that was to indicate each 10 men who died. He had to account for the rations and he added: "We're very efficient here."

We proceeded to the small courtyard. The wall adjoined what had been a stable or garage. We entered. It was floored with concrete. There were two rows of bodies stacked up like cordwood. They were thin and very white. Some of the bodies were terribly bruised; though there seemed to be little flesh to bruise. Some had been shot through the head, but they bled but little.

I arrived at the conclusion that all that was mortal of more than 500 men and boys lay there in two neat piles. There was a German trailer, which must have contained another 50, but it wasn't possible to count them. The clothing was piled in a heap against the wall. It appeared that most of the men and boys had died of starvation; they had not been executed.

But the manner of death seemed unimportant. Murder had been done at Buchenwald. God alone knows how many men and boys have died there during the last 12 years. Thursday, I was told that there were more than 20,000 in the camp. There had been as many as 60,000. Where are they now?

I pray you to believe what I have said about Buchenwald. I reported what I saw and heard, but only part of it. For most of it, I have no words.

If I have offended you by this rather mild account of Buchenwald, I'm not in the least sorry.

"They Died 900 a Day in 'the Best' Nazi Death Camp," *PM*, April 16, 1945.

Document 4: Rudolf Hoss, Commandant of Auschwitz

In Commandant of Auschwitz—the Autobiography of Rudolf Hoss, *Hoss recalls the day he was told that his camp would become the principal extermination center.*

In the summer of 1941, I cannot remember the exact date, I was suddenly summoned to the *Reichsfuhrer* SS [Heinrich Himmler], directly by his adjutant's office. Contrary to his usual custom, Himmler received me without his adjutant being present and said in effect:

The Fuhrer has ordered that the Jewish question be solved once and for all and that we, the SS, are to implement that order.

The existing extermination centers in the East are not in a position to carry out the large *Aktionen* which are anticipated. I have therefore earmarked Auschwitz for this purpose, both because of its good position as regards communications and because the [camp] can easily be isolated and camouflaged. . . .

The Jews are the sworn enemies of the German people and must be eradicated. Every Jew that we can lay our hands on is to be destroyed now during the war, without exception. If we cannot now obliterate the biological basis of Jewry, the Jews will one day destroy the German people.

. . . Shortly afterwards [Adolf] Eichmann came to Auschwitz and disclosed to me the plans for the operations as they affected the various countries concerned. . . .

We discussed the ways and means of effecting the extermination. This could only be done by gassing, since it would have been absolutely impossible to dispose by shooting of the large numbers of people that were expected, and it would have placed too heavy a burden on the SS men who had to carry it out, especially because of the women and children among the victims.

Eichmann told me about the method of killing people with exhaust gases in lorries, which had previously been used in the East. But there was no question of being able to use this for the mass transports that were due to arrive in Auschwitz. Killing with showers of carbon monoxide while bathing, as was done with mental patients in some places in the Reich, would necessitate too many buildings. . . . We inspected the area in order to choose a like spot. We decided that a peasant farmstead situated in the north-west corner of what later became the third building sector at Birkenau would be the most suitable. It was isolated and screened by woods and hedges, and it was also not far from the railway. The bodies could be placed in long, deep pits dug in the nearby meadows. We had not at that time thought of burning the corpses. We calculated that after gas-proofing the premises then available, it would be possible to kill about 800 people simultaneously with a suitable gas. These figures were borne out later in practice.

Document 5: Truman and the Harrison Report

In 1945, President Harry S. Truman dispatched Earl Harrison, the U.S. representative on the Intergovernmental Committee on Refugees and the president's personal envoy, to Europe to investigate the conditions and needs of the displaced persons and, especially, those of the Jewish refugees. Harrison's report shockingly described the terrible conditions of the refugees and recommended that the Jews be allowed to immigrate to Palestine. The following letter, which is found on the Jewish Student Online Research Center website, was sent by Truman to General Dwight D. Eisenhower, along with the Harrison Report.

My Dear General Eisenhower:
   . . . While Mr. Harrison makes due allowance for the fact that during the early days of liberation the huge task of mass repatriation required main attention he reports conditions which now exist and which require prompt remedy. These conditions, I know, are not in conformity with policies promulgated by SHAEF [Supreme Headquarters, Allied Expeditionary Forces of World War II], now Combined Displaced Persons Executive. But they are what actually exists in the field. In other words, the policies are not being carried out by some of your subordinate officers.

For example, military government officers have been authorized and even directed to requisition billeting facilities from the German population for the benefit of displaced persons. Yet, from this report, this has not been done on any wide scale. Apparently it is being taken for granted that all displaced persons, irrespective of their former persecution or the likelihood that their repatriation or resettlement will be delayed, must remain in camps—many of which are overcrowded and heavily guarded. Some of these camps are the very ones where these people were herded together, starved, tortured and made to witness the death of their fellow-inmates and friends and relatives. The announced policy has been to give such persons preference over the German civilian population in housing. But the practice seems to be quite another thing.

We must intensify our efforts to get these people out of camps and into decent houses until they can be repatriated or evacuated. These houses should be requisitioned from the German civilian population. That is one way to implement the Potsdam policy that the German people "cannot escape responsibility for what they have brought upon themselves."

I quote this paragraph with particular reference to the Jews among the displaced persons:

> As matters now stand, we appear to be treating the Jews as the Nazis treated them except that we do not exterminate them. They are in concentration camps in large numbers under our military guard instead of S.S. troops. One is led to wonder whether the German people, seeing this, are not supposing that we are following or at least condoning Nazi policy.

. . . I know you will agree with me that we have a particular responsibility toward these victims of persecution and tyranny who are in our zone. We must make clear to the German people that we thoroughly abhor the Nazi policies of hatred and persecution. We have no better opportunity to demonstrate this than by the manner in which we ourselves actually treat the survivors remaining in Germany.

I hope you will report to me as soon as possible the steps you have been able to take to clean up the conditions mentioned in the report.

I am communicating directly with the British Government in an effort to have the doors of Palestine opened to such of these displaced persons as wish to go there.

Very sincerely yours,
Harry S. Truman

Document 6: The Law for the Protection of German Blood and German Honor

In 1935 two measures were announced at the annual Nazi Party rally in Nuremberg, becoming known as the Nuremberg Laws. The first law, the Law for the Protection of German Blood and German Honor, is cited here. It prohibited marriages and extramarital intercourse between Jews (the name was now officially used in place of "non-Aryans") and Germans and also the employment of German females under forty-five years of age in Jewish households. This excerpt is from Documents on Nazism, 1919–1945, *by Jeremy Noakes and Geoffrey Pridham.*

Entirely convinced that the purity of German blood is essential to the further existence of the German people, and inspired by the uncompromising determination to safeguard the future of the German nation, the Reichstag has unanimously resolved upon the following law, which is promulgated herewith:

Section 1

1. Marriages between Jews and citizens of German or kindred blood are forbidden. Marriages concluded in defiance of this law are void, even if, for the purpose of evading this law, they were concluded abroad.

2. Proceedings for annulment may be initiated only by the Public Prosecutor.

Section 2

Sexual relations outside marriage between Jews and nationals of German or kindred blood are forbidden.

Section 3

Jews will not be permitted to employ female citizens of German or kindred blood as domestic servants.

Section 4

1. Jews are forbidden to display the Reich and national flag or the national colors.

2. On the other hand they are permitted to display the Jewish colors. The exercise of this right is protected by the State.

Section 5

1. A person who acts contrary to the prohibition of Section 1 will be punished with hard labour.

2. A person who acts contrary to the prohibition of Section 2 will be punished with imprisonment or with hard labour.

3. A person who acts contrary to the provisions of Sections 3 or 4 will be punished with imprisonment up to a year and with a fine, or with one of these penalties.

Section 6

The Reich Minister of the Interior in agreement with the Deputy Fuhrer and the Reich Minister of Justice will issue the legal and administrative regulations required for the enforcement and supplementing of this law.

Section 7

The law will become effective on the day after its promulgation; Section 3, however, not until 1 January 1936.

Document 7: The Reich Citizenship Law

The second Nuremberg law, the Reich Citizenship Law, cited below, stripped Jews of their German citizenship and introduced a new distinction between "Reich citizens" and "nationals." The law is reprinted in Documents on Nazism, 1919–1945, *by Jeremy Noakes and Geoffrey Pridham.*

Article 1

1. A subject of the State is a person who belongs to the protective union of the German Reich, and who therefore has particular obligations towards the Reich.

2. The status of subject is acquired in accordance with the provisions of the Reich and State Law of Citizenship.

Article 2

1. A citizen of the Reich is that subject only who is of German or kindred blood and who, through his conduct, shows that he is both desirous and fit to serve the German people and Reich faithfully.

2. The right to citizenship is acquired by the granting of Reich citizenship papers.

3. Only the citizen of the Reich enjoys full political rights in accordance with the provision of the laws.

Article 3

The Reich Minister of the Interior in conjunction with the Deputy of the Fuhrer will issue the necessary legal and administrative decrees for carrying out and supplementing this law.

Document 8: The Testimony of Albert Speer

Albert Speer was the minister of armaments in the Third Reich, and one of Hitler's closest confidants. He was among the Nazis tried for war crimes at Nuremberg and was sentenced to thirty years in prison for his actions. In Six Million Did Die, *by Arthur Suzman and Denis Diamond, Speer recalls Hitler's attitude toward the Jews.*

Hatred of the Jews was Hitler's motor and central point, perhaps even the very element which motivated him. The German people, the German greatness, the Empire, they all meant nothing to him in the last analysis. For this reason, he wished in the final sentence of his testament, to fixate us Germans, even after the apocalyptic downfall in a miserable hatred of the Jews.

I was present at the session of the Reichstag of 30th January 1939, when Hitler assured us that in case of a war, not the Germans, but the Jews would be annihilated. This dictum was pronounced with such certainty that I would not have felt permitted to question his intention to carry it through. He repeated this announcement of his intentions on 30th January 1942, in a speech I also know of: The war would not end, as the Jews imagined, by the extinction of European-Aryan peoples, but it would result in the annihilation of the Jews. This repetition of his words of 30th January 1939 was not unique. He would often remind his entourage of the importance of this dictum.

When speaking of the victims of the bomb raids, particularly after the massive attacks on Hamburg in Summer 1943, he again and again reiterated that he would avenge these victims on the Jews; just as if the air-terror against the civilian population actually suited him in that it furnished him with a belated substitute motivation for a crime decided upon long ago and emanating from quite different layers of his personality. Just as if he wanted to justify his own mass murders with these remarks. . . .

Hitler's method of work was that he gave even important commands to his confidants verbally. Also in the leader's records of my interviews with Hitler—completely preserved in the German Federal Archives—there were numerous commands even in important areas which Hitler clearly gave by word of mouth only. It therefore conforms with his method of work and must not be regarded as an oversight, that a written order for the extermination of the Jews does not exist.

Document 9: Hitler on the Annihilation of the Jews

Adolf Hitler made no secret of his contempt for Jews and his belief that they should be exterminated. Documentation of his views can be found predating his joining the Nazi Party. Hitler's following letter to Adolf Gemlich, dated September 16, 1919, is found in Lucy S. Dawidowicz's A Holocaust Reader.

Anti-Semitism as a political movement should not and cannot be determined by factors of sentiment, but only by the recognition of the facts. These are the facts:

To begin with, Jewry is unqualifiedly a racial association and not a religious association. . . . Its influence will bring about the racial tuberculosis of the people.

Hence it follows: Anti-Semitism on purely emotional grounds will find its ultimate expression in the form of pogroms. Rational anti-semitism, however, must lead to a systematic legal opposition and elimination of the special privileges which Jews hold, in contrast to the other aliens living among us (aliens' legislation). Its final objective must unswervingly be the removal of the Jews altogether. Only a government of national vitality is capable of doing both, and never a government of national impotence.

Document 10: Jews Disbelieve Reports of the Extermination

With the benefit of hindsight, it is difficult to understand how it could be that the Jews did not know what the Nazis planned to do to them. The truth was that no one could believe the Germans could or would try to exterminate the Jews of Europe. The following report came out of Warsaw in March 1944 and was forwarded to London by the Polish underground. It makes clear that even as mass murders were being perpetrated, Jews still could not believe the reports they were hearing.

The liquidation of the Jews in the Government-General began at Passover 1942. The first victims were the Jews of the city of Lublin, and shortly after that the Jews of the whole District of Lublin. They were evacuated to Belzec, and there they were killed in new gas-chambers that had been built specially for this purpose. The Jewish Underground newspapers gave detailed descriptions of this mass slaughter. But [the Jews of] Warsaw did not believe it! Common human sense could not understand that it was possible to exterminate tens and hundreds of thousands of Jews. They decided that the Jews were being transported for agricultural work in the parts of Russia occupied by the Germans. Theories were heard that the Germans had begun on the productivization of the Jewish lower-level bourgeoisie! The Jewish press was denounced and charged with causing panic, although the *descriptions* of the "rooting out" of the population corresponded accurately to the reality. Not only abroad were the crimes of the Germans received with disbelief, but even here, close by Ponary, Chelmno, Belzec and Treblinka, did this information get no hearing! This unjustified optimism developed together with the lack of information, which was the result of total isolation from the outside world and the experience of the past. Had not the Germans for two and a half years carried out many deportations of Jews—from Cracow, from Lublin, from the Warsaw District and from the "Reich?" Certainly there had been not a few victims and blood had been shed during these deportations, but total extermination?

There were some people who believed it, however. The events at Ponary and Chelmno were a fact, but—it was said—"that was just a capricious act of the local authorities." For, after all, the German authorities in the Government-General did not have the same attitude to the ghettos in the cities and the small towns, not until death brought an equal fate to all. More than once, in various places, the reaction to the information we had about the liquidation of the Jews was: "That cannot happen to us here."

It was of course the Germans themselves who created these optimistic attitudes. Through two and a half years they prepared the work of exterminating the three and a half million Jews of Poland with German thoroughness. They rendered the Jewish masses helpless with the aid of individual killings, oppression and starvation, with the aid of ghettos and deportations. In years of unceasing experiments the Germans perfected their extermination methods. In Vilna they had needed several days to murder a thousand Jews, in Chelmno half an hour was enough to kill a hundred, and at Treblinka ten thousand were murdered every day!

"Jews Disbelieve Reports of the Extermination," March 1944. Available at the Jewish Student Online Research Center, www.us-israel.org/jsource/Holocaust/disbelief.html.

Document 11: *Kristallnacht* Order

On the nights of November 9 and 10, rampaging mobs throughout Germany and the newly acquired territories of Austria and Sudetenland freely attacked Jews in the street, in their homes, and at their places of work and worship. At least ninety-six Jews were killed and hundreds more were injured, more than one thousand synagogues were burned, almost seventy-five hundred Jewish businesses were destroyed, cemeteries and schools were vandalized, and thirty thousand Jews were arrested and sent to concentration camps. The official German position on these events, which were clearly orchestrated by propaganda minister Joseph Goebbels, was that they were spontaneous outbursts. The following message, however, from the archives of Yad Vashem, was sent from SS leader Reinhard Heydrich before the pogrom.

Secret

Copy of Most Urgent telegram from Munich, of November 10, 1938, 1:20 A.M.

To
All Headquarters and Stations of the State Police
All districts and Sub-districts of the SD
Urgent! For immediate attention of Chief or his deputy!
Re: *Measures against Jews tonight*

Following the attempt on the life of Secretary of the Legation vom Rath in Paris, demonstrations against the Jews are to be expected in all parts of the Reich in the course of the coming night, November 9/10, 1938. The instructions below are to be applied in dealing with these events:

1. The Chiefs of the State Police, or their deputies, must immediately upon receipt of this telegram contact, by telephone, the political leaders in their areas—*Gauleiter or Kreisleiter*—who have jurisdiction in their districts and arrange a joint meeting with the inspector or commander of the Order Police to discuss the arrangements for the demonstrations. At these discussions the political leaders will be informed that the German Police has received instructions, detailed below, from the *Reichsfuehrer* SS and the Chief of the German Police, with which the political leadership is requested to coordinate its own measures:

a) Only such measures are to be taken as do not endanger German lives or property (i.e., synagogues are to be burned down only where there is no danger of fire in neighboring buildings).

b) Places of business and apartments belonging to Jews may be destroyed but not looted. The Police is instructed to supervise the observance of this order and to arrest looters.

c) In commercial streets particular care is to be taken that non-Jewish businesses are completely protected against damage.

d) Foreign citizens—even if they are Jews—are not to be molested.

2. On the assumption that the guidelines detailed under para. 1 are observed, the demonstrations are not to be prevented by the Police, which is only to supervise the observance of the guidelines.

3. On receipt of this telegram Police will seize all archives to be found in all synagogues and offices of the Jewish communities so as to prevent their destruction during the demonstrations. This refers only to material of historical value, not to contemporary tax records, etc. The archives are to be handed over to the locally responsible officers of the SD.

4. The control of the measures of the Security Police concerning the demonstrations against the Jews is vested in the organs of the State Police, unless inspectors of the Security Police have

given their own instructions. Officials of the Criminal Police, members of the SD, of the Reserves and the SS in general may be used to carry out the measures taken by the Security Police.

5. As soon as the course of events during the night permits the release of the officials required, as many Jews in all districts—especially the rich—as can be accommodated in existing prisons are to be arrested. For the time being only healthy male Jews, who are not too old, are to be detained. After the detentions have been carried out the appropriate concentration camps are to be contacted immediately for the prompt accommodation of the Jews in the camps. Special care is to be taken that the Jews arrested in accordance with these instructions are not ill-treated. . . .

signed Heydrich,
SS *Gruppenfuehrer*

"*Kristallnacht* Order." Available at the Jewish Student Online Research Center, www.us-israel.org/jsource/Holocaust/kristallnacht_order.html.

Document 12: Hans Frank on the Jews

Hitler could not have implemented his policies against the Jews without having willing, often enthusiastic subordinates who shared his anti-Semitic views. One such man was Hans Frank, the governor general of Nazi-occupied Poland. On December 16, 1941, Frank gave the following speech, found in the online documents of the Nizkor Project, before a session of the cabinet.

As far as the Jews are concerned, I want to tell you quite frankly that they must be done away with in one way or another. The Führer said once: "Should united Jewry again succeed in provoking a world-war, the blood of not only the nations which have been forced into the war by them, will be shed, but the Jew will have found his end in Europe." I know that many of the measures carried out against the Jews in the Reich at present are being criticized. It is being tried intentionally, as is obvious from the reports on the morale, to talk about cruelty, harshness, etc. Before I continue, I want to beg you to agree with me on the following formula: We will principally have pity on the German people only, and nobody else in the whole world. The others, too, had no pity on us. As an old National-Socialist, I must say: This war would only be a partial success if the whole lot of Jewry would survive it, while we would have shed our best blood in order to save Europe. My attitude towards the Jews will, therefore, be based only on the expectation that they must disappear. They must be done away with. I have entered negotiations to have them deported to the East. A great discussion concerning that question will take place in Berlin in January, to which I am going to delegate the State Secretary Dr. Buehler. That discussion is to take place in the Reich Security Main Office with SS-Lt. General [Reinhard] Heydrich. A great Jewish migration will begin, in any case.

But what should be done with the Jews? Do you think they will be settled down in the "Ostland," in villages? This is what we were told in Berlin: Why all this bother? We can do nothing with them either in the "Ostland" nor in the "Reich kommissariat." So liquidate them yourself.

Gentlemen, I must ask you to rid yourself of all feeling of pity. We must annihilate the Jews, wherever we find them and wherever it is possible, in order to maintain there the structure of the Reich as a whole. This will, naturally, be achieved by other methods than those pointed out by Bureau Chief Dr. Hummel. Nor can the judges of the Special Courts be made responsible for it, because of the limitations of the framework of the legal procedure. Such outdated views cannot be applied to such gigantic and unique events. We must find at any rate a way which leads to the goal, and my thoughts are working in that direction.

The Jews represent for us also extraordinarily malignant gluttons. We have now approximately 2,500,000 of them in the General Government, perhaps with the Jewish mixtures and everything that goes with it, 3,500,000 Jews. We cannot shoot or poison those 3,500,000 Jews, but we shall nevertheless be able to take measures, which will lead, somehow, to their annihilation, and this in connection with the gigantic measures to be determined in discussions from the Reich. The General Government must become free of Jews, the same as the Reich. Where and how this is to be achieved is a matter for the offices which we must appoint and create here. Their activities will be brought to your attention in due course.

Hans Frank, "Hans Frank on the Jews." Available at the Jewish Student Online Research Center, www.us-israel.org/jsource/Holocaust/frank_on_jews.html.

Document 13: Himmler Orders Completion of the Final Solution

Perhaps the closest thing we have to a direct order for the extermination of the Jews is the July 19, 1942, order from Heinrich Himmler, excerpted from the archives of Yad Vashem.

I herewith order that the resettlement of the entire Jewish population of the Government-General be carried out and completed by December 31, 1942.

From December 31, 1942, no persons of Jewish origin may remain within the Government-General, unless they are in collection camps in Warsaw, Cracow, Czestochowa, Radom, and Lublin. All other work on which Jewish labor is employed must be finished by that date, or, in the event that this is not possible, it must be transferred to one of the collection camps.

These measures are required with a view to the necessary ethnic division of races and peoples for the New Order in Europe, and also in the interests of the security and cleanliness of the German Reich and its sphere of interest. Every breach of this regulation spells a danger to quiet and order in the entire German sphere of interest, a point of application for the resistance movement and a source of moral and physical pestilence.

For all these reasons a total cleansing is necessary and therefore to be carried out. Cases in which the date set can not be observed will be reported to me in time, so that I can see to corrective action at an early date. All requests by other offices for changes or permits for exceptions to be made must be presented to me personally. Heil Hilter!

"Himmler Orders Completion of the Final Solution." Available at the Jewish Student Online Research Center, www.us-israel.org/jsource/Holocaust/Himorder.html.

Document 14: Himmler on Evacuating the Jews

In the following document from Yad Vashem, dated October 4, 1943, Himmler boasts about stealing the Jews' wealth and calls the extermination of the Jews a "page of glory" in German history.

I also want to speak to you here, in complete frankness, of a really grave chapter. Amongst ourselves, for once, it shall be said quite openly, but all the same we will never speak about it in public. Just as we did not hesitate on June 30, 1934 [referring to the Night of the Long Knives], to do our duty as we were ordered, and to stand comrades who had erred against the wall and shoot them, and we never spoke about it and we never will speak about it. It was a matter of natural tact that is alive in us, thank God, that we never talked about it amongst ourselves, that we never discussed it. Each of us shuddered and yet each of us knew clearly that the next time he would do it again if it were an order, and if it were necessary.

I am referring here to the evacuation of the Jews, the extermination of the Jewish people. This is one of the things that is easily said: "The Jewish people are going to be exterminated," that's what every Party member says, "sure, it's in our program, elimination of the Jews, extermination—it'll be done." And then they all come along, the 80 million worthy Germans, and each one has his one decent Jew. Of course, the others are swine, but this one, he is a first-rate Jew. Of all those who talk like that, not one has seen it happen, not one has had to go through with it. Most of you men know what it is like to see 100 corpses side by side, or 500 or 1,000. To have stood fast through this and—except for cases of human weakness—to have stayed decent, that has made us hard. This is an unwritten and never-to-be-written page of glory in our history, for we know how difficult it would be for us if today—under bombing raids and the hardships and deprivations of war—if we were still to have the Jews in every city as secret saboteurs, agitators, and inciters. If the Jews were still lodged in the body of the German nation, we would probably by now have reached the stage of 1916–17.

The wealth they possessed we took from them. I gave a strict order, which has been carried out by SS *Obergruppenfuehrer* Pohl, that this wealth will of course be turned over to the Reich in its entirety. We have taken none of it for ourselves. Individuals who have erred will be punished in accordance with the order given by me at the start, threatening that anyone who takes as much as a single Mark of this money is a dead man. A number of SS men—they are not very many—committed this offense, and they shall die. There will be no mercy. We had the moral right, we had the duty towards our people, to destroy this people that wanted to destroy us. But we do not have the right to enrich ourselves by so much as a fur, as a watch, by one Mark or a cigarette or anything else. We do not want, in the end, because we destroyed a bacillus, to be infected by this bacillus and to die. I will never stand by and watch while even a small rotten spot develops or takes hold. Wherever it may form we will together burn it away. All in all, however, we can say that we have carried out this most difficult of tasks in a spirit of love for our people. And we have suffered no harm to our inner being, our soul, our character.

"Himmler on 'Evacuation of the Jews.'" Available at the Jewish Student Online Research Center, www.us-israel.org/jsource/Holocaust/himevac.html.

Document 15: Banning References to the Final Solution

Though Hitler frequently spoke about his intent to exterminate the Jews, he issued the following order on July 11, 1943, specifically banning any reference to the Final Solution. The order is excerpted from the archives of Yad Vashem.

National-Socialist German Workers' Party

Party Secretariat

Head of the Party Secretariat

Fuhrer Headquarters, July 11, 1943

Circular No. 33/43 g.

Re: *Treatment of the Jewish Question*

On instructions from the Fuhrer I make known the following:

Where the Jewish Question is brought up in public, there may be no discussion of a future overall solution (*Gesamtlosung*).

It may, however, be mentioned that the Jews are taken in groups for appropriate labor purposes.

Signed M. Bormann

Distribution: *Reichsleiter*

Gauleiter

Group leaders

File Reference: Treatment/Jews

"Hitler Bans Public Reference to the 'Final Solution.'" Available at the Jewish Student Online Research Center, www.us-israel.org/jsource/Holocaust/hitban.html.

Document 16: Hitler the "Prophet"

On January 31, 1939, Hitler gave the following speech predicting the annihilation of the Jewish people. It was reprinted in Trials of War Criminals Before the Nuremberg Military Tribunals.

Today I will once more be a prophet: If the international Jewish financiers in and outside Europe should succeed in plunging the nations once more into a world war, then the result will not be the bolshevization of the earth, and thus the victory of Jewry, but the annihilation of the Jewish race in Europe!

Adolf Hitler, "Statements by Leading Nazis on the 'Jewish Question,'" January 31, 1939. Available at the Jewish Student Online Research Center, www.us-israel.org/jsource/Holocaust/nazi_statements.html.

Document 17: The Complete Annihilation of the Jews

In a January 30, 1942, speech, Hitler forecasts how the war will end. This excerpt is from The Holocaust, *by Martin Gilbert.*

And we say that the war will not end as the Jews imagine it will, namely with the uprooting of the Aryans, but the result of this war will be the complete annihilation of the Jews.

Document 18: Avoiding "Squeamish Sentimentalism"

The Reich's propaganda minister, Joseph Goebbels, wrote in his diary on February 14, 1942, the fate intended for the Jews. His diary entries were later reprinted as the book The Goebbels Diaries, 1942–1943.

World Jewry will suffer a great catastrophe at the same time as Bolshevism. The Führer once more expressed his determination to clean up the Jews in Europe pitilessly. There must be no squeamish sentimentalism about it. The Jews have deserved the catastrophe that has now overtaken them. Their destruction will now go hand in hand with the destruction of our enemies. We must hasten this process with cold ruthlessness.

Document 19: Wannsee Protocol

On January 20, 1942, a group of Nazi bureaucrats met at a villa along Wannsee Lake to discuss the final solution to the "Jewish question." The meeting was run by Reinhard Heydrich, the chief of the Nazi secret police. The minutes, which came to be known as the Wannsee Protocol, were taken by Heydrich's subordinate, Adolf Eichmann. The following excerpts are from volume 11 of The Holocaust: Selected Documents in Eighteen Volumes, *edited by John Mendelsohn.*

At the beginning of the discussion Chief of the Security Police and of the SD, SS Obergruppenführer Heydrich, reported that the Reich Marshal had appointed him delegate for the preparations for the final solution of the Jewish question in Europe. . . . The Chief of the Security Police and the SD then gave a short report of the struggle which has been carried on thus far against this enemy, the essential points being the following:

    a) the expulsion of the Jews from every sphere of life of the German people,

    b) the expulsion of the Jews from the living space of the German people.

    In carrying out these efforts, an increased and planned acceleration of the emigration of the Jews from Reich territory was started, as the only possible present solution.

    By order of the Reich Marshal, a Reich Central Office for Jewish Emigration was set up in January 1939 and the Chief of the Security Police and SD was entrusted with the management. Its most important tasks were

    a) to make all necessary arrangements for the preparation for an increased emigration of the Jews,

    b) to direct the flow of emigration,

c) to speed the procedure of emigration in each individual case. The aim of all this was to cleanse German living space of Jews in a legal manner. . . .

Another possible solution of the problem has now taken the place of emigration, i.e. the evacuation of the Jews to the East, provided that the Führer gives the appropriate approval in advance.

These actions are, however, only to be considered provisional, but practical experience is already being collected which is of the greatest importance in relation to the future final solution of the Jewish question.

Approximately 11 million Jews will be involved in the final solution of the European Jewish question. . . .

Under proper guidance, in the course of the final solution the Jews are to be allocated for appropriate labor in the East. Able-bodied Jews, separated according to sex, will be taken in large work columns to these areas for work on roads, in the course of which action doubtless a large portion will be eliminated by natural causes.

The possible final remnant will, since it will undoubtedly consist of the most resistant portion, have to be treated accordingly, because it is the product of natural selection and would, if released, act as the seed of a new Jewish revival (see the experience of history.)

In the course of the practical execution of the final solution, Europe will be combed through from west to east. . . .

State Secretary Dr. Bühler stated that the General Government would welcome it if the final solution of this problem could be begun in the General Government, since on the one hand transportation does not play such a large role here nor would problems of labor supply hamper this action. Jews must be removed from the territory of the General Government as quickly as possible, since it is especially here that the Jew as an epidemic carrier represents an extreme danger and on the other hand he is causing permanent chaos in the economic structure of the country through continued black market dealings. Moreover, of the approximately 2½ million Jews concerned, the majority is unfit for work. . . .

He had only one request, to solve the Jewish question in this area as quickly as possible.

Document 20: Establishing the Warsaw Ghetto

The Warsaw ghetto was established in November 1940. Surrounded by a wall, the ghetto confined nearly five hundred thousand Jews. The following order, found in the archives of Yad Vashem, was issued by the head

of the Warsaw District on October 2, 1940, and outlines the plan to cre-
ate the ghetto.

1. On the basis of the Regulation for Restrictions on Residence in the Government-General of September 13, 1940 . . . , a Jewish quarter is to be formed in the city of Warsaw, in which the Jews living in the city of Warsaw, or still to move there, must take up residence. The [Jewish] quarter will be set off from the rest of the city by the following streets: [here follows a list of streets and sections of streets]. . . .

2. Poles residing in the Jewish quarter must move their domicile into the other part of the city by October 31, 1940. Apartments will be provided by the Housing Office of the Polish City Hall.

Poles who have not given up their apartments in the Jewish quarter by the above date will be forcibly moved. In the event of a forcible removal they will be permitted to take only refugee [style] luggage (*Fluechtlingsgepaeck*), bed-linen, and articles of sentimental value.

Poles are not permitted to move into the German quarter.

3. Jews living outside the Jewish quarter must move into the Jewish area of residence by October 31, 1940. They may take only refugee luggage and bed-linen. Apartments will be allocated by the Jewish Elder (*Judenaeltester*).

4. The Appointed Mayor of the Polish City Hall and the Jewish Elder are responsible for the orderly move of the Jews to the Jewish quarter, and the punctual move of the Poles away from the Jewish quarter, in accordance with a plan yet to be worked out, which will provide for the evacuation by stages of the individual Police districts.

5. The Representative of the District Governor of the city of Warsaw will give the necessary detailed instructions to the Jewish Elder for the establishing and permanent closure of the Jewish quarter.

6. The Representative of the District Governor of the city of Warsaw will issue regulations for the execution of this Decree.

7. Any person contravening this Decree, or the Regulations for its execution, will be punished in accordance with the existing laws on punishment.

> *Head of the Warsaw District*
> *Dr. Fischer*
> *Governor*

"The Establishment of a Ghetto in Warsaw." Available at the Jewish Student Online Research Center, www.us-israel.org/jsource/Holocaust/fischer.html.

Document 21: The Call for Resistance in the Warsaw Ghetto

From April 19 to May 16, 1943, a revolt took place in the Warsaw ghetto when the Germans, commanded by General Jürgen Stroop, attempted to raze the ghetto and deport the remaining inhabitants to Treblinka. The uprising, led by Mordecai Anielewicz, was the first instance in occupied Europe of an uprising by an urban population. In January 1943 the following call for resistance was issued by the Jewish underground in the ghetto. This excerpt is from the archives of the Jewish Historical Institute in Poland.

To the Jewish Masses in the Ghetto

On January 22, 1943, six months will have passed since the deportations from Warsaw began. We all remember well the days of terror during which 300,000 of our brothers and sisters were cruelly put to death in the death camp of Treblinka. Six months have passed of life in constant fear of death, not knowing what the next day may bring. We have received information from all sides about the destruction of the Jews in the Government-General, in Germany, in the occupied territories. When we listen to this bitter news we wait for our own hour to come, every day and every moment. Today we must understand that the Nazi murderers have let us live only because they want to make use of our capacity to work to our last drop of blood and sweat, to our last breath. We are slaves. And when the slaves are no longer profitable, they are killed. Every one among us must understand that, and every one among us must remember it always.

During the past few weeks certain people have spread stories about letters that were said to have been received from Jews deported from Warsaw, who were said to be in labor camps near Minsk or Bobruisk. *Jews in your masses, do not believe these tales. They are spread by Jews who are working for the Gestapo.* The blood-stained murderers have a particular aim in doing this: to reassure the Jewish population in order that later the next deportation can be carried out without difficulty, with a minimum of force and without losses to the Germans. They want the Jews not to prepare hiding-places and not to resist. Jews, do not repeat these lying tales.

Do not help the [Nazi] agents. The Gestapo's dastardly people will get their just desserts. *Jews in your masses,* the hour is near. You must be prepared to resist, not to give yourselves up like sheep to slaughter. *Not even one Jew must go to the train. People who cannot resist actively must offer passive resistance, that is, by hiding.* We have now received information from Lvov that the Jewish Police there

itself carried out the deportation of 3,000 Jews. Such things will not happen again in Warsaw. . . . Now our slogan must be:
Let everyone be ready to die like a man!

"Call to Resistance in the Warsaw Ghetto." Available at the Jewish Student Online Research Center, www.us-israel.org/jsource/Holocaust/call.html.

Document 22: Goebbels on the Ghetto Revolt

The Germans were surprised by the ability of a small band of Jews to revolt in the Warsaw ghetto. The grudging respect and sense of fear of Jews with guns can be seen in the May 1, 1943, entry from the diary of Joseph Goebbels, which was later reprinted in the book Goebbels' Diaries for the Years 1942–1943, *and Other Documents.*

There is nothing sensational in the reports from the Occupied Territories. The only thing noteworthy is exceptionally sharp fighting in Warsaw between our Police, and in part even the Wehrmacht, and the Jewish rebels. The Jews have actually succeeded in putting the ghetto in a condition to defend itself. Some very hard battles are taking place there, which have gone so far that the Jewish top leadership publishes daily military reports. Of course this jest will probably not last long. But it shows what one can expect of the Jews if they have arms. Unfortunately they also have some good German weapons in part, particularly machine-guns. Heaven only knows how they got hold of them.

Document 23: The Destruction of the Warsaw Ghetto

On February 16, 1943, Heinrich Himmler issued the following order to destroy the Warsaw ghetto. The order is excerpted from the Yad Vashem archives.

Reichsfuehrer SS Field Command
Journal No. 38/33/43 g. February 16, 1943
Secret!
To:
   Higher SS and Police Leader (*Hoeher SS- und Polizeifuehrer*), East SS *Obergruppenfuehrer* Krueger, Cracow
   For reasons of security I herewith order that the Warsaw ghetto be pulled down after the concentration camp has been moved: all parts of houses that can be used, and other materials of all kinds, are first to be made use of.
   The razing of the ghetto and the relocation of the concentration camp are necessary, as otherwise we would probably never establish quiet in Warsaw, and the prevalence of crime cannot be

stamped out as long as the ghetto remains.

An overall plan for the razing of the ghetto is to be submitted to me. In any case we must achieve the disappearance from sight of the living-space for 500,000 sub-humans (*Untermenschen*) that has existed up to now, but could never be suitable for Germans, and reduce the size of this city of millions—Warsaw—which has always been a center of corruption and revolt.

signed H. Himmler

"Himmler Orders the Destruction of the Warsaw Ghetto." Available at the Jewish Student Online Research Center, www.us-israel.org/jsource/Holocaust/himmord.html.

Document 24: The Last Letter from Mordecai Anielewicz

Mordecai Anielewicz led the Jewish resistance forces. The Nazis greatly outnumbered the resistance in soldiers and weapons, so that the hundreds of fighters, with only hand revolvers, had no chance of victory. Still, the Jews would not surrender. On May 8 Anielewicz was killed. The following excerpt is from the last letter he wrote, dated April 23, 1943, and is found in the archives of Yad Vashem.

It is impossible to put into words what we have been through. One thing is clear, what happened exceeded our boldest dreams. The Germans ran twice from the ghetto. One of our companies held out for 40 minutes and another—for more than 6 hours. The mine set in the "brushmakers" area exploded. Several of our companies attacked the dispersing Germans. Our losses in manpower are minimal. That is also an achievement. Y. [Yechiel] fell. He fell a hero, at the machine-gun. *I feel that great things are happening and what we dared do is of great, enormous importance. . . .*

Beginning from today we shall shift over to the partisan tactic. Three battle companies will move out tonight, with two tasks: reconnaissance and obtaining arms. Do you remember, short-range weapons are of no use to us. We use such weapons only rarely. What we need urgently: grenades, rifles, machine-guns and explosives.

It is impossible to describe the conditions under which the Jews of the ghetto are now living. Only a few will be able to hold out. The remainder will die sooner or later. Their fate is decided. In almost all the hiding places in which thousands are concealing themselves it is not possible to light a candle for lack of air.

With the aid of our transmitter we heard the marvelous report on our fighting by the "Shavit" radio station. The fact that we are remembered beyond the ghetto walls encourages us in our struggle. Peace go with you, my friend! Perhaps we may still meet again! *The dream of my life has risen to become fact. Self-defense in the ghetto will have been a reality. Jewish armed resistance and revenge are facts. I have been a witness to the magnificent, heroic fighting of Jewish men in battle.*

"Mordecai Anielewicz, "The Last Letter from Mordecai Anielewicz." Available at the Jewish Student Online Research Center, www.us-israel.org/jsource/Holocaust/Anielewiczlet.html.

Document 25: Auschwitz and the "Resettlement Action"

The following document is excerpted from a report made to Himmler after one of his subordinates conducted an inspection at Auschwitz in May 1943. It is reprinted in G. Fleming's Hitler and the Final Solution.

The Auschwitz camp plays a special role in the resolution of the Jewish question. The most advanced methods permit the execution of the Führer-order in the shortest possible time and without arousing much attention. The so-called "resettlement action" runs the following course: The Jews arrive in special trains (freight cars) toward evening and are driven on special tracks to areas of the camp specifically set aside for this purpose. There the Jews are unloaded and examined for their fitness to work by a team of doctors, in the presence of the camp commandant and several SS officers. At this point anyone who can somehow be incorporated into the work program is put in a special camp. The curably ill are sent straight to a medical camp and are restored to health through a special diet. The basic principle behind everything is: conserve all manpower for work. The previous type of "resettlement action" has been thoroughly rejected, since it is too costly to destroy precious work energy on a continual basis.

The unfit go to cellars in a large house which are entered from outside. They go down five or six steps into a fairly long, well-constructed and well-ventilated cellar area, which is lined with benches to the left and right. It is brightly lit, and the benches are numbered. The prisoners are told that they are to be cleansed and disinfected for their new assignments. They must therefore completely undress to be bathed. To avoid panic and to prevent disturbances of any kind, they are instructed to arrange their clothing neatly under their respective numbers, so that they will be able to find their things again after their bath. Everything proceeds in a perfectly orderly fashion. Then they pass through a small corridor and enter a large cellar room which resembles a shower bath. In this room are three large pillars, into which certain materials can be lowered from outside the cellar room. When three- to four-hundred people have been herded into this room, the doors are shut, and containers filled with the substances are dropped down into the pillars. As soon as the containers touch the base of the pillars, they release particular substances that put the people to sleep in one minute. A few minutes later, the door opens on the other side, where the elevator is located. The hair of the corpses is cut off, and their teeth are extracted (gold-filled teeth) by specialists (Jews). It has been discovered that Jews were hiding pieces of Jewelry, gold, platinum etc., in hollow teeth. Then the corpses are loaded into elevators and brought up to the first floor, where ten large crematoria are located. (Because fresh corpses burn particularly well, only 50–100 lbs. of coke are needed for the whole process.) The job itself is performed by Jewish prisoners, who never step outside this camp again.

The results of this "resettlement action" to date: 500,000 Jews. Current capacity of the "resettlement action" ovens: 10,000 in 24 hours.

Document 26: The Jager Report

The following report was written by a commander of one of the Einsatzgruppen *(special task forces) that were in charge of liquidating Jews, communist leaders, partisans, and others in the Soviet Union. In it, Commander Jager details the killing of 137,346 people. This is for one* Einsatzgruppe, *in a five month period, in one area. The following is the conclusion of the "Jager Report" taken from Ernst Klee, et al.,* The Good Old Days.

Today I can confirm that our objective, to solve the Jewish problem for Lithuania, has been achieved by EK 3. In Lithuania there are no more Jews, apart from Jewish workers and their families. . . .

I consider the Jewish action more or less terminated as far as Einsatzkommando 3 is concerned. Those working Jews and Jewesses still available are needed urgently and I can envisage that after the winter this workforce will be required even more urgently. I am of the view that the sterilization programme of the male worker Jews should be started immediately so that reproduction is prevented. If despite sterilization a Jewess becomes pregnant she will be liquidated.

(signed) Jager
SS-Standartenfuhrer

Chronology

1932

German national elections for delegates to the Reichstag (parliament) result in Nazis attaining 230 seats, or 38 percent. Social Democrats receive 21 percent; Communists, 15 percent; Catholic Center, 12 percent; and numerous other parties combine to receive 14 percent.

1933

President Hindenburg appoints Adolf Hitler chancellor (prime minister). The Reichstag building is burned. The first concentration camp, Dachau, is established. The Law for Removing the Distress of People and Reich (commonly known as the Enabling Act) is passed, giving the chancellor (Hitler) legislative authority. A boycott of all Jewish shops in Germany is instigated by the SA. This action was also directed against Jewish physicians and lawyers. Jewish students were forbidden to attend schools and universities. A decree is issued defining a non-Aryan as "anyone descended from non-Aryan, especially Jewish, parents or grandparents. One parent or grandparent classifies the descendant as non-Aryan . . . especially if one parent or grandparent was of the Jewish faith." Books written by Jews and opponents of Nazism are burned. The Nazi Party is declared the only party in Germany.

1934

The "Night of the Long Knives" occurs when Hitler's rivals in the SA leadership are murdered. President Hindenburg dies. Offices of president and chancellor are combined. Hitler becomes sole leader (führer) and commander in chief of the armed forces.

1935

National Day of the NSDAP. The Reichstag passes, during a special session, the anti-Semitic Nuremberg Laws, the Reich Citizenship Law, and the Law for the Protection of German Blood and Honor. These laws were the basis for the exclusion of Jews from all public business life and for the reclassification of the political rights of Jewish citizens.

1936
The opening of the Olympic Games in Berlin. Anti-Semitic posters are temporarily removed.

1937
The start of the Aryanization of the economy; Jewish owners are forced, without legal basis, to sell their businesses, in most cases considerably below the value of their goods.

1938
"Annexation" (*Anschluss*) of Austria and start of persecution of Austrian Jews. An international conference is held in Évian-les-Bains, France, and is attended by delegates from thirty-two countries, including the United States, Great Britain, and France, to discuss the problem of Jewish refugees from Germany results in no effective help for Jewish refugees. The Munich Agreement: Britain and France accept German annexation of Sudetenland, part of Czechoslovakia. *Kristallnacht:* The Government-organized pogrom against Jews in Germany. It destroys synagogues, businesses, and homes. More than 26,000 Jewish men are arrested and committed to concentration camps—Dachau, Buchenwald, and Sachsenhausen. At least 91 Jews are killed, 191 synagogues are destroyed, 7,500 shops are looted. Jewish children are expelled from German schools.

1939
Hitler predicts in the Reichstag the "extermination of the Jewish race in Europe" in the event of war. Passengers board the USS *St. Louis* in Hamburg for trip to Cuba. Nazis sign the Pact of Steel with Italy. Germany attacks Poland; World War II begins. Numerous pogroms in Poland. Curfews for Jews in Germany (9:00 P.M. in the summer, 8:00 P.M. in the winter). Britain and France declare war on Germany. Germans and Soviets divide Poland. More than 2 million Jews live in the German area and 1.3 million in the Soviet-controlled territory. Nazis begin euthanasia on sick and disabled in Germany. The first ghetto (unguarded and unfenced) is established in Piotrków, Poland.

1940
The establishment of the Warsaw ghetto is ordered.

1941
German Jews are inducted into forced labor. Germany attacks the Soviet Union. Göring assigns to Heydrich the task for "a complete

solution of the Jewish question in the German sphere of influence in Europe," beginning the Final Solution. A police order decrees that, effective September 19, all Jews age six and older in Germany must wear the Star of David. The first gassing tests take place in Auschwitz using Zyklon B. The mass murder of Jews occurs at Babi Yar near Kiev (thirty-four thousand victims). German Jews are ordered to be deported from Germany, as defined by its 1933 borders. Start of deportation of the Jews from the Reich. *Einsatzgruppen* mass killings of Jews occur all over southern Russia. The Japanese attack Pearl Harbor. Hitler issues Night and Fog Decree. The United States and Britain declare war on Japan. Chelmno extermination camp is opened near Lodz, Poland; by April 1943, 360,000 Jews had been murdered there. Germany declares war on the United States; America declares war on Germany.

1942

Wannsee Conference is held to solidify plans for deportation and extermination of European Jewry (Final Solution). Extermination of Jews begins at Sobibor; by October 1943, 250,000 Jews had been murdered there. Start of Operation (Aktion) Reinhard, the code name for the operation that had as its objective the physical destruction of the Jews in the interior of occupied Poland within the framework of the Final Solution. Jewish schools are closed in Germany. Mass gassings start at Auschwitz. Himmler grants permission for sterilization experiments at Auschwitz. Himmler orders Operation Reinhard, the mass deportation of Jews in Poland to extermination camps. Hitler publicly repeats his forecast of the destruction of Jewry. The Allies solemnly condemn the extermination of the Jews and promise to punish the perpetrators.

1943

The first armed resistance against deportation takes place in the Warsaw ghetto. Germans order all Gypsies arrested and sent to concentration camps. German Sixth Army surrenders at Stalingrad. (This marks the turning point in the war.) Nazis arrest White Rose leaders in Munich. American Jews hold a mass rally at Madison Square Garden in New York to pressure the United States to aid European Jewry. The Bermuda Conference: fruitless discussions by U.S. and British delegates on deliverance of Nazi victims. Revolt in and destruction of the Warsaw ghetto. Benito Mussolini is arrested and the fascist government in Italy falls; Marshal Pietro Badoglio takes over and negotiates with Allies. An order calls for the expulsion of Danish Jews; due to the rescue operations by the Danish underground, some 7,000 Jews were evacuated to Sweden. Only 475 were captured by the Germans. Italy declares war on Germany. A revolt occurs in Sobibor.

1944

Roosevelt creates the War Refugee Board. Rudolf Vrba and Alfred Wetzler escape from Auschwitz and carry detailed information about the death camp to the outside world. A Red Cross delegation visits Theresienstadt. D day, the Allied invasion in Normandy, begins. Swedish diplomat Raoul Wallenberg arrives in Budapest, Hungary, and begins to issue diplomatic papers to save Hungarian Jews. Anne Frank's family is arrested by the Gestapo in Amsterdam. Gassings in Auschwitz are terminated. Himmler orders the destruction of the crematorium at Auschwitz-Birkenau, as Nazis try to hide evidence of the death camps.

1945

Auschwitz is evacuated; the death march of prisoners begins. Soviet troops liberate Auschwitz. Hitler orders the destruction of all German military, industrial, transportation, and communications facilities to prevent them from falling into enemy control. The Allies discover stolen Nazi art and wealth hidden in salt mines. Buchenwald is liberated by American troops. President Roosevelt dies; Truman becomes president. American troops liberate Dachau. Hitler commits suicide. Germany concedes to unconditional surrender, ending the war in Europe. The first atomic bomb is dropped on Hiroshima. Japan surrenders, ending World War II. Nuremberg trials start. They end January 10, 1946, with twelve defendants sentenced to death, three to life imprisonment, four to various prison terms, and three acquitted.

For Further Research

Books

Robert H. Abzug, *Inside the Vicious Heart: Americans and the Liberation of the Nazi Concentration Camps.* New York: Oxford University Press, 1987.

American Jewish Historical Society, *When the Rabbis Marched on Washington.* Waltham, MA: American Jewish Historical Society, 1999.

Yitzhak Arad, *Belzec, Sobibor, Treblinka: The Operation Reinhard Death Camps.* Bloomington: Indiana University Press, 1987.

Mitchell G. Bard, *Forgotten Victims: The Abandonment of Americans in Hitler's Camps.* Boulder, CO: Westview, 1994.

Yehuda Bauer, *A History of the Holocaust.* New York: Franklin Watts, 1982.

——, *Jews for Sale? Nazi-Jewish Negotiations, 1933–1945.* New Haven, CT: Yale University Press, 1994.

Michael Berenbaum, *The World Must Know: The History of the Holocaust as Told in the United States Holocaust Memorial Museum.* Boston: Little, Brown, 1993.

Michael Berenbaum and Abraham J. Peck, eds., *The Holocaust and History.* Bloomington: Indiana University Press, 1998.

Mary Berg, *Warsaw Ghetto.* New York: L.B. Fischer, 1945.

Richard Breitman, *Official Secrets: What the Nazis Planned, What the British and Americans Knew.* New York: Hill & Wang, 1998.

Christopher Browning, *Ordinary Men: Reserve Police Battalion 101 and the Final Solution in Poland.* New York: HarperCollins, 1992.

Harry James Cargas, *When God and Man Failed.* New York: Macmillan, 1981.

Richard Chesnoff, *Pack of Thieves: How Hitler and Europe Plundered the Jews and Committed the Greatest Theft in History.* New York: Doubleday, 1999.

Robert E. Conot, *Justice at Nuremberg.* New York: Harper & Row, 1983.

David Cornwell, *Hitler's Pope: The Secret History of Pope Pius XII.*

New York: Viking, 1999.

Lucy S. Dawidowicz, *The War Against the Jews, 1933–1945.* New York: Bantam Doubleday Dell, 1991.

Ruth Elias, *Triumph of Hope.* New York: John Wiley & Sons, 1998.

Henry Feingold, *The Politics of Rescue: The Roosevelt Administration and the Holocaust, 1938–1945.* New Brunswick, NJ: Rutgers University Press, 1970.

Benjamin Ferencz, *Less than Slaves.* Cambridge, MA: Harvard University Press, 1979.

Jack Fishman, *Long Knives and Short Memories.* New York: Richardson & Steirman, 1987.

Anne Frank, *Anne Frank: The Diary of a Young Girl.* New York: Bantam Books, 1967.

Saul Friedländer, *Nazi Germany and the Jews.* Vol. 1. *The Years of Persecution 1933–1939.* New York: HarperCollins, 1997.

Varian Fry, *Surrender on Demand.* Boulder, CO: Johnson Books, 1997.

Martin Gilbert, *The Boys: The Untold Story of 732 Young Concentration Camp Survivors.* New York: Henry Holt, 1997.

Daniel Jonah Goldhagen, *Hitler's Willing Executioners: Ordinary Germans and the Holocaust.* New York: Alfred A. Knopf, 1996.

Israel Gutman, *Resistance: The Warsaw Ghetto Uprising.* Boston: Houghton Mifflin, 1994.

Kitty Hart, *Return to Auschwitz.* New York: Atheneum Books, 1982.

William E. Helmreich, *Against All Odds: Holocaust Survivors and the Successful Lives They Made in America.* New York: Simon & Schuster, 1992.

Robert Edwin Herzstein, *Roosevelt and Hitler.* New York: Paragon House, 1989.

Raul Hilberg, *Perpetrators, Victims, Bystanders: The Jewish Catastrophe, 1933–1945.* New York: HarperPerennial, 1993.

Eva Hoffman, *Shtetl.* Boston: Houghton Mifflin, 1997.

Marion Kaplan, *Between Dignity and Despair: Jewish Life in Germany.* New York: Oxford University Press, 1998.

Eugen Kogon, *The Theory and Practice of Hell: The German Concentration Camps and the System Behind Them.* Trans. Heinz Norden. 1950. Reprint. New York: Berkley, 1980.

Gerd Korman, ed., *Hunter and Hunted: Human History of the Holocaust*. New York: Viking, 1973.

Ota Kraus and Erich Kulka, *The Death Factory*. London: Pergamon, 1966.

Lucette Matalon Lagnado and Sheila Cohn Dekel, *Children of the Flames: Dr. Joseph Mengele and the Untold Story of the Twins of Auschwitz*. New York: Penguin, 1992.

Lawrence Langer ed., *Art from the Ashes*. New York: Oxford University Press, 1995.

Primo Levi, *Survival in Auschwitz and the Reawakening*. New York: Summit Books, 1965.

Alan Levy, *The Wiesenthal File*. Grand Rapids, MI: William B. Eerdmans, 1993.

Guenter Lewy and John Snoek, "The Christian Churches," *Holocaust*. Jerusalem: Keter, 1974.

Deborah E. Lipstadt, *Beyond Belief: The American Press and the Coming of the Holocaust, 1933–1945*. New York: Free Press, 1986.

———, *Denying the Holocaust: The Growing Assault on Truth and Memory*. New York: Free, 1993.

Haskel Lookstein, *Were We Our Brothers' Keepers? The Public Response of American Jews to the Holocaust, 1938–1944*. New York: Hartmore House, 1985.

Jane Marks, *The Hidden Children*. New York: Fawcett Books, 1995.

Michael Marrus, *The Holocaust in History*. Hanover, NH: University Press of New England, 1987.

Arno Mayer, *Why Did the Heavens Darken?* Buffalo, NY: Pantheon Books, 1988.

Ernest Michel, *Promises to Keep*. New York: Barricade Books, 1993.

Judith Miller, *One by One by One: Facing the Holocaust*. New York: Simon & Schuster, 1990.

Arthur D. Morse, *While Six Million Died: A Chronicle of American Apathy*. New York: Random House, 1968.

Peter Novick, *The Holocaust in American Life*. New York: Houghton Mifflin, 1999.

Carol Rittner and John Roth, eds., *Different Voices: Women and the*

Holocaust. New York: Paragon House, 1993.

Richard Rubenstein and John Roth, *Approaches to Auschwitz: The Holocaust and Its Legacy*. Atlanta: John Knox, 1987.

Abram Sachar, *The Redemption of the Unwanted*. New York: St. Martin's, 1983.

Tom Segev, *Soldiers of Evil*. New York: McGraw-Hill, 1987.

Eric Silver, *The Book of the Just*. New York: Grove, 1992.

Jean-Francois Steiner, *Treblinka*. New York: Simon & Schuster, 1967.

Nechama Tec, *When Light Pierced the Darkness: Christian Rescue of Jews in Nazi-Occupied Poland*. New York: Oxford University Press, 1986.

John Toland, *Adolf Hitler*. New York: Anchor Books, 1976.

Isaiah Trunk, *Jewish Responses to Nazi Persecution*. New York: Stein and Day, 1979.

Elie Wiesel, *Night*. New York: Bantam Books, 1960.

Simon Wiesenthal, *Justice Not Vengeance*. Trans. Ewald Osers. New York: Grove Weidenfeld, 1989.

————, *The Sunflower*. New York: Schocken Books, 1998.

E. Thomas Wood and Stanislaw M. Jankowski, *Karski: How One Man Tried to Stop the Holocaust*. New York: John Wiley & Sons, 1994.

David S. Wyman, *The Abandonment of the Jews*. New York: Pantheon Books, 1984.

Mark Wyman, *DP—Europe's Displaced Persons, 1945–1951*. London: Associated University Presses, 1989.

Shalom Yoran, *The Defiant*. New York: St. Martin's, 1996.

Susan Zuccotti, *The Holocaust, the French, and the Jews*. New York: BasicBooks, 1993.

Periodicals

Yitzhak Arad, "Operation Reinhard," *Yad Vashem Studies*, vol. 16, 1984.

Mitchell G. Bard, "Holocaust Museum Gives Portrait of World Gone Awry," *Women's World*, Spring 1993.

Maria Júlia Cirurgião and Michael D. Hull, "Aristides de Sousa Mendes: Angel Against the Blitzkrieg," *Lay Witness*, October 1998.

Stuart Erdheim, "Could the Allies Have Bombed Auschwitz-Birkenau?" *Holocaust and Genocide Studies*, vol. 11, no. 2, Fall 1997.

Internet Sources

Ben S. Austin, "An Introduction to the Holocaust," Holocaust/Shoah Page. www.mtsu.edu/~baustin/holo.html.

Yale Edeiken, "An Introduction to the Einsatzgruppen." www.pgonline.com/electriczen/index.html.

Ron Greene, "Visas for Life: The Remarkable Story of Chiune and Yukiko Sugihara." www.hooked.net/users/rgreene/Sug.html.

Gary M. Grobman, "Resisters, Rescuers, and Bystanders," *The Holocaust—A Guide for Teachers*, 1990. www.remember.org/guide/wit.root.wit.res.html.

Harry Herder Jr., "The Liberation of Buchenwald: The Forgotten Camps." www2.3dresearch.com/~June/Vincent/Camps/CampsEngl.html.

The History Place, www.historyplace.com/.

Holocaust Memorial Center, www.holocaustcenter.com/.

Jacob G. Hornberger, "The White Rose," Future of Freedom Foundation. www.execpc.com/~jfish/fff/.

Internet Modern History Sourcebook, www.fordham.edu/halsall/mod/modsbook.html.

Albert J. Kosiek, "Liberation of Mauthausen," KZ Mauthausen-Gusen Info-Page. www.linz.orf.at/orf/gusen/kosiek1x.htm.

Ruediger Lautmann, "Gay Prisoners in Concentration Camps as Compared with Jehovah's Witnesses and Political Prisoners," Nizkor Project. www.nizkor.org/ftp.cgi/micellany/homosexuals/homosexual.002.

David Metzler, Raoul Wallenberg website. www.raoul-wallenberg.com/.

Per Anger website, "The History of a Swedish Hero." www.raoul-wallenberg.com/per-anger/history.html.

Jennifer Rosenberg, "The Tragedy of the Steamship *St. Louis*," About.com. www.history1900s.about.com.education/history1900s/library/holocaust/aa103197.htm.

William Shapiro, "A Medic Recalls the Horrors of Berga,"

Jewish Student Online Research Center. www.us-israel.org/jsource/ Holocaust/Shapiro.html.

Southern Institute for Education and Research at Tulane University, "Schindler's List Teaching Guide." www.tulane.edu/~so-inst/slindex.html.

James Steakley, "Homosexuals and the Third Reich," *Body Politic*, January/February 1974. People with a History: An Online Guide to Lesbian, Gay, Bisexual, and Trans History, www.fordham.edu/halsall/pwh/.

U.S. Holocaust Memorial Museum, "Children and the Holocaust." www.ushmm.org/education/children.html.

———, "The Nazi Olympics." www.ushmm.org/olympics/zch002.html.

Watchtower Bible and Tract Society, www.watchtower.org/.

Robert S. Wistrich, *Who's Who in Nazi Germany*. Routledge. www.routledge.com/routledge/who/germany/hitler.html.

Yad Vashem, "The 'Righteous Among the Nations' Program." www.yad-vashem.org.il/righteous/index.html.

Websites

About.com Guide to the Holocaust (http://holocaust.about.com/). Contains many original articles related to the Holocaust, news about current events, and links to other sites.

American-Israeli Cooperative Enterprise (AICE) (www.us-israel.org/). One of the most extensive collections of documents, articles, and photographs on the Holocaust.

The Anne Frank House (www.annefrank.nl/). This is the official website for the museum in the house where Anne Frank was hidden.

Auschwitz—Gate to Hell (http://home8.inet.tele.dk/aaaa/Auschwitz.htm). Offers a good collection of photos and brief descriptions of events during the Holocaust.

The Avalon Project (www.yale.edu/lawweb/avalon/avalon.htm). This Yale University project has a collection of World War II and Holocaust-related documents, including transcripts from the war crimes trials.

C.A.N.D.L.E.S. Holocaust Museum (www.candles-museum.com/frmain01.htm). Provides information about survivors—

especially twins—lesson plans, and general information on the Holocaust.

Cybrary of the Holocaust (http://remember.org/). One of the best collections of materials and links on all aspects of the Holocaust.

The Einsatzgruppen (www.pgonline.com/electriczen/einsatz.html). A site devoted to material related to the Nazi mobile killing squads.

The Forgotten Camps (www2.3dresearch.com/~June/Vincent/Camps/CampsEngl.html). Contains detailed information on some of the lesser-known concentration camps.

Forgotten Victims: The Abandonment of Americans in Hitler's Camps (http://members.aol.com/bardbooks/index.htm). A site with a synopsis of study on what happened to American civilians and prisoners of war captured during World War II.

Hell of Sobibor (http://home.wirehub.nl/~mkersten/shoa/sobibor.html). A site devoted to telling the story of one of the Nazi death camps, which also was the scene of the most dramatic escape.

The History Place (www.historyplace.com/index.html). An excellent collection of materials on all aspects of the Holocaust.

Holocaust Educational Digest (http://idt.net/~kimel19/digest.html). Offers an excellent series of articles prepared by a survivor on all aspects of the Holocaust.

The Holocaust History Project (www.holocaust-history.org/). An archive of documents, photographs, recordings, and essays regarding the Holocaust, including direct refutation of Holocaust-denial.

Holocaust Memorial Center (www.holocaustcenter.com). A museum in Michigan that maintains a website with a good overview of the Holocaust and a chronology of events.

Holocaust Pictures Exhibition (www.fmv.ulg.ac.be/schmitz/holocaust.html). A collection of digitized Holocaust photographs.

The Holocaust\Shoah Page (www.mtsu.edu/~baustin/holo.html). An excellent collection of essays and documents on virtually every aspect of the Holocaust.

Internet Modern History Sourcebook (www.fordham.edu/ halsall/mod/modsbook.html). A good collection of links to documents and articles on the Holocaust.

Jewish Student Online Research Center (JSOURCE) (www. us-israel.org/jsource/). A comprehensive encyclopedia of Jewish history and culture that includes an extensive collection of Holocaust material.

KZ Mauthausen-GUSEN Info-Pages (http://linz.orf.at/orf/ gusen/index.htm). A collection of material related to the Mauthausen death camp and its subcamps.

March of the Living (Canada) (www.bonder.com/march. html). A site that organizes an annual student trip to Israel and eastern Europe.

Moreshet Mordechai Anilevich Memorial (www.inter.net.il/ ~givat_h/givat/moreshet/moreshet.htm). A museum website devoted to the leader of the Warsaw Ghetto Uprising.

The Nizkor Project (www.nizkor.org). One of the largest collections of Holocaust documents, specializing in material aimed at debunking Holocaust deniers.

Raoul Wallenberg Website (www.raoul-wallenberg.com/). A site dedicated to telling the story of the Swedish diplomat who rescued thousands of Jews in Hungary before being arrested by the Soviets.

Schindler's List Teaching Guide (www.tulane.edu/~so-inst/ slguide.html). An excellent website covering the story of Oskar Schindler, the rescuer featured in the movie *Schindler's List*.

Shamash (http://shamash.org/trb/judaism.html). An excellent collection of materials on a broad variety of topics related to Jewish history, Judaism, and the Holocaust.

The Simon Wiesenthal Center (www.wiesenthal.com). This site, named after the famed Nazi hunter, has an extensive collection of Holocaust material and entries from the *Encyclopedia of the Holocaust*. One of the three best sources of information on all aspects of the Holocaust.

A Teacher's Guide to the Holocaust (http://fcit.coedu.usf.edu/ holocaust/default.htm). A comprehensive overview of the Holocaust with photos, maps, and links to other related sites.

United States Holocaust Memorial Museum (www.ushmm. org/). One of the best sources of Holocaust information. The site has a growing number of online exhibits and provides access to many of the museum's photographs.

Women and the Holocaust (www.interlog.com/~mighty/). A collection of articles related to women in the Holocaust.

Yad Vashem (www.yad-vashem.org.il/). Israel's Holocaust museum has a number of online exhibitions and document collections. One of the three best sources of information on the Holocaust.

Index